Paul + Noreen
Good meeting you
both. May you always
find peace + love in
your hearts

FINDING

The story of a young boy who becomes his adoptive mother's greatest
spiritual teacher

Kim Fuller

ISBN: 1539494152
ISBN 13: 9781539494157
Library of Congress Control Number: 2016917217
CreateSpace Independent Publishing Platform
North Charleston, South Carolina

TABLE OF CONTENTS

CHAPTER 1

CONNECTION

"Remember that sometimes not getting what you want is a wonderful stroke of luck."

—Dalai Lama XIV

Summer, 2007

Keydell is fourteen now, and I feel like I can tell my story. He arrived in our lives like a hurricane blowing in off the coast, ripping out trees, shredding the wiring, and drenching my safe and peaceful shore. My version of how our son came into our lives, however, is my own; it is different from that of the rest of our family, different from his. That is what makes each of our worlds so unique: we can experience the same event but have profoundly different versions of how it went down.

My journey with Keydell began, not with his arrival, but almost two years before, when I was blessed to meet His Holiness the Dalai Lama.

1

November 3, 2005

I drove onto the campus of Salve Regina University, where His Holiness the Fourteenth Dalai Lama was scheduled to speak, and felt the excitement in the air. I was there for an extraordinary assignment and, as it always does before a big photo shoot, my stomach felt like a television screen full of static. I knew that once I started shooting my internal "channel" would lock in—but for now, I was buzzing.

The security guards, who were directing traffic, sent me to a parking lot for journalists. I grabbed my camera bag out of the car, and headed toward Ochre Court. There was a long security line at the gate to the university mansion; I hoped that Deb, my contact, could get me through the line quickly. Honestly, I didn't understand the tight security. Who would want to harm the Dalai Lama? He is all about love and compassion right? But then, I never understood why anyone would harm someone intentionally.

As I reached the security line, Deb was there to greet me with a big hug.

"This is so exciting," I said. "Thanks for the assignment."

"Are you kidding? I wouldn't have asked anyone else. Besides, I knew you'd want to hear the Dalai Lama talk."

She was right. I didn't know much about Buddhism—or any other religion, for that matter—but was extremely curious to know more. My dad always thought sailing on our boat was a much better option for a Sunday afternoon than church, so the water, wind, and the contemplative silence out at sea became my spiritual environment. Now, though, as much as I loved those quiet times in nature, I was searching for spiritual teachings that made sense to me.

During my years at Salve, Deb and I had often chatted about spirituality, relationships and other fulfilling topics. I have always appreciated someone who speaks honestly, and can get "deep" with me. Maybe growing up as a Navy brat taught me to get to the point in conversations because if I waited out the small talk, my dad might get stationed to a new town before I ever finished the conversation.

"Thanks Deb. You're the best." I replied, as my equipment was checked by a guard, "Can I move around freely during the event?"

"You've been given permission to walk around since you're with Salve," Deb explained. "The front row is for all the newspaper journalists and once the talk starts they're not allowed to leave their seats, so you won't have to fight anyone for a shot."

I was super psyched. "Where's the Dalai Lama right now?"

"He's with Sister Therese," she replied, referring to the president of the university. "They're having a private meet-and-greet."

"Can I go over there now and snap a few images?" I was feeling star-struck, which is unusual for me. I had photographed many celebrity events in the past with little interest in meeting the stars, but now I was thinking how great it would be to get closer—and possibly get a personal introduction.

"I think we're all set. Sister Therese's assistant hired some guy he knew to shoot them together, and a few journalists from the papers are over there, too."

I felt instantly deflated, like someone had popped me with a pin. I had been shooting for Salve for more than twenty years. When I started freelancing, the University had been one of my first clients. They knew I was coming—but instead, "some guy" had been given the best part of the job? What was up with that?

Deb outlined what would happen once the program began. His Holiness would enter from the back to make his way to the podium. He would greet Sister Therese on the stage, where some students would present him with a Salve shirt and hat. Then, he would speak.

"It would be great to get shots of the students as they present him with the Salve gear, and of course of him speaking," said Deb.

Okay, not as interesting as the candid shots I imagined during his meeting with Sister Therese, but I had my assignment. I nodded to Deb that I understood. She walked off to check on the other journalists, and I was left standing there with my deflated ego.

3

The tent was enormous, with close to 4,000 seats set up for the audience. Salve students and staff got first dibs on seats at the front of the tent and then the remaining tickets for the area in the back were sold to the public. A giant monitor hung from the roof, which would allow those in the back sections to see and hear the lecture.

As the tent began to fill, I sensed a distinct energy of anticipation in the crowd. Everyone seemed excited and happy and it felt like that moment just before the bride walks into the church for her wedding. They were all jostling around to make sure they wouldn't miss anything. Salve is a Catholic university, but I wondered if the students would have been as excited to see the Pope.

After I had been under the tent for an hour or so, talking with photographers and journalists from various Rhode Island newspapers and catching up with a few friends I'd seen milling around, a kind of hush came over the crowd. His Holiness was entering the back of the tent.

Suddenly, Deb rushed over to me in a panic. "Kim, bad news. You have to sit down during this whole event. You won't be allowed to leave your seat."

"What? Are you kidding me? I can't even move when the Dalai Lama is coming in?" How was I supposed to get my key shots of him walking down the aisle? I'd really been hoping to capture images of His Holiness greeting people, seeing their smiling faces—something more engaging than just his talking head at the podium.

"I just got word from security," Deb replied sadly.

"It's not your fault." But inside I was seething. This had felt like the assignment of a lifetime, and now it was crashing and burning. This was *not* how things should be going for me.

"The front row is full of journalists, but I got you a seat in the second row right at the end," Deb said, trying to soothe me while pointing to where I needed to stay put. "You'll be sitting right here in front of the students who are going to present the gifts."

Well, I would just have to do my best. What choice did I have?

As I sat down and looked back at the students, I thought I might actually get a good shot here if I popped on my wide angle lens and focused on them watching the Dalai Lama in awe when he came down the aisle. I changed my lens, made sure all my settings were where I wanted them and that my flash was ready to fire. Maybe this would work out after all.

The crowd shifted in their chairs, creating a low rumble as they turned, smiling to see.

I caught a glimpse of His Holiness through the sea of heads and the security guards that surrounded him. That other photographer—the guy who had the job that should have been mine—was also by his side, flash popping every few seconds as he snapped away. "Damn it," I thought. "He's getting all the good shots. Why does *he* get to move around?"

I felt like a prisoner in my chair. How come I had to miss all the good stuff?

As the Dalai Lama moved along, however, I began to feel more at peace. Here I was, obsessing about my seat situation, when I'd been given this great opportunity to see a major religious and spiritual leader. "Let it go and do your job," I reminded myself.

As the Dalai Lama continued up the aisle, he greeted audience members with handshakes and smiles. I found myself delighted by the childlike looks on everyone's faces as they stared at His Holiness, beaming from ear to ear. He moved from side to side along the aisle, trying to greet as many people as he could, so it took a while for him to get to the front. Excited butterflies danced in my stomach as I checked and rechecked my equipment to make sure I was ready.

When he was three rows back, greeting some people on my side of the aisle, I couldn't stand it anymore, and stood up to capture a wide shot of him amidst the excited crowd, all of whom were hoping for a single touch from his hand. I got my shot and sat back down, not wanting to get in trouble.

He was just behind me now, pausing at the row full of students. Those butterflies were doing the conga line now in my belly but I was focused, ready: camera up, framing the moment, waiting for the perfect interaction between the students and His Holiness. His gold robes leaned into the left edge of my frame. His hand reached toward the awestruck students who filled the right side of the frame, and I got a beautiful shot of two bright-eyed, joyful kids looking up at the Dalai Lama's smiling face. They were both wearing their Salve sweatshirts. Perfect.

After spending a few moments with the students, he moved across the aisle to the other side. I felt compelled to put my camera down for a minute and just watch him. He was so graceful and calm, so *present* for each person. His simple gold and burgundy robes hung on his slightly hunched, but relaxed seventy-plus-year-old shoulders.

Then, it happened. He turned back toward my side of the aisle and we locked eyes.

Time slowed down as I realized he was coming toward me to shake my hand. The butterflies in my stomach paused in mid-air as I took a deep breath and smiled at him. His footsteps were slow and carefully placed. I reached out my hand to meet his warm touch as his gaze pierced right through to my inner being.

In those few moments, everything was just as it should be. Pure love was staring right at me, and I felt like I had been seen for the very first time. It was so powerful and beautiful that I began to cry.

I come from a very loving family. I have dear and amazing friends, and am married to the love of my life, but this feeling was new. My ego receded. All my frustrations about my stupid seat, my assignment, my life—everything—just melted away. I felt infinitely blessed. I didn't want to let go. My heart was swollen with love, and that was all that mattered.

He did not even know me; how was he able to connect like that? Had everyone else experienced that same feeling as he shook their hands? How did he so easily love all the beings he touched? How could he move me so deeply with just a look and a handshake?

He probably only held on for a few seconds, but it felt like an hour. He was so present for me in those three or four heartbeats, and his inner peace seemed to pass through his hand and into me.

How could I learn to be more like this man? How could I learn to be present, peaceful, and ooze happiness?

I wanted to know everything about him. I wanted to know what he ate for lunch.

Once on stage with Sister Therese, he conversed with his translator for a moment, then looked out at the audience. As he put on the Salve ball cap, he giggled, and his eyes twinkled like a kid with a big secret to share. I felt that, when he did tell us that secret, I was going to have the answers to every question I'd ever asked in life.

I snapped back to my assignment and took more photos as I listened to His Holiness talk about cultivating love and compassion for all sentient beings. He spoke about looking at our reality in the present moment, instead of getting caught in our past or our expectations for the future, and how we must become aware of our attachments to the self—a self separate from others—and the material attachments that bring us suffering. He assured us that human beings universally want to be happy and relieved from suffering, and that there is a path to that relief; opening ourselves to compassion, empathy, and love toward others would bring us the greatest peace.

Well, heck, I wanted the guidebook for *that* path.

The Dalai Lama told us that he was no different than us. He was a simple monk who had a mother and a father, and missed his country of Tibet. He suffered when his mother died, and he suffered when he lost his country (he was exiled to India by the Chinese). He had suffered like all of us, but he had studied and practiced Buddhism for most of his life, and understood that we all have the potential to reach enlightenment and the state free from suffering, just as the original Shakyamuni Buddha had. We might even reach enlightenment in this lifetime—but, he added, as though reading my mind, if that feels like too much to handle, we can simply practice compassion and kindness toward all sentient beings.

As he spoke, I realized that this notion of enlightenment felt possible. I started to grasp that peace and happiness was my own responsibility, not something in the hands of a higher power. That made a lot of sense to me. *My* thoughts, *my* decisions, *my* actions … These created my happiness or suffering. I wondered if I could be with people without judging—if I could just be present with them, as the Dalai Lama was present with all of us; full of openness and love, not expecting anything in return.

I sure wanted to try. But I needed to know more.

Despite all my initial whining, I got the photographs I needed that day. I realized, as I was packing up, how much energy I had wasted getting upset. I had been so attached to my ideas of what was acceptable, and fair, and right—but after hearing the Dalai Lama speak, I understood that these were not based in reality. I had dreamed up what "should" happen and when it didn't, I was let down because of my own delusions. If I had stayed more present, instead of expecting something that was not happening, I wouldn't have suffered as I did around the situation. Most of what happened had been out of my control anyway, except for my state of mind. Wow.

Maybe I hadn't been there just to take good photos. Maybe I was there to have my life changed forever. The gift His Holiness gave me that day was beyond measure.

My spiritual journey had begun.

⟞⊹⊹⟝

After that day, I embarked on a learning curve unlike any I've ever experienced. I began to read as many books about Buddhism as I could find, mainly books written by the Dalai Lama himself. I realized that understanding my mind, and how it guided me through the day, was going to be a big part of the practice.

Meditation was recommended to slow me down enough to watch my mind, but I wasn't sure how to do it. My husband Jim had tried meditation a while back for stress relief, but I'd never joined him in his sits because I didn't consider myself a "stressed" person. I began looking for a meditation teacher. It was clear to me that, if I truly wanted to become a *Bodhisattva*—a person who aspires to become enlightened—I needed to learn to slow down my churning mind and work on cultivating the thoughts that brought me happiness, which would then lead to feeling more peaceful. Then, my actions would reflect that state of mind and maybe, just maybe, I could affect others like the Dalai Lama had affected me.

Whew. I needed a few more lifetimes.

Over the next two years, I also dove headfirst into the Buddhist teachings. I went to the Dalai Lama's week-long teachings at Lehigh University in Pennsylvania where he taught from the Lam Rim, the sacred texts that contain the keys to enlightenment. Most of it went right over my head, but I took copious notes and studied them over and over again. At the end of the week, His Holiness taught us how to meditate. I was so excited to learn from him that I called my mom screaming with joy that I had been taught how to meditate by none other than the Dalai Lama. "No better teacher than him," I squealed.

I wasn't sure where all of my explorations would lead me, or if I could grasp even half of what I was learning—but I knew that, in order to be present and helpful for others, I had to have some peace within myself. I reflected often on that feeling of being seen that I had experienced that day at Salve, and it kept me going in my practice. It reminded me of what was possible. As I continued to learn, grow and find some peace, I began to reach out more to others as well. I practiced staying calm with my family and friends, and got back into some volunteer work.

That's when I met Keydell. If there was ever going to be someone who would keep me on my toes, it was him. My newfound enlightenment was about to be challenged in a *big* way.

⇥⊹⇤

There he was: a tiny brown-skinned boy, fresh from his shower with water droplets still clinging to his head. I've always loved how wet kinky hair sparkles in the sunlight as though adorned with sequins. He came bounding out of the group home, leaping completely over the front steps to join the other boys on the lawn. They teased him for being late; I could tell it annoyed him.

"Shut up, you guys!" His six-year-old voice carried the full weight of his forty-five-pound body behind it. He flopped down on the grass at the edge of the group of boys, scowling at each of them. I, and the other women in the "Adopt-a-Home Moms" volunteer group, hadn't even been introduced to the boys yet, but I fell instantly in love with this spunky little guy. He was going to be part of my life, somehow. I just knew it.

It was the same feeling I'd had when I saw my husband for the first time, back in 1983.

He was jogging down a cobblestone street in Newport, Rhode Island, wearing gym shorts with white piping that showed off his muscular legs. His sandy blonde, stick-straight hair bounced as he ran by.

"Who's that tall drink of water?" I asked my gal pal and co-worker, who was trolling out the store window with me. When business was slow, we'd sit there watching for hot guys walking around Newport. It was the America's Cup summer, so the ships' store was *the* place to meet sexy sailors from around the world. This

10

American guy stood out, however. I was going to meet him, I just knew it. It was like a spotlight suddenly went on over his head that read, "Future influence in your life. Walk this way!"

This young boy squirming on the grass was no different.

On that warm afternoon in August 2006, I watched him settle on the grass, keeping a safe distance between himself and the other boys. They were not allowed to touch each other: house rules. He looked to be the youngest in a group that ranged in age from six to twelve years old. Although they all came from Rhode Island— which, like most of New England, is predominantly white—only one of them was blond, blue-eyed, and WASP-y looking. The rest were of varying ethnicities.

As volunteers, we were not privy to any information about these boys or how they came to be here at the Trout Drive Group Home. Honestly, I didn't want to think about it. I wanted to accept each of them simply as a child—not a child of color, or a child of abuse, just a child who needed love, attention, and a little bit of fun.

"They must be so scared and confused when they arrive here for the first time," I thought. This place was a home, but not their own home.

When I was a kid, and my family would get transferred to the next Naval station, my sisters and I would get so excited to pick out our new bedrooms, and arrange our toys in a new space. The walls would be bare, fresh for decorating. It was thrilling.

I guessed that these munchkins had much different experiences. One boy's gaze darted around the volunteers like a ping-pong ball, as if gauging which of us was the most trustworthy. The tension in his little body made me sick to my stomach. Had he been abused? Had someone hurt him?

"Change your thoughts, Kim," I told myself. "Get back to the task at hand. Smile. They don't want your pity."

Denise, the house manager, came out to introduce us to the boys. A light-hearted woman with dark hair and freckles, she beamed at us while fanning her shirt over her large bosom. "It's so nice of you ladies to do this."

She seemed relieved we were there. I could only imagine how stressful it must be to manage a house full of troubled young boys.

"What kinds of things would you like to do here?" she asked.

She was asking us? We had been hoping that she would have suggestions! "Um, how about an ice cream social?" I suggested.

That got the boys' full attention. The littlest boy, the one with the wet hair, seemed particularly excited. When I pointed this out to Denise, she told me that he loved ice cream, and did his best to display good behavior so that he wouldn't have to miss Ice Cream Wednesdays.

"A man after my own heart," I said.

I wondered if the little guy had already had a bar of chocolate, or something caffeinated, because he could not sit still. He looked like he was ready to lift off to the moon. As we wrapped up our introductions, he yelled out to anyone who was listening, "Want to see my cartwheel?" He was so wiggly and cute. He and Kelly, one of the volunteers who'd come with me, proceeded to do cartwheels on the lawn while the other boys got up to shoot hoops or ride on their scooters. The rest of us milled around in the yard talking to Denise—or, in my case, attempting to play basketball with some of the kids. Not my greatest talent, but I gave them something to laugh at.

My sister came up to me as I dodged off the driveway court for a break. "I already know who you're drawn to. You like that little blonde boy."

"He's cute," I said, trying to catch my breath. "But that little black boy, the one who came out from the house last ... He's some kind of special." I gestured as if pinching his cheeks. "He's so feisty and smart, I can just tell."

Amy laughed at me like only a sister would. "Yeah," she agreed. "Feisty."

I drove home that night thinking about each of the boys' faces; so beautiful, diverse and eager. I have always loved faces, especially the eyes. They say so much without uttering a sound. They can smile, or look sad, distant, or tired. Those boys' eyes held many untold stories, and I was curious to unravel a few of them.

Over my years as a portrait photographer, I have practiced tuning into the subtle expressions in the eyes of my subjects; in their body language, and their voices, many things come through. My talent lies in my ability to let go of any expectations I have for the photo shoot and watch carefully for what is possible. My clients often show me their natural inner beauty when we are between takes—when they are fixing their hair, or waiting for me to adjust my camera. Since I began studying Buddhism, I've learned to be even more present for my subjects, and pause before shooting, so that I can really listen to them and see who they are beneath the nervousness or discomfort of the photo shoot.

When I looked at these boys on the lawn that day, I knew that I wanted to have that same presence for them; to really see them for who they were, deep down, and not just their current circumstances or where they came from.

In those boys' eyes I saw their eagerness to please, to be accepted or stand out—but those eyes also carried the weight of fear. It must feel very scary when the uncertainty of your family life overshadows everything. Perhaps by applying the mindfulness I acquired through photography to these boys, I could give them some ease and make them feel accepted for who they were, in all their perfection. I was going to try letting go of any expectations about each of them. Maybe our volunteer group could help them feel like things would be okay, at least for the hours we were there at the group home with them.

Coincidentally, it was through my photography work that I and the other "Adopt-a-Home Moms" ended up at Trout Drive. A few weeks earlier, Child and Family, the sponsors of this home, had hired me to photograph each of their six group homes for a brochure they were putting together. They hoped to entice community groups from the Newport, Middletown, and Portsmouth areas to "adopt" one of the homes for a year. The brochure would showcase what the homes looked like and explain what needed to be done within each.

Through that assignment, I became inspired to adopt one of the homes myself. Looking at the rooms in each house, all I could see were big blank walls like canvases waiting to have color added. I saw myself making those spaces more homey and inspiring for the kids who lived there. I had served on various volunteer boards before, but this seemed like it would be more hands-on.

After completing my photo assignment, I called Keith, who'd hired me to do the shoot, and asked if I could put together a group to adopt one of the homes. I think we were the first group to approach him and he was very excited to get us started.

I e-mailed several of my best girlfriends, many of whom were mothers, and asked if they would form a volunteer group with me. They all said yes. I invited them all to my house one evening, and Keith explained what our one-year commitment might look like. We were tasked with raising one thousand dollars, or finding donations in the form of supplies, repairs, and household items that equaled that amount.

At first, I envisioned us working with the teen girls' home. We could teach them photography and meditation, and mentor them as they moved on in school. Keith, however, thought that the Trout Drive home for young boys needed us most.

"I think the boys could really use some mother figures," he explained.

We divvied up the tasks among the ten of us so no one had to work too hard. Every one of the Adopt-a-Home Moms played to her skill set. For example, my sister Amy (who is not a "kid person" or a mom in real life) took on fundraising. The Rays (as in, Rays of Light, my posse of three close female friends) stepped up to do the tasks which involved hands-on house projects and interacting with the boys.

We had a good group. And, although Keith had given us an idea of what to expect, having seen the real needs of the Trout Drive kids, our hearts were dedicated to it now.

I sat down to dinner at the kitchen table that evening with my own beautiful children, Henry and Ella, and my husband Jim, the guy with the great legs. Our bright orange kitchen, with its 1950s green tiling, made for a much cozier and more colorful setting than I'd experienced earlier today.

"How was the group home, Mom?" Henry asked through a large wad of food in his cheek; he looked like a squirrel storing food for the winter. Lately, he couldn't get enough food into that fifteen-year-old body of his.

"It was sad to see all those young kids away from their parents. But they are safe. The house is big, and they've got a great yard."

"The boys must be so cute, Mom," Ella piped in. "They're, like, middle school and younger, right?" She had started babysitting at age eleven, and couldn't get enough of kids and babies.

"Oh, they're cute, Boo," I agreed. "And they're so young to have gone through so much already. Some of them just have that look of sadness that comes from deep down. They have those dark circles that tell you there's something going on. I mean, I get dark circles, but I'm an old lady." I smiled. I was only forty-four.

"What about the staff?" Jim asked.

"Denise, the house manager, is really cool. Not sure how she went from being an artist to managing the group home, but I think I'm going to like her. You can tell she loves the kids. But the rest of them … They look like college students, for Christ's sake. There was one older lady there, too, who seems to do a lot of the cooking. She's a big, cuddly, mother type, but her hair was stringy and she kind of smelled." I wrinkled my nose.

"Wow, Mom. Super judgmental," Ella smirked. "You always say not to judge people by the way they look."

Jim eyeballed me to watch my reaction. I looked down at my food for a shameful pause. "You're right. I just noticed. Her appearance made me think about how selfless the job must be, that's all."

Henry rescued me. "Do the boys get to just hang out, or is it really structured?" he asked.

"From what I can tell, it looks like some of the boys are shadowed by a staff member the whole day, but then others have more freedom. I think it depends on their behavior, and how long they've been there. I mean, the rules are obviously tight. The boys couldn't just walk inside when it was time for dinner. They had to ask, 'Can I go in?' Then the next one would say, 'Can I go in?' It was pretty funny."

My kids normally scattered after dinner, but tonight they both lingered for a few minutes. Then Henry asked, "Can I go there with you, Mom, and play lacrosse or soccer with the boys?"

I turned toward him, balancing two plates and stacked silverware in my hand. "Yeah, I think that's possible. The boys would love it. Not sure if you have to get a background check like I did since you're only fifteen, but we can figure that out."

"Can I could go, too?" Ella asked, her wide-set eyes brimming with ideas. "I can do some arts and crafts, or sports with Henry."

"Alright, you two, slow down. I've only been there once. Let me check it out. I'm happy you're asking, though."

I suppose if you lead by example, the kids will follow.

≍⊹⊱

As I did my usual back scratches and good nights that evening (I still loved putting my two teenagers to bed), I wondered who was saying good night to the boys at Trout Drive. Was there a staff person who read stories, or gave them each a big hug?

Bedtime at my home growing up was filled with stories. My dad would create funny voices for each character. My mom would then rub our heads, soothing us to sleep. She woke us up that way, too. I fell asleep safe and cozy, without a fear in my mind.

With Henry and Ella, I followed the same pattern. After reading and catching up on the day's events, I'd start their music boxes and tuck them in. I wanted to be there at night for those boys at the group home, and imagined myself going into each room, reading a bedtime story, and giving each one a kiss on the cheek. I wanted them to feel safe, too. Without a steady adult in their lives, they must live with a lot of fear, I thought.

At that point, I had no idea what bedtime was actually like at the Trout Drive group home, but later I found out that it was the most difficult time of the day for most of the boys. Before coming to Trout, bedtime had been a time when "things" used to happen. Some were awakened in the middle of the night by an unwanted man on top of them; others by screaming fights. I wanted to hold each of them and tell them everything would be okay, but I did not know if it would. I was grateful for Child and Family for providing a safe place for these kids to go. It might not be perfect, but it was something.

So many people were already involved in the care of those six boys; could I, one woman, make a difference? Could the Adopt-a-Home Moms, ten women, make a difference?

"I still have some good mothering in me," I thought. "If I could make a difference in even one of those children's lives, that would be enough."

On ice cream social day, the Adopt-a-Home Moms and I showed up after dinner with a couple of gallons of various flavors and toppings. We wanted to start off with a bang. Denise greeted us with her happy smile as we set up in the kitchen and invited the boys to sit at the dining room table. Denise told us that this was an agreeable bunch who got along for the most part.

"Do you sometimes get a group that fights?" I asked.

"It's not so much that they fight but, boys come and go from here all the time. Some stay for a few weeks and some for up to a year. With each new arrival or when a boy leaves it changes the dynamic or can upset a boy if one of his friends leaves. You just never know. They all come with different issues and behaviors as well, so it can get pretty crazy at times. These guys are good though. We're in a groove." she smiled.

As I started scooping ice cream one of the boys, whom I played with on our first visit, saw me and his eyes lit up with joy. I went to give him a big hug.

One of the staff darted over. "You can't do that."

"I'm not allowed to hug him?" I asked. "Just him, or all of them?"

"You can, but you have to ask, or they have to ask you," was the reply.

I got it, but I had a pit in my stomach. Hugging is something I do a lot, and for a child to not be able to hug naturally seemed awful. Still, I suspected that, for some of these boys, physical contact might have a very different meaning than it did for me.

It was not a carefree social, but the boys seemed to understand the rules. Each boy was asked into the kitchen separately to get his ice cream. They sat an arm's length apart from each other, hands folded on the table, and waited as quietly as they could, considering their excitement. The staff worked on the boys' table manners and reminded them to say please and thank you.

Once the boys' bowls were loaded up, I looked around the kitchen and noticed a behavior chart on the wall made from a big piece of poster paper. It listed the names of the boys with various stars next to each. The stars represented the number of days of good behavior.

Seth, 15 good days; Juan, 45 good days; Carlos, one good day. Then I noticed one boy who had what looked like two hundred-plus good days.

"Which boy is this?" I asked Denise. "Keydell? Am I saying that right?"

"It's that little guy over at the end of the table," she said, pointing to the young black boy I'd been so drawn to that first day on the lawn, "and you say his name 'Ky-dell.' Funny story about his name," Denise continued. "When we were doing his initial paperwork, I asked Matt, his DCYF caseworker, how to pronounce his name. Matt told me that originally his name was spelled 'Kydell,' but the hospital messed it up on his birth certificate and his mom never fixed it."

"That's weird," I agreed. "You'd think his mom would want it to be right."

"Who knows? But it's pronounced 'Ky-dell.'"

I nodded, and went to the table. "Hey, Keydell! I hear you're a big ice cream lover, just like me."

He looked up without saying anything.

"I noticed on the behavior chart that you've had a ton of good days. Nice work."

He was very focused on his ice cream but managed to say, "Thank you."

I squatted down so I could be at his eye level. "My name is Kim."

"I'm Keydell," he replied in his raspy little voice. His brown eyes were as rich as the chocolate sauce on his ice cream; the same sauce was smeared all around his mouth. He closed his eyes in delight with each bite. It was really funny. This kid was passionate about his ice cream.

I was startled out of my observation when one of the other kids yelled, "Can I clear?"

A staff member said, "Yes," giving the young boy permission to get up to clear his bowl.

"Can I go in?" as he got to the door of the kitchen.

"Yes."

"Can I clear?"

"Yes."

And so it went. Keydell asked for seconds but there were none to be had.

As the boys started their nighttime routine of homework and showers, the Adopt-a-Home Moms cleaned up and gathered outside before heading home.

"What a great bunch of boys," I said. "I am so in love with all of them."

"I just want to take Seth home," said Kelly. Seth was the cute little blonde kid who looked like he could be Kelly's son.

"They're so innocent," I added. "It's hard to imagine what they must have been through to end up here."

As we stood in the warm September evening saying our good-byes, I felt so grateful for these women: my "Rays of Light," Lisa, Lorraine, and Kelly, and my other dear friend, Rachel. I had never been the type to hang with a gaggle of girls, but these like-minded ladies had become my closest confidants, walking buddies, dance partners and my source of comfort in hard times. They knew me so well that I didn't even have to explain myself anymore.

Growing up, I'd moved around so much that it had been hard to establish deep ties; my husband, also a Navy brat, had had similar experiences. We had now been here in Rhode Island longer than anywhere else we'd ever lived.

I reflected on the fact that, between all the moves with my officer father and artist mother (who were more hippies than formal military), I had learned to morph into whoever I needed to be for any occasion. I would go from being a bell-bottom-wearing, Volkswagen-bus-riding flower child to pressed, dressed, and standing at attention at a Navy change of command. I could put on a Southern drawl or a New England twang, depending on who I was with. In high school, I transformed myself into a surfer chick in Virginia Beach after being a kick-ass marching band flag twirler in Norfolk, where I was also the only white girl on the track team. (The team girls called me the White Shadow but they also taught me to dance. I loved it.)

It wasn't until I got to the Rhode Island School of Design (better known as RISD) that I really found my people. There, I didn't need to morph anymore; everyone was doing their own thing, and finding their own voice. I'd met a variety of people over the course of my childhood, but in my case, this was a good thing. Each move was an opportunity to get curious about the people I'd met and how they behaved. I carried this curiosity into my photography practice and it gave me an extra dose of awareness around how unique we all are. Besides, no matter where we'd ended up, I always had my loving parents, and my sisters Lisa and Amy who knew me best. The houses may have changed, but when I walked through any of our front doors it was like an exhale from the crazy day. I always felt safe and grounded with a happy place to come back to and now Rhode Island and these girls felt that way for me as well.

The boys at Trout Drive had moved around many times in their lives, too. But what made them feel safe and happy? Who were the adults they could count on? Did the group home provide a sense of security—even if it was short-term—or was security only a dream for them?

Sadly, I thought it might be the latter.

In that moment, standing in the group home's driveway with my best ladies, I vowed to show those kids that there *were* adults on whom they could rely—and that I was one of them.

CHAPTER 2
POSSIBILITY

*"If you think you are too small to make a difference, try
sleeping with a mosquito."*

—*Dalai Lama XIV*

I came back within the next few days by myself to scope out
the house and talk more with Denise about some projects we
might do for the place. I parked my Prius on the street in case
the boys played basketball in the driveway when they came home
after school. I opened the slightly torn screen door and knocked.
A young man, about thirty, answered the door. He had a round
face with large features and a crew cut that made him look tough.
He had on a short-sleeved T-shirt and I could see he had quite a
few tattoos. He told me later that he covered them up when the
boys were around. He didn't want to give a bad impression, which
I considered extremely thoughtful even though I found tattoos to
be artful. He smiled, and let me in.

I headed up the stairs to the main floor of the split-level house.
It was quiet, which I imagined was rare when all the boys were

home. I was sensitive to the residual energy, however. When spaces are quiet and empty, I see them better because I'm not distracted by any people or faces in the room.

"Do you mind if I look around?" I asked.

"Sure. Denise is in the basement when you're ready to see her. She knew you were coming," he replied.

I thanked him and, as he left me to mill around, I started to get nosy. Right away I noticed a few holes in a wall and made a mental note to see if any of the women had connections with a contractor.

I walked down the long hallway of the main floor and looked in the three bedrooms. The first room was large, with two sets of bunk beds and a fair amount of space left over. There was one big closet enclosed with crappy wooden doors that were dappled in old Scotch tape from bygone posters and drawings. One of the doors was dangling on its hinge. I visualized a wrestling match where one of the boys rammed into the door after rolling away from the grip of another boy and that thing fell on him. Perhaps the wrestling match caused the door to break in the first place. Hopefully, it wasn't from a fight that had gone wrong.

I went back to happier thoughts, imagining painting the walls like I had done with my kids' rooms. Henry's was painted light blue with a big silver wave design that wrapped around two walls, and Ella had gold stars painted on her midnight-blue ceiling. Maybe I could do something fun and personal like that in here.

I continued down the hall past the other bedrooms to the only bathroom on this floor. It was in bad shape. The fixtures looked old and partly broken and the toilet had no lid. It would be one of our first orders of business to make sure everything worked.

I noticed a pack of pull-up diapers in the cabinet and wondered why these boys, ages six and up, needed them. I'd have to ask Denise about that.

The kitchen, which I had examined the night of the ice cream social, needed new appliances and a paint job at the very least. I continued my big circle into the dining room and through to the living room at the front of the house. It had a big bay window, which was great for letting light in, and made the room feel homier. Each room was bare of décor, with just the basics. The living room held tables, chairs, two couches, a television, an open cabinet with a few papers on it, and one locked cabinet that I guessed held a computer or games. I assumed good behaviors were rewarded with things from behind the locked cabinet.

The place was clean, but uninspiring. I was ready to add some life to it.

After surveying the first floor and making my notes on how the Adopt-a-Home Moms could best serve this place, I went downstairs to say hi to Denise. Her office was in the back room of a very large, finished basement, which was being used as a playroom. It had a big red corduroy couch, a bookshelf holding games and books, and a television with a video game station underneath it. (Note to self: it needed a new floor.)

I poked my head in her door, and Denise greeted me with a welcoming smile from behind a heavy desk that held toys, snow globes, photos and the kids' artwork. I was wondering if the kids were allowed to visit her in here—and, if they were, would they consider it a special treat? I think Denise tried to make the boys feel special in any way she could.

I gave her a quick hug over the desk and sat down across from her. I mentioned my thoughts about some projects I had in mind, and asked about the bathroom in particular. Denise sat back in her chair and leaned against the back wall. The office was very narrow— more like a storage space than office space—but she was making the best of it. I am sure they couldn't spare a bedroom for an office.

"Oh, yeah. The bathroom," she groaned. "That's the one place the boys can go alone and shut the door. Some of them, after we get to know them, have to leave the door open even when they go number two."

She explained how, in the past, some of the boys had taken their own feces and rubbed them all over the walls. They snuck markers in and wrote all over the place, or stuffed things like socks and underwear in the toilet. It was a way for them to feel in control of their body, especially if they had been abused.

"Are there things we women should worry about when we visit?" I asked with some hesitation.

"No, this current group is pretty good," she assured me. "No one is too inappropriate or wild."

"What do you mean by inappropriate? Like, swearing or something?"

"Like grabbing people or making rude gestures—and yes, sometimes swearing or using foul language," she explained. "For the most part, a staff member will be with you or nearby so just always ask before you interact with one of the boys alone. There are some who will be very engaging, and some not so much."

I could tell she really loved these boys and didn't want to make them look bad. I noticed that one of the drawings on the wall behind her looked like a rendition of Denise and one of the boys standing together. They were holding hands.

"Why are some of these boys here?" I asked.

"I can't give many details, but some have their own issues, and some have parents with issues, and some both," Denise replied. "DCYF tries hard to reunite them with their parents if, for example, the parent has a drug or drinking problem and gets help for it. Sometimes they end up with a relative instead."

"I guess it's best if they can be with a parent as long as they're safe, huh?" I couldn't imagine not being with my parents growing up.

"DCYF feels it's best," she said.

"I'm getting the impression you don't think so, Denise."

"Not always."

"Do you just get so sad sometimes hearing their stories?" I asked.

"Yes, sometimes, but we just do the best we can to make this a good home for them," she answered.

"You do good work here, Denise. Our group is excited to get started and help you out."

⚓

Over the next few weeks, our group painted walls, installed new flooring, donated from the Home Depot, in the basement play-room, collected games, toys, and new bedding donations, and built a homework desk in the dining room. I was very proud of the team. Three or four of us from the group continued to visit on a fairly regular basis, just as I had promised I would. Once or twice a week, while Henry and Ella were at soccer, lacrosse practice, or other after-school events, I would just drop by and knock on the door. The staff got to know me pretty quickly and didn't seem to mind me hanging out. Hopefully I was a welcome break for some of them.

I really enjoyed my time with the boys but never knew what I was walking into with each visit. There could be one boy in a corner facing the wall with a staff member by his side, screaming or moaning to be released from a "time-out," while another boy was trying to do homework amidst the chaos. Keydell often played video games in the basement by himself. There were obvious levels of behavioral privilege.

⚓

The first Christmas we were a part of the home was fun. We each picked a boy to shop for, and I chose Keydell. Henry, Ella and my sister, Amy, helped me pick out games and sporting equipment for him. I think he got more presents than my own kids because, in addition to our gifts, several charities donated over the holidays.

27

_ us went over one evening just before Christmas to de-
_ie gifts. It was also family visiting day, so I met some of the
ʋoys' parents for the first time.

I remember sitting in the living room, watching carefully as some of the boys grabbed their mothers' hands and led them around the house, showing them all the places they ate, did homework, or hung out. The boys' eyes were filled with hope, as if this would be the day they might go home—but the parents seemed stiff, foreign, and often bored.

I asked if Keydell was around, and Rob told me he was in his room with his mom. I walked down the hall and peeked quietly into the room that Keydell shared with his roommate, Dante. Tiny Keydell was sitting on the floor next to his large and very attractive mother. Keydell looked a lot like her. As they played a video game on the TV, his mom's face flickered and glowed in the light of the screen; she wore a kind of blank look that could have been either boredom or sadness.

I watched for a moment as Keydell laughed and wiggled against his mom as they played the game. He was obviously beating her. I let them be and went back to join the holiday party in the living room.

Soon, it was time for dinner, and the families gathered in the dining room. As Keydell and his mom came out of his room, I noticed she looked pregnant. It made me wonder again why Keydell was here, and what his family's story was. Did his mom have other children? Was Keydell her first, and now she was having another? Would she be able to keep that baby? My mind was racing with questions that I knew might never be answered because of the kids' privacy issues. Keydell seemed so good and stable, minus a few anger issues; I just assumed he was angry because he had to be at the group home and not with his mom. With more than 300 good days now, he had either figured out the system here at the home or he really was a very good boy.

I started to make so many assumptions in my head. "Oh, his mom must be this, his mom must be that." What did I know? I decided not to go there with my thoughts when the important thing was to be present for them in a kind and compassionate way.

The Buddhists teach that one of the first steps toward a compassionate heart is to develop empathy. We do this by realizing the suffering of others so that we feel concerned for their well-being. Remembering this, I tried to keep an open mind as I watched Keydell and his mother. She must be suffering greatly if she had to put her child into another's care. That is not an easy thing to do. I tried not to make any assumptions beyond that.

I believe that most people do their best to be kind, but some have so many other issues that they use up all their energy just surviving. Our actions reflect our emotions, so if we feel alone, helpless, or even angry about our lives, we act based on those feelings. Perhaps I needed to focus on ways to help myself through times of suffering, I reflected, so I could help others—like Keydell's mom—through theirs.

I found out later from Denise that Keydell had an older brother and sister—and that, yes, his mom was pregnant again.

The summer of 2008 was upon us, and Ella thought it would be fun to make tie-dyed T-shirts with the boys one day. "Do you think I can volunteer over there yet, Mom?" she asked. "Henry has been able to go." Her brother had come a few times to play lacrosse with the boys.

"Yes, actually, I did get permission, now that you're a little older, so you can do your project."

Ella was now a beautiful, blossoming fourteen-year-old girl. I wondered how the boys would view her. It was one thing to bring Henry, who was just another guy, but Ella might be interesting in other ways. She always carried herself with grace, so I was pretty sure she could handle herself. The day we went was an unusually hot June afternoon so we set up under a shady tree next to the kickball field.

We gathered the boys in the yard, and Ella asked them each to pick out a white T-shirt from the pile. Then, she laid out bottles of dye, rubber bands, and rubber gloves.

"First, tie the rubber bands around different parts of the T-shirt like this," Ella demonstrated. "Then, squirt some dye on each section."

We quickly realized it was better to ask them which color they wanted to use; otherwise, they would just pick up a bottle and go nuts with it, squirting dye all over the place. They seemed to be enjoying the project, and Ella was happy to be a part of the group.

The boys were winding down from the project when I looked over at Keydell, whose shirt was already covered in colors. "Are you done, buddy?" I asked.

"No, I want more dye," he said with some urgency in his voice.

We still had some dye left so I asked Ella if we had enough for him to use.

"Sure, what the heck, let him go wild," she said with an encouraging look toward Keydell. He squirted that shirt until it was dripping with dye. His hands were covered in colors, despite the gloves, but he was happy. "He's an all-or-nothing kind of guy," I thought.

Ella and I then collected the shirts to dry. We told the boys that we would bring them back another day and hand them out.

That never got to happen for Ella.

She was finishing up middle school that year and some of the group home boys attended the same school a grade below her.

"Mom, guess who's dating me?" she asked, making air quotes with her fingers around the word "dating."

"Who?"

"James, from the group home. Apparently, he's been going around school telling everyone he and I are going out, and that we kissed. I don't really care, but I thought you should know."

"Yeah, I wondered if something like this might happen," I said. "James, from what I know, has a tendency to lie a lot and really create an imaginary world for himself as an escape mechanism. His reality is one of abuse, fear, and shame, so I get it. Sorry about that sweetie."

"It's fine. I understand, actually. I know no one believes that we're dating or have kissed, but he kind of follows me around at school. I don't want to get him in trouble and I asked him to stop—so, whatever," she said with a tilt of her head. She was so great at handling things like this with kindness and firmness at the same time.

"I'll let Denise know, Ella, and tell her how you're handling it. I'm proud of you for being so kind. I think you get how much these boys have been through, but I want you to feel safe, too."

"I do," she insisted. "He's never tried to touch me or anything."

Of course, when I told Denise this story we both agreed it was best that Ella not come over any more.

"I am sorry, Kim," Denise said apologetically. "Ella was so great with the boys. It's so tough because these kids sometimes just don't have appropriate behaviors in situations like this and James really can get lost in his make-believe."

"The mind is a beautiful place to create your world," I said with some sarcasm.

"Tell Ella I'll take a photo of all the boys with their tie-dyed shirts on and send her a copy."

When the photo arrived, it showed all the boys sitting on the couch, one body length apart from each other, and some standing in the back, proudly wearing their shirts. Keydell's shirt was a pattern of muddy thunder clouds, but his smile was as bright as the sun.

Keydell's "all-in" personality was becoming more apparent with each activity I did with him. When I hung out with him while he played on the X-Box, he was so focused that I couldn't get his attention. He tried to teach me how to use the controller, but I was hopeless and I think it frustrated him.

One late summer afternoon during a kickball game, little Keydell was on my team. We had the staffer, Rob, out there, too, and perhaps four other boys. The game was close, and we were up to kick. Keydell got up for his turn and I, being the "rah-rah" girl that I am, cheered him on. (I *had* gotten the best sportsmanship award for my entire town softball league, after all.)

"Okay, Keydell, get on base, sweetie. Give us a good kick."

One of the boys, Tony, rolled the ball toward home plate and Keydell swung his leg with all his might. Again, he showed that he never did anything halfway. His foot missed the ball and his tiny little body fell to the ground, raising a cloud of dirt from the worn, dusty field.

Tony laughed and taunted, "Ha! We're going to win for sure now. Keydell can't kick."

Keydell got up with an angry look on his face and brushed himself off. He looked so focused and determined to get the next pitch. He pulled up the legs on his jeans and readied himself for the ball. It bounced over the tufts and divots in the grass and made it to Keydell's foot this time. He gave the ball a wallop and it sailed to the outfield. Keydell bolted to first base. He was fast for such a little guy. He started off for second, determined to make it around to win the game, when just then, James, who was playing in the outfield, threw the ball at him and tagged him out.

Most kids would have been upset, as it was our third out and last chance to score, but Keydell reacted in a way I had not expected. He rolled on the ground, grabbing his head, then reached for the ball that had landed beside him and threw it back at James with angry force. His furrowed brow was tight. His once loose and athletic posture turned stiff and knotted, ready to pounce. Rob recognized this, and went over to stop him.

"Keydell, it's okay. They played a good game, and sometimes we lose."

"Shut up and leave me alone!" Keydell screamed. He stomped over to the bushes at the side of the house and started ripping the leaves off.

I walked over, thinking I could give him some motherly support.

"Hey, buddy, I had fun even though we lost. You're so fast, and you're extremely athletic. I was honored to be on your team."

He turned his head, and looked right into my eyes with a glare of threatening proportions. Then, he stormed away into the house.

"Wow, that was intense," I said turning to Rob.

"Keydell is really hard on himself. He gets angry like this a lot."

"Should I go check on him?" I asked.

"You can if you want, but don't expect too much," Rob replied.

As he said that, I reflected on the times I had come by for visits and been excitedly welcomed by some of the other boys, while Keydell kept to what he was already doing, clinging to his independence. However, it was almost dinner time at the home, so I decided to go in for a quick goodbye anyway. The angry little man was sitting on the couch, arms crossed, bottom lip out.

"You okay, Keydell?" I asked. "You seemed very upset outside."

"I don't want to talk about it," he said, without looking at me. His feet dangled, not touching the floor. The large couch was swallowing his tiny body, but he oozed the negative energy of a much larger person. I tried not to smile at his determined anger.

"Well, I had fun today, and will see you next week. Maybe I'll practice my kicking until then and we'll beat them next time. Are you okay sitting here by yourself?"

"Yes," he answered, as if I should know that by now. "I have the best behavior so I get to be alone."

I wanted to laugh at his insistence. It was as passionate as his desire to soak his T-shirt with dye and score a run in the kickball game.

"Oh, yes, of course," I said. "You do have a ton of good days. I'll see you later, then."

As I was leaving I heard, "Can I come in?" "Can I go out?" as some of the boys entered and left various rooms in the house.

⇒⊣⊢⇐

As August 2008 came to a close, so did our Adopt-a-Home Moms commitment. I met with the other women and thanked them for all they had done for the house and the boys, but if they wanted, they could take a break now. I, on the other hand, didn't want it to end.

Denise and I had become very good friends over that past year, and I continued visiting with her and the boys regularly. Keydell was allowed to play in the basement near her office on the video game unit, so I would often pass him on the way to Denise's office. One time he followed me in. He stood there staring at Denise for a bit, until she asked, "Keydell, do you want a hug?"

A big smile spread across his face as he snuggled into her large bosom. He held her for about three seconds and then pulled away and started examining all the things on her desk. She finally told him he had to go back out so we could chat. He didn't listen and continued to fiddle with some things in a box nearby. "What is this, Denise?" he asked. "Can I have it? Where did you get this?"

"Keydell, I asked you to please go back to the play room," Denise repeated.

"Why, why can't I stay? Can I have some candy?"

I can't say I blame him for not wanting to leave. I would have come in just for hugs, too, if no one touched me all day long.

Finally, with some effort, Denise managed to get him to leave. I told him I would play a game with him shortly and that seemed to please him.

I leaned against the side wall, smiling. Denise took a seat on the edge of her desk. She looked thoughtfully at me, and I knew she had something to discuss.

"Kim, you've been coming here for a while now, and I know Keydell really likes you," Denise began. "He loves your dog Edo, too, and has fun playing with Henry."

"I really like Keydell, too. He's such a cutie."

"Well," said Denise, "I thought you'd like to know that he's up for adoption."

"Oh, really?" I said, dragging the question out. "I bet *you're* thinking of adopting him aren't you? I see how much he loves you, and you him."

It did happen sometimes that staff would bond with certain kids and end up adopting them. I could never work at an animal shelter because of that. I would be that crazy cat lady in no time.

"Oh, I wish I could," said Denise, shaking her head no. "But I'm barely getting by myself. I can't take care of a child."

I was suddenly very grateful not to be raising my children as a single mother.

"There's a man in New York City who is looking at Keydell," she continued. "He's a single dad, African-American, who has one adopted son already and is looking for a brother for him. My concern is that if Keydell has to move out of Rhode Island, he might not do very well. He needs a home that makes him feel stable; that allows him to stay at his school and with his friends."

"But what about his mom?" I asked. "She's going to live with her baby, right?"

"Yes, and her two other children, but she can't keep him, either."

"Wait, I don't get it. Is his mom giving him up, or has the state decided he can't go back? Why can't he live with her?"

"She's been asked if she's ready to take him back, because he's been here almost two years. She said she wasn't, so he is being placed for adoption," replied Denise.

"So she's keeping all the other kids but not Keydell?" I asked in amazement, hearing the judgment in my voice. "I don't get it. What about a foster home until she feels ready?"

"He already did that before he came here. He got kicked out for hurting the family's young daughter and kicking their cat."

"Oh, that's not good. I hope the New York guy can handle him. I'm going to miss him, though."

"Well, the thing is, the guy started the process, but then his mom got sick and he had to put it on hold," Denise explained. "When I heard that, I thought of you and your family, and wondered if you might consider adopting him?"

I stared at Denise, trying to take in what she had just said. The weight of her question took me off guard. The room went still; my body felt numb, and my mind was racing. I was looking at the kitten behind the glass, staring at me with those big kitten eyes, asking me to take him home. I was melting.

Did I already know the answer?

I reached for the chair behind me and sat down. The room suddenly felt even smaller, and every sound was crystal clear. Denise watched me without saying a word.

"Wow." I breathed. "I've never thought of adopting a child, Denise. This is big. My children are almost fourteen and seventeen. They're easy now. I have some freedom to do things like come here to volunteer, and Henry will be going to college in two years. Keydell is only in second grade!"

"I know," said Denise, "but just think about it. You have the perfect setup for this. You are happily married, have a farmhouse with five acres of land, and the dog. Keydell would have a brother and sister. He could stay at his school, too."

"God, Denise, you are killing me. You know what a sap I am about kids. You sure know how to do your job."

"Well, talk to Jim and the kids and see what they think."

I walked out of the office, still feeling numb, like everything else was but a cloud around me. My heart was open and beating fast. I looked over at Keydell, now happily playing his video game, and thought, "Can I do this?"

Keydell, focused on his video game, barely noticed me coming out of the office. For him, that game was what existed in his life right then and there. He was perfectly focused.

I, on the other hand, was feeling all my emotions at once, and I saw him in all his innocence. My thoughts had shifted around who he was. He was no longer just some boy, but one who might be my son one day. Funny how quickly our minds can do that.

Could I be his mom? Did he even want to have me as his mother? Denise had warned me not to say anything to him because DCYF liked to sort things out before they let kids know where they might be going. He knew he was up for adoption, but he knew nothing of the New York man, or of the possibility of me and my family swooping him up and making him a bigger part of our lives.

I sat down next to him and grabbed the other game controller. Its buttons and control stick were as foreign to me as something out of Star Trek. Neither of us knew, as he proceeded to beat me at every round, that both of our lives were about to change in a big way.

"When we are motivated by compassion and wisdom, the results of our actions benefit everyone, not just our individual selves or some immediate convenience. When we are able to recognize and forgive ignorant actions of the past, we gain strength to constructively solve the problems of the present."

— Dalai Lama XIV

CHAPTER 3

A DECISION

*"It's not a terrible thing that we feel fear when faced with
the unknown. It is part of being alive, something
we all share. Fear is a natural reaction to moving
closer to the truth."*

—Pema Chodron

September 2008

The bluestone gravel crunched under my tires as I pulled into
my driveway after the short drive home from Trout. Denise's
whopper of a question was weighing on my mind. Did I want to
adopt Keydell? Would Jim want to adopt him? When Ella reached
the age of five, and we knew that we didn't want any more children,
we agreed that Jim would get "neutered." So, clearly, we were done
having kids. Weren't we?

As I opened the back door of our 160-year-old farmhouse, I
thought, "What are a few more years?"

Jim was in the kitchen cooking, like he often does, wearing his manly apron with blue and white pin stripes. His broad shoulders and graceful hands were sexy as he moved the spatula in the pan.

I hugged him from the back as he faced the stove, and I said in my best sing-song voice, "I have something to tell you."

Because he was turned from me, I didn't have to look him in the eye with my news and tell him what Denise had just proposed. I was nervous.

"First, how was your day?" I began, trying to get a sense of his mood.

"Good," he said, the typical answer. "What's up?"

"Well," I began, dragging it out with a touch of drama. "You know I've been visiting the group home for a while and have bonded with some of the boys and Henry and Ella and Edo have been coming ...?"

"Mm-hmmm," Jim said as he turned the stove top off and looked at me, knowing more was to come.

"Well, apparently Keydell, the youngest boy there, is up for adoption."

Jim's face didn't change, so I continued.

"Denise sat me down today and asked if *we* would consider adopting him," I said with squinted eyes, waiting for his response.

"What did you say?"

"I told her I had to talk to you about it."

"Well, let me meet him," Jim said. Just like that, no hesitation. I have always loved him for his open heart.

"Really?" I said smiling from ear to ear. "You would be up for this? Because honestly, her request threw me for a loop."

On the one hand, his response scared me because I thought adopting Keydell could actually happen and his acceptance put us one step closer. I mean, this was a *big deal*. Once I set my mind on something like this, I knew I would not back out. How could I?

This was a young boy's life we were talking about, a life that was already fragile from the trauma of moving from family to family, house to house.

But … If Jim was on board, we could do this; I knew we could.

He answered, "Yeah, why not? One thing you and I have done very well in this life is raise two great kids. Why not throw another one in the mix, especially one who needs parents?"

I stared into his beautiful blue eyes and pulled him in for a hug.

"Really?" I said again, holding back tears, "You would consider doing this?"

"Sure," he said, "I've thought about adopting a child before."

"You have? I didn't know that."

This was no surprise, really. Jim kept a lot of thoughts to himself. He was sharing in this moment though, and I was grateful. He had my full attention.

Jim passively pushed out of our hug and turned back to the stove. "You know my Mom was adopted, and she fostered a lot of babies when I was younger, too. So, yeah, I've been thinking about it."

His mother Jean found out she was adopted at the age of sixty-two, when she went to apply for Social Security. It shocked Jim's entire family, especially his oldest sister, who had just finished an extensive genealogy that was now invalid. I think that in some ways Jim and his siblings, after hearing this news, began to question their own identities and connection to that side of the family—and to the cousins, aunts, and uncles whom, they now realized, were not blood relatives. It was a startling discovery, but in the end, Jim decided that he wanted to feel connected to family, no matter who that family was made up of. Hopefully, Keydell would feel the same.

"What's Keydell like?" Jim continued. "I should meet him before we decide and, of course, we have to talk to Henry and Ella."

Jim turned, and put his arms around my waist again. "You are a nut, you know that, right? Leave it to you to go volunteer and want to bring a kid home. You're being a good *bodhisattva*."

"Yes, I suppose I am," I admitted, and gave him a sweet kiss to say thank you.

The next day we went over to meet Keydell together. I wasn't excited or anything. Jim had done all of his background checks when he was a Boy Scout leader for Henry's troop years before, so he was clear to visit. Jim made a delicious pan of shepherd's pie for the boys and we brought it over for dinner.

We walked into the house, and I introduced the staff and some of the boys to Jim. We all laughed when the boys teased us in unison, "Ooooohhhh, Kim has a *husband*. La de *dah*."

Jim's introduction to Keydell was brief and impersonal because Keydell was busy with homework, but Jim thought he was articulate, and saw that same sparkle in his eyes that I had noticed when I first met him. He made Jim happy at dinner though by devouring every bite of his shepherd's pie, and continually asking for more.

Denise came upstairs to see us, and she and Jim instantly connected. She reached out for a big hug like she knew him well.

"Kim's told me a lot about you," she said. "Thanks for sharing her with us."

After dinner, she invited us downstairs to talk. As I followed her down the steps to the basement office, I knew this was it. This was the beginning of the process, and I was all in. I was frightened—but I had Jim, my partner in crime, with me, so I knew it would be fine.

We could do this, couldn't we?

We sat down in Denise's now-crowded office, and shut the door. The air was still in that basement room, but I was stirring with emotion. I sat on the edge of my chair to start the conversation.

"So, Denise," I said, as she looked at me with anticipation, "if we decide to adopt Keydell, what happens next? What is the process?"

I wondered if we would have nine months to process, like we had with my two pregnancies.

"Well, first off, I am so glad you are considering it," she began. "Very exciting. First, we will have to talk with DCYF to let them know you are interested, and then get the go-ahead to start some visits with Keydell outside the group home. You can take him for ice cream or pizza, and just get to know each other better. You can all keep visiting here, too, Kim, but the home visits are a good way for your family to see how it might feel to have Keydell in *your* lives."

"Yeah, that makes sense," I said. "Jim and I will keep talking about this—and, of course, talk with our kids. When we decide for certain, I'll let you know."

"Are we the only family looking to adopt Keydell right now?" Jim asked. "Kim mentioned something about a guy in New York?"

"He is still considering adopting, but he's on the fence, so let me know soon what you guys decide."

"Oh, I thought his mom was sick so he was backing out," I said in surprise.

"I thought so, too, but DCYF likes to find placements when they can, so they've been working on him," Denise said. "I'll keep you posted."

I was getting competitive with this guy, and I didn't even know him. Didn't he know that Keydell was mine? I had set my mind to doing this, and now Mr. New York was throwing a curve ball at me. There was that quick shift in perception again.

When Denise first mentioned the guy, I thought it was great of him to want another child. Now, I hoped he wouldn't want to follow through. I had to be careful not to get too attached to my belief that we would have Keydell in our lives, just in case it didn't happen. The Buddha taught that all things are impermanent, including our thoughts and beliefs, so we shouldn't get too attached to them. We can hang on to things—but not too tightly, or we will feel great suffering when they inevitably change.

In that moment, I decided to silently pray that Keydell would have a loving home, whether it was with Mr. New York, or with us.

"Okay, thanks Denise," I said, reining in my drifting thoughts. "We will talk to the kids tonight and get back to you. I hope you realize you've been a catalyst for great change in our lives." I stood up and walked around the desk to give her a big hug.

"You're the best," she said.

Jim and I collected the empty shepherd's pie pan said goodbye to the boys (with a little extra goodbye for Keydell) and left for home.

"You ready to talk to the kids, Jim?" I asked after a few contemplative minutes in the car.

"Sure," he said. I waited for more.

"Sure?" I said.

"Sure."

⇒⊢⊣⇐

Our current home life was smooth. In the mornings, after the kids left for school, I meditated, while Jim headed to the pool for an early swim. Sporting events and my visits to the group home filled the afternoons. Henry and Ella were independent enough that I was able to take evening photo shoots without getting a sitter. I basically had more freedom from my mothering duties. We had a good rhythm going, and we were happy.

Raising Henry and Ella had been a breeze in the grand scheme of things. Their easygoing behavior made bringing them to galleries, parks, and even my photo shoots, occasionally, easy and fun. Jim and I took them camping, went hiking in Maine and the Grand Canyon, and they even enjoyed long sits by the ocean.

Yes, I was grateful for our peaceful home life—but, as I had learned; all things are impermanent. Now, we were going to ask Henry and Ella to change things up by bringing in a third child.

We could come up with lots of reasons we shouldn't adopt Keydell—like, "The economy is tanking," or "Our two kids are almost adults"—but Jim and I decided that our reasons were not as important as the good we might do for this young boy and our family. We could help him, and he could become another cool kid in our house. Win, win.

We called the kids down from their homework chambers (their bedrooms), saying that we needed to talk about something.

"Be right there," they yelled. A few minutes later, they came bounding down the stairs into the kitchen. We gathered around our wooden farm table, and Jim and I took a deep breath.

"You want to start. Jim?" I asked, hoping he would say yes. I always started.

"Okay, guys," Jim said folding his hands on the table. "If there's one thing your mom and I did really well, it was raise you two, so what do you think about bringing Keydell from the group home into our family?"

The question lingered out there for a few moments. Henry stared up toward the sky, like he usually did when he was thinking, and Ella wiggled with excitement.

Then, with all of her teen wisdom, she said, "You mean, adopt him? We'd be like Angelina Jolie and Brad Pitt!" She loved pop culture and seemed to think it would be a pretty cool thing to do. I nodded yes, grinning at her excitement.

Henry said, "Keydell's an awesome kid. He's super athletic, so I think he will fit in great with us. Let's do it."

And there it was. We would be five, as long as everything worked out.

"You guys are going to be old when he graduates high school!" Ella said with a sheepish grin.

"Thanks for pointing that out," I said dryly.

I think they both appreciated the life they had and thought it would be fun to have a little brother. "This is not like bringing an animal into the house, guys. If we do this, it's forever and he will require all of our attention," I explained. "I know none of us really knows how it'll be, but are you sure you're okay with this? I want you both to know that we love you and are so proud of you. We wouldn't ask this if we didn't think you were in good places yourselves."

"I just don't want to be like my friend Carla, Mom," said Ella. "She has to babysit her little brother and sister all the time. She misses things, and I don't think I can do that."

"I understand," I assured her. "There may be times when I need a little help, but I won't let it interfere with what you guys have going on. I would always ask and make sure you are willing."

I understood Ella's request. She was a busy high schooler, and had already done plenty of babysitting; it would not be fair to expect her to watch Keydell all the time. It did get me thinking about my work schedule again, however. I'd have to go back to juggling babysitters or after-school care. Jim's job had allowed him to work from home sometimes, so we've always managed somehow, and he assured me we would manage again. We could only act in each moment, and figure it out as we went.

We were decided: we could do it. We could ride blind together into this uncharted territory.

"Would you guys have wanted to do this if Keydell were a baby?" Ella asked.

"No," I said emphatically. "I don't have the energy for another baby, but I think I can handle a 7-year-old."

Boy, was I in for a surprise.

Over the weekend, we all sat with our decision. I wanted to give it a few days before I told Denise. In the back of my mind, I thought the universe would really be settling this for us anyway. Maybe

Mr. New York would want Keydell in the end, and that would be that. I was nervous about our decision, but also excited.

The following week, I went in early one morning to see Denise.

"Hey, can I talk to you?" I asked.

Denise was out in the yard, having just put all the kids on the bus for school. We went into the house and down to her office.

"How did it go this weekend with your family?" she asked me.

I smiled and said, "We asked the kids what they thought about having Keydell in our family."

"And?"

"We are in. We would love to adopt Keydell!" I opened my arms wide.

Denise was so happy as she came around the desk to receive my hug. She gently pulled away, and looked me right in the eye.

"I am so psyched, Kim, because I just got news that the New York guy has decided he cannot adopt again right now," Denise confided. "He's going to wait a year or so, until his life settles a bit."

"Oh, my God, that is so great," I exclaimed. "I mean, I hope things are okay with his mother and all, but that is great. That is so great."

"You are going to change Keydell's life," she said.

All I could think about was how much our lives would change, too—and hopefully in a good way, for all of us. I trusted that life was putting in front of me just what I needed, and I had to trust my heart.

"I will contact Matt, Keydell's DCYF case worker," said Denise, "and let him know you have decided."

Every child who comes through the foster care system, or the group home, has a "Matt" in their lives. Case workers are the ones who help place a child when he or she is removed from their home, and continue to check on them every week to make sure they are safe. They act as a go-between with birth parents and caregivers. It's a tough job, filled with emotional dealings.

"Can I tell Keydell? I asked. "I feel like I should spend more time with him when I visit. Or will that give away the fact that we want to adopt him?"

"You can't tell him yet, but it's fine to spend as much time as you want with him," said Denise. "I'll let the staff know to let you do that, and will work on getting some visits approved outside of Trout."

My head started whirling with ideas. It had been a while since we'd had a little guy around, and I was looking forward to doing some of the things I used to do with Henry and Ella, like ride bikes, or walk to the small airport at the end of our street to watch the planes take off and land. We could walk to Frosty Freeze, the infamous local ice cream shop, which was about a half a mile from our house. I knew he would like that.

"You and Jim are going to have to take adoption classes at DCYF, too," said Denise. "It's a six-week course, once a week, and it will go over all the things you need to know about adoption. There's a lot of paperwork to go over, too, but we'll get to that."

"Do you think I can get a little more background on him now that we're at this stage?" I asked.

"Sure," said Denise. "I'll let you talk with Michele, the house counselor. I'll buzz her that you'll be coming over."

Denise sent me over to Michelle's office, which was across the basement hallway next to the steamy, dimly lit laundry room. My heart felt like the old dryer that was bumping around with sneakers in it. I had just committed to adopting a child—and now I was wondering what the hell I had just done. Would Keydell's past make a difference in our decision? I had the distinct feeling I was headed for a wild ride.

Michelle told me some things I already knew about Keydell, like how angry he could get. She also told me that he once inappropriately grabbed down her shirt during one of her counseling sessions with him. I remembered Denise explaining why the hugging rules were in place, telling me that some of the boys who asked for hugs would start rubbing on you or squeezing too hard. The staff had to be careful who they hugged, and who hugged them. The boys were definitely not allowed to touch each other; between the physical abuse done to some, and the inappropriateness of others, it was just too risky. Was Keydell experimenting with what was appropriate? Was inappropriate grabbing something he had seen before and was re-enacting?

She clarified that Keydell had been living with his great aunt just before coming to Trout, and that he had been difficult for her to manage. After her own health issues worsened, she asked his birth mom to take him back while she got medical attention, but birth mom said she couldn't do it, and so he was placed in the system. Keydell, who'd believed that his siblings' father was also his father since he'd spent so much time with him, was very confused when he couldn't go live with him or his birth mom—especially since his brother and sister still lived with them.

I was confused as well. It was a no wonder Keydell was angry.

"What about his birth father?" I asked.

"Unknown," Michele replied. "Birth Mom apparently had a few boyfriends at the time Keydell was conceived, so whoever he is, we can't contact him to see if he would care for Keydell. We're pretty sure Mom didn't really want the pregnancy from the beginning, so she was disconnected emotionally from Keydell even before he was born."

"So does she have drug or alcohol issues?" I asked. "Is she battling depression or some other mental issue? I mean what's her situation?"

"I can't really give you too much more about Mom right now, but it's all in his folder for you later," said Michele.

"Okay, I get it. Thanks for what you have given me."

Keydell needed a steady home life, so maybe this was the best thing for his birth mom to do. I knew she loved him on some level, because she still visited him every week. Maybe her love was what made her put him up for adoption.

Michele closed with, "I don't want to freak you out with too much information, but I think it's important to understand what you are getting into," she said gently.

I thought I was getting a chance to do something good, a chance to learn and grow together—a chance to develop a relationship with a child who needed to be loved just like I and my kids needed to be loved. Even this new knowledge of Keydell's anger issues and inappropriate behaviors did not close my heart down; if anything, it expanded in that moment.

I stood up, thanked Michelle again and left the group home. The wheels had been set in motion for our wild ride. I didn't know how this would be for us—but, hey, I didn't know what I was having for dinner that night. Life is like that. We don't know what the next moment will bring. We just have to take it one bite at a time.

CHAPTER 4

MOM

"We don't set out to save the world; we set out to wonder how other people are doing and to reflect on how our actions affect other people's hearts."

—*Pema Chodron*

My visit to the group home that week fell on awards night. The boys had been back to school for a month or so, and it was time to reward them for good school and home behaviors. Now that I knew we were going to adopt Keydell, I couldn't stay away.

Before the awards began, the boys sat the proper distance apart on the couch, waiting impatiently. Keydell, who'd been reading, had a book in his lap, so I sat next to him to check it out. It was a great opportunity to do more bonding.

"Want to hear me read?" Keydell asked, looking up at me with hopeful doe-like eyes. His full, perfectly shaped lips smiled, revealing his chicklet-sized baby teeth and a gap in front where one was missing.

"Definitely," I said, scooching in as close as I thought I could get away with.

"The dog and boy played in the yard," Keydell read. "The boy threw the ball for the dog."

"Awesome," I said, trying to make eye contact. "Oh, it looks like we're getting started with the awards. Let's take a break."

We turned our attention to Denise, who proceeded to hand out the awards. "Michael: best bedtime behavior this week. Good job buddy," she began. The boys clapped for one another. They were each other's family while they lived here.

"Seth, you have done all your chores without being asked, so you get the award for best chore guy."

Keydell was awarded best overall behavior. He leaped up from beside me to collect his finely crafted construction paper award and proudly bounced back down next to me. I could see by the looks on the boy's faces that this awards night boosted their self-esteem. Denise wrapped up the ceremony, and the boys were set free to play before dinner.

Keydell looked up at me again. "Want to hear me read still?" he asked in his deep raspy voice.

"Of course I do. You're great at it."

He was having a hard time sitting still. After reading only a page, he jerked his head up toward me and blurted out, "I might not be here much longer. I'm getting adopted."

"Really?" I said, "That's wonderful!"

Inside, I was all in knots. I wanted to blurt right back and say, "It's me, it's me! I'm adopting you!" I wanted to pick him up in my arms and hug him and swing him around.

Then Keydell shocked me out of my thoughts by abruptly asking, "Will *you* adopt me?"

His face was locked in a giant, hopeful smile, which looked as if he had been practicing. What a charmer this kid was. Had someone said something to him? Did he think of this question on his own, or was he so desperate for a new home that he was going to ask the first person he saw?

"I don't know. Would you like that?" I didn't know what else to do. My desire to say yes was hard to hide.

Keydell replied, "I love your dog and I would have a brother and a sister."

I couldn't speak. I had a lump in my throat. I was so happy that this was a two-way street.

"Well, wherever you end up, Keydell, I am sure the family will love you so much. You are a very special boy."

That seemed to satisfy him for the moment. He went back to reading his book. I sat with him until it was time to leave, but I didn't hear another word he said. I was in love.

As we waited for clearance to do outings with Keydell, I continued to visit him at the group home. I noticed that his mom and siblings were still coming by as well. It was awkward: we were adopting Keydell, but she didn't know who I was. The most heart-wrenching day for me, however, was when Keydell's mom brought over her new baby. I watched them from afar as they sat on the couch together and Mom held her new baby girl with pride. As Keydell touched her tiny fingers and looked at her lovingly, I wondered what he was thinking about. He knew he was getting adopted—but did he really know what that meant? Did he think he would live with his mother again someday? I mean, she had the baby so of course she would take him back, right?

Keydell and she didn't touch much, and I barely heard them say two words to each other— but I was not really in earshot, so who knows? I watched them as long as I could stand it.

I didn't understand why she still had the right to visit him. Was she expecting an open adoption? Would she have a choice in the matter, or would it be up to us? Did she even know that a family had been found for him?

Many of my questions were answered by Angela, the support person for Keydell from Adoption Rhode Island. I met her in October, about a week after I told Denise our intentions, and she quickly became one of my favorite people.

Angela's job was to help us navigate Keydell's move out of the group home and into ours. Where Matt from DCYF was the nuts and bolts of the operation, Angela was the warm and fuzzy. She made an appointment with us at Trout Drive to talk about her role in his adoption, so Jim and I went over to meet her.

I started right in. "So, Angela, are you the person who can tell us what will happen with Keydell's relationship with his mom when we adopt him? I have so many questions about that."

"Yes, I guess I am," she replied. "I've been in touch with her through the process of termination."

That sounded so brutal. A *termination.*

"Do you think we should meet Keydell's mom soon? Do you think she'll want to stay in touch after we adopt him?" I asked.

"Well, she's hard to reach. She doesn't always answer my calls." Angela replied. "Would you consider an open adoption?"

"Yes, I think we would, as long as Keydell is okay with it. Right, Jim?" He nodded his head yes.

I continued, "As long as she's a fairly stable woman then we would definitely consider it."

Angela agreed. "I will keep you updated as things go along, but I want you to know that you will always have the final say in this. It's your choice. You will be his parents and you can do what you think is best for him."

"Since we know we want to adopt him, what is the foster period all about? Can't we go straight to adoption?"

"You will want to foster first, trust me." said Angela, "We call those first few weeks together the 'honeymoon period.' Everything usually goes well for about six weeks or so, and everyone is happy. Then, sometimes, things start to go really badly. The parents and child are not always a good fit, and the child gets put back into the system."

How awful, I thought. I couldn't imagine us giving Keydell back. We were in it for the long haul. "We won't be giving him back Angela. We couldn't." Jim nodded his head in total agreement.

"Well, either way, that is the process," she said. "You have to foster for a few months before you can make the adoption official."

"Okay. In the meantime, when can we start outside visits with Keydell? I thought Matt was going to let us know, but we haven't heard from him. I feel like those visits will give us some indication as to whether we 'fit' or not."

I could hear the sarcasm in my voice. I didn't like that word, "fit." I wasn't trying on a new kid like I would a new jacket. This was a human being we were talking about.

"I spoke with Matt the other day," said Angela. "He said you guys can do visits now if you like, but you can't tell Keydell you're adopting him, just in case something goes wrong. We want to protect him from that disappointment. I will be with you more toward the transition from here to your home, but in the meantime, I will try to keep in touch with his birth mom."

Birth mom. Birth mom. I said it in my head a couple of times. I would just be Mom. *Just* Mom. I suppose any woman can birth a child, but not all can be called *just* moms. Same goes for the dads. I wanted to be Keydell's mom. Birth or not, I wanted to care for him the way I cared for Henry and Ella.

We said our goodbyes to Angela. Jim and I sat looking at each other, thinking the same thing. Oh, nothing will go wrong, we're great parents and we've got this. We will just get through these classes, do the fostering and give this boy a nice home. Everything will be hunky dory.

These thoughts overrode our fears, at least for the time being.

⊰ ⊱

I was excited to pick up Keydell for our first scheduled home visit. I came alone to get him, but we were all going to go for pizza after sports practices and work. I was happy to have some quiet time with him before that.

It was the beginning of November, 2007, and Keydell would be seven years old in a few weeks. I had known him for a year and three months now, but felt I didn't really *know* him. I knew he was athletic, and that he loved video games and ice cream—but I was interested in his dreams and fears, his sleeping habits, whether he liked a bath or a shower, things like that. The kinds of things you learn about someone when you live with them.

When I arrived at Trout, Keydell was abnormally quiet, but hopped in my back seat and buckled up without hesitation. He was so little that I could only see the top of his head in my rear view mirror. I wanted so badly to tell him that everything was going to be okay. I wasn't sure if leaving the group home felt liberating and fun, or scary as hell. I was guessing a little bit of both.

Keydell looked out the window as we drove. I tried to break the ice with some questions. "What did you do in school today?"

"Not much," he answered.

"What's your favorite subject?" I asked.

Oh, so dumb, Kim. He's only in first grade. Don't you have a better question than that? I was so nervous. I don't know why. I wanted him to like me. It was just crazy that now he was coming over to see my home life.

He said he liked recess and math.

"How are you doing on your video game?" I asked, with better results. It opened the floodgates of conversation. Keydell started talking all about his game, what level he had gotten to and used terminology I had no clue about. Henry and Ella grew up just before gaming became popular, so I didn't know much about the systems or what any of the games were called. (There was a play box and an X station or something like that.)

It was okay by me. I just wanted to hear him talk. I was so into him, and wanted him to have a good time without worrying about strict rules. In our home, you didn't have to ask to go through a door.

"What do you want to do at my house?" I asked. I wanted to say "at home," but couldn't yet.

"Will Edo be there?" I could see his head lift a little higher in my mirror.

"Yes, we can take him for a walk if you want to. He's going to be very excited to see you, ya know."

We pulled up to our farmhouse, passing through the old stone wall opening, and I could see Keydell's eyes light up.

"Is this where you live?" he asked.

"Yep, this is home," I said. Oops, I'd said "home."

"Cool." He jumped out of the car as soon as it stopped and started exploring.

We walked around the yard and I gave him the ten-cent tour. Our tiny 1,500-square-foot house sits on five acres of land that was once a gentleman's farm. We have three outbuildings, one of them a barn that I use for my photography studio and our offices. We're very lucky to have found this property; there aren't too many houses with land like this in Middletown any more. I was excited to show it off to Keydell.

Keydell and I grabbed the dog from the house and walked around the back field. I could see he was happy, and that made me happy. We put Edo on his leash, and decided to walk down the street to the airport. Keydell was so small, but determined to walk Edo by himself. He almost got pulled off his feet.

"Here, I can help you, buddy."

"I've got it," he said, and tied the leash around his waist so Edo couldn't pull the leash from his hands.

"That's pretty smart, Keydell. Great idea."

I held my hand at my side to see if Keydell might take it. He slipped his small, brown, youthful hand into my contrasting white-adult one.

As different as we looked, we were the same in that moment. We both needed that connection. I gripped him lightly as we walked, talking about everything and nothing.

CHAPTER 5
DORITOS

"In the beginner's mind there are many possibilities, but in the expert's there are few."

—Shunryu Suzuki, Zen Mind, Beginner's Mind: Informal Talks on Zen Meditation and Practice

"Oh, God, Jim. It's Tuesday again. These freakin' DCYF classes are going to kill me," I whined.

Those classes were like a scary scene in a movie that I couldn't unsee. We learned, in graphic detail, what happens to some children—and frankly, it made us sick.

Arriving at the first foster/adoption class together, Jim and I wondered why we even had to be there. We knew how to raise children! Wasn't this just for new parents-to-be? I was all puffed up, having parented two amazing children already—but after a few classes, we realized there was so much we didn't know about the issues that children in the foster care system had. We were overwhelmed by what we heard, and my ego deflated quickly.

We had to walk through the dingy DCYF offices to get to the classroom space. Most of the lights were out over the rows and rows of cubicles, but a few glowed from behind their walls where a desk lamp that had been left on. There was an air of hopelessness in the building. I couldn't see any personal items on the walls, or flowers on the desks; I sensed it was not a great working environment. The job of the workers here was to help people live better lives, but their office environment felt dead. Honestly, I felt like I did when I saw the group homes for the first time: I wanted to perk up the place with some fresh paint and a happy mural.

We signed our names in the roll-call book at the front of the classroom, and each took a bag of Doritos from the snack table before we sat down. Those stinking, orange-finger-causing bags of chips became the highlight of our Tuesday nights; that's how bad the classes were. The green glow of the florescent lights gave me a headache after about two minutes. What a place.

Jim and I found seats at one of the two big tables at the back of the long room, and started cracking jokes to lighten our mood. (We really should not take classes together or at least be allowed to sit near each other. I mean, we were almost kicked out of Lamaze class for laughing too much during the breathing exercises. Jim could not stay focused, and his breaths are so shallow compared to my long, deep ones that we just couldn't get in sync. All the other "serious" couples glared at us.)

After a few introductions, we were asked to fill out paperwork that would help DCYF match us with a child. It was like Match.com for adoption. I think we were the only ones who already knew who we were adopting, and I was really grateful for that. I had not thought much about the "type" of child I would want if we hadn't known Keydell. I didn't get to pick Henry or Ella so it seemed funny to have a choice in the matter. The questionnaire asked if we wanted a boy or girl, what ages we were willing to take and if we were interested in siblings. Somehow I felt that, no matter how someone answered these questions, the right child would come—that everything would be just as it should, even if the adoption itself didn't work out. The intention to take in any child was what felt important. I instantly felt respect for the other people in the class. Adopting or fostering a child is a brave thing to choose to do. In my case, it chose me.

Then, the instructors gave us The Binder.

The Binder became the butt of many jokes between Jim and me; the thing was *so* big.

"Did you put the seat belt on The Binder?" We would joke as we drove to the class. "Did you feed The Binder tonight?"

This three-inch book was filled with "resources" and forms to be completed with questions about our childhoods, how we were raised, how we were disciplined, and our thoughts on whether we would act the same way with our child. There were personal questions about our physical and mental health, and about our backgrounds (criminal or otherwise).

I don't think Jim or I had ever investigated our lives so thoroughly. I learned a lot more about Jim's childhood than I had ever known before. For example, Jim got backhanded and smacked around by his father, who favored his sisters.

My parents never hit us. If anything, we were told to go to our rooms, pull our pants down, and wait for a spanking that Dad never actually came to give us. The waiting was the actual punishment. We three girls were mainly talked to when we did something wrong. I remember listening to the words coming from my father's moving lips, nodding my head, acknowledging the punishment or words of advice, and moving on. My sister and he, on the other hand, would talk for hours, which drove me crazy. I just wanted the lectures to be over—but, according to my sisters, I was the perfect child, so I guess I tended to keep my behaviors on the down-low. Jim, not so much; he was a rascal.

That first week of class was all paperwork, information about fostering versus adoption, and questions about ourselves. The classes that followed got tougher. The two instructors began to tell us about the children who were in the foster care system, and why. Some were there because their young mothers couldn't take care of them, or because the parents had mental illnesses that prevented them from caring for their child. Those stories I understood. The other stories—the ones about children who had been beaten, abandoned, neglected, or sexually abused—were harder to take. I felt sick listening to these stories, and chewed away on my Doritos for comfort.

We dreaded going to class each week, knowing we would have to hear more. I mean I wasn't so naive that I didn't know some of this went on, but my heart just wept for these children. How could adults do these kinds of things to kids?

So many people don't know what to do once their child is born. "Where's the handbook for this baby?" they wonder. I always thought there should be parenting classes for everyone in high school, before couples started having children. Anyone can have a baby in this country without training or a license—but here we were, experienced parents, having to go through six weeks of training to be able to have a child. Something didn't make sense here.

These helpless kids in the foster care system had been through tons of trauma—and, I suspected, so had their parents. It was a vicious cycle of abuse leading to more abuse, neglect bringing more neglect. Maybe, by adopting Keydell, we could stop one cycle, but I wasn't sure which one since I didn't fully understand what his past traumas had been.

The instructors prepared us by explaining some of the behaviors to expect from our adopted or foster children next. Hording food, lying, tantrums, stealing, and perhaps some violence could be expected; such behaviors were reactions to the trauma they had been through. It was so disturbing; all of it. I blocked a lot of it out, crunching on my chips.

I found it odd that there were no lessons at any point in these six weeks of classes about how to parent a child who was violent or destructive. I guess we just had to wing it.

At the time of these classes, I had not heard or seen Keydell behaving in any of the above ways—at least, not to the extremes the instructors mentioned. But, then again, I only saw him once a week for an hour or two. I guess that's what the pre-adoptive fostering phase would be about, to see how Keydell would behave in our home.

At the end of the six weeks, I let out a big sigh of relief. I was ready to move on to the good stuff, like visiting more with Keydell and ultimately having him stay with us. We were feeling sad and concerned for all the kids out there who needed homes, yet encouraged by the other class members and future parents who were willing to take a child in. Our classmates who consisted of gays and lesbians, single future parents, blacks, whites, and Hispanics, all of whom were there to do one thing: love a child. If there is love from a parent, there is a family, no matter what that family looks like from the outside.

Hopefully Jim, Henry, Ella and I could be that family for Keydell. I knew we cared and had plenty of love—but after all we heard in the past six weeks, we had to be strong, too. Keydell needed us, and he was going to show us what we were made of. I knew that meeting Keydell was no accident. With or without AdoptionMatch.com, we were destined to find each other.

CHAPTER 6
TESTING

*"You can discover more about a person in an hour of play
than in a year of conversation."*

—Plato

One Saturday morning, I stopped by to play with Keydell. He had been to our house a few times now and, I think, was beginning to realize something was up. We were almost done with all our adoption paperwork, and were waiting for a home inspection to check all of our fire alarms and make sure we hadn't ripped our mattress tags off. (Yes, it was that detailed and silly, especially since we had lived there safely for so long with two other children. I got it, though; it was part of the deal if we wanted Keydell to be able to sleep over.)

The staff at Trout knew we were in the process of adopting, so I was given a lot more leeway around playing with Keydell one-on-one. We ended up playing a game of hide and seek in his room one day. There wasn't anywhere for Keydell to hide, really, except under his covers or in the closet, but for a seven-year-old the fun was in *thinking* he was hidden, and waiting to be found. The anticipation made Keydell scream before I "found" him anyway, so it was quite entertaining. I hadn't seen this happy, playful side of him before.

I thought that, somehow, he knew we were adopting him. He is a smart boy, and it was kind of obvious because of all the time we were spending with him, but for the boys at the group home, uncertainty was a constant. Whatever the reason, though, his energy was sky high, like he'd downed a Red Bull before we started playing.

"Okay, you go hide, Keydell, and I'll find you," I said.

"Count to twenty, okay?" He twirled away from me as I covered my eyes, and I heard him climbing up the bunk bed ladder.

"One, two, three …"

When I got to twenty, I waited quietly for about three seconds. I could see the bump of his body on the top bunk. He was lying just under the covers, against the wall. I pretended not to see him. I looked in the closet and got down on my knees to look under the bed. He couldn't stand it and screamed with excitement and jumped from the top bunk to the floor.

"Whoa, Keydell, careful," I told him. "That's a pretty high jump you just made. Maybe use the ladder next time."

At this point, I was still on my hands and knees and he was facing me. Suddenly, he jumped over my head and on to my back with his head toward my rear end. What happened next really took me by surprise. He stuck his hand down the back of my pants.

"Hey!" I said firmly, as I pulled him off of me. "No, Keydell, that is *not* okay. You startled me, and that is not appropriate play."

I sat back on my heels to look him in the eyes, so he would know I was serious. He jammed his hand down the front of my shirt this time.

"Keydell," I snapped. "That is not okay either. If you want to touch someone, you're supposed to ask—and it's for a hug, not to touch them somewhere private."

I wasn't sure what to say because I didn't even know if he knew what "private areas" were. Was that something they talked about at the home? It must have been; he had done this to Michelle, and I'm sure she went over it with him when it happened. It was funny, though, because he was grabbing in such an excited kind of way that I felt he was testing me to see what I would do. I had to be careful with my responses.

"Keydell, I want to play hide and seek with you, but if you keep grabbing me like that I'm not going to. You are a smart boy, and I know that you know better."

He dashed away from me and said, "Count again, count again," like nothing had happened.

"Okay, but remember what I said," I cautioned.

We played one more round where I found him in his closet. He screamed so loudly that Rob, the counselor, came in to see what was up. Keydell began to throw all the toys out of his closet in a panic, saying he had no good hiding spots. I could tell he was getting upset. He'd been caught by the staff.

Rob said, "Hey, Keydell, let's quiet down in here and maybe give Kim a break."

I said, "I have to get going anyway, Keydell, so can I have a hug goodbye?" I wanted to give him an opportunity to touch appropriately.

He snapped back, "No!" and hid in his closet.

"Okay," I said, "I guess I will see you another time then. I had a good time playing hide and seek with you."

He dashed out and tried to pull my pants down just as I was walking out the door. It totally took me by surprise, but Rob yelled, "Hey, cut it out!" and told him to go sit in the time-out chair.

"It's okay, Rob, I think I got him a bit wound up with the game. I shouldn't have done that." I felt so ashamed. I had bent the rules of the house just because he was going to be my son. I understood now why they had such rules around touching. It must have been very confusing for Keydell, me playing so freely with him and in his room. Who knows what kinds of feelings were coming up for him around all that? He seemed to know that touching people in that way was not appropriate, though, so I wondered if there was more to it.

That evening, I told Jim about what had happened. "What do you think was going on?" he asked me.

"I don't know," I replied honestly. "I think he was just excited and wound up, but it was weird that he went right for my rear end and chest rather than just jumping on me or hugging me hard or something. I don't know where grabbing like *that* came from. Maybe he was testing me to see how I would react. Maybe that's how he thinks you show affection. It wasn't like he was trying to wrestle and his hands accidentally went to the wrong spot. It was very intentional, and very shocking." I continued.

All I wanted to do was get this adoption settled, get him into our home for good, and let him know we loved him. That would "fix" everything, I thought.

Little did I know, this incident was a sign of much more unusual behavior to come.

⊰┼⊱

Just before Thanksgiving, Keydell came over for a visit. It wasn't long after the grabbing incident so I was nervous about how he might act. He didn't seem to remember it, and never said anything about it, so I decided to let it go for the moment.

He showed up wearing a shiny, two-piece tracksuit. It was red with black trim, his favorite colors. He looked so stinking cute in it, like a little man strutting around the gym.

"You look so sharp." Ella told him. She came bounding down the stairs from her bedroom to greet him on her way to a babysitting job. "Where did you get that suit, Keydell?"

"We go shopping once in a while at Walmart, and I picked it out myself," he answered proudly. The state provides a stipend for the kids each month so they can buy things they need.

"You picked that out yourself? You've got style, Keydell." Ella gave him the once over, looking him up and down with approval. He loved it.

She took off for her job, so Keydell, Edo and I headed out for a walk to the airport. Keydell found a small rock and started kicking it along the road. It bounced ahead, skipping over cracks and fallen leaves. Edo pulled on the leash with excitement and jumped around, waiting for Keydell to kick again. Keydell had as much energy as our crazy border collie, and Edo loved herding him around as if he were a sheep. They made a great pair.

While seemingly focused on the rock, and without a pause in his kicking, Keydell blurted out, "You guys are adopting me aren't you?"

Okay, here we go, I thought.

I knew he knew, and I was kind of glad he asked. I didn't care anymore what DCYF said. I knew we were committed to the adoption, and I could tell he had had enough of this charade. I was ready to tell him our intentions. Maybe it would give him some peace.

"You know what, Keydell, it's not like you couldn't figure it out by now. You're a bright kid, and we do really like you—and, yes, we *really* want to adopt you. We are working on it right now, buddy."

"Really?" he said, finally pausing to look up at me.

"Yep, we've just finished taking some classes to learn about fostering and adopting, done lots of paperwork and, of course, visited with you to make sure you like it here, so we are almost done. We are very excited to have you be our son soon."

Without much response beyond a quick forced grin, Keydell turned back toward his rock, and we continued our walk. I thought it best to let this news just sink in without much talking. He must have agreed, because he returned his focus to kicking. He had gotten his answer; there was no need to ask anything else. He probably didn't know what else to ask anyway. His mission was to find a home, and he had.

We paused at the chain link fence at the edge of the airport runway, and watched as the airplanes took off and landed. Edo stared at the boy in the shiny red track-suit, waiting for his next move, as Keydell and I stood quietly, unified in thought, knowing our lives were about to change.

What the hell were we thinking? Christmas Eve as the first sleepover with Keydell at our house? I thought the Tasmanian Devil had energy, but he had nothing on Keydell. This was one of the most fun visits I can remember, though.

We all went to pick up Keydell from the group home on Christmas Eve. He had his little backpack of clothes all zipped up and ready to go when we arrived. He was so curious to know where he would sleep. Could Edo sleep with him? Could he take a bath in our big tub before bed? I loved all the questions. Having a little guy in the house again was fun. What a great Christmas present for all of us!

We walked into the kitchen and Keydell bolted upstairs to Henry's old bedroom, Edo close at his heels. Henry had moved downstairs to our den and made that his new bedroom so Keydell could be upstairs, across from Jim and me. Our upstairs is very small, with half-walls and a very narrow hallway, so it would be tight, but we would be close to him if need be.

For the time being we had a twin mattress and box spring on the floor for Keydell (for which we got the finger wag during the home inspection) but he thought it was great. He threw his backpack on the bed and bounced on it, trying out the springs. With a huge smile on his face, he took out a blanket he had brought from the group home that was made out of some gross polyester material, and spread it on the bed, smoothing it out, claiming his territory. We were told that letting kids keep items like this is very important, because it is something that is theirs and only theirs. They don't have much, so any small thing felt important.

I remembered when our family used to move to a new place. I couldn't wait to put my things in my room to make it feel personal. I knew that once my dad's certain coffee cup and Mom's art supplies were unpacked, we were home. I hoped that was the feeling Keydell was having in this moment.

He bolted back down the stairs after his unpacking, actually sliding down the stair railing, never touching any of the stairs. He was a quick little bugger. Edo was tripping trying to keep up.

It was already past dinnertime, so I asked him if he wanted to do his bath. This was his first time taking a bath or showering at our house, so I was not quite sure how he would feel about me helping him get undressed. He had just turned eight years old, and I kind of remembered Henry at that age feeling okay with me seeing him naked, so I ran the water, added a bunch of bubbles, and started to help Keydell get undressed with a careful awareness to his reaction. He didn't seem to care one bit, which I thought was hopeful. I figured if something had happened to him sexually in the past, he would have flinched or resisted my help.

I picked up his tiny, wiry body and plunked him in the warm water. His smooth, brown skin was so beautiful next to the bright white bubbles in the tub. He was up to his chest in foamy suds. I gave him a pair of swim goggles so he could go under—and, with that; he disappeared under the surface. We had a little fish on our hands.

We found an old rubber ducky, some submarine toys that sunk to the bottom, so you could dive for them, and other bath toys that hadn't been used in a while. After a few minutes, I left Keydell alone with the door cracked, and sat on the couch with Jim to give him time to bathe in private.

Soon, some unfamiliar noises started coming from the bath-room, so Jim and I went up to check on him. We opened the door and burst out laughing. There was water *everywhere*. It looked like someone had given him a turkey baster to play with. Somehow, he'd squirted water all over the newly renovated walls, onto the slate floor, into the laundry basket, and onto the ceiling.

"Wow, Keydell. You really went to town in here," I said in sur-prise. My favorite room in the house was a mess.

"Yeah! Watch me dive under the water," he said as he dove down, head first. His tiny little bubble-butt popped above the surface.

"Well, here we go, babe," I said to Jim. "We are in for some fun with this one."

After Keydell got out of the tub, we explained that he had to help dry the place off a bit.

"I love that you enjoyed your bath," I said with a chuckle, "but next time let's keep the water in the tub, okay?"

He seemed not to know what I was talking about. His aware-ness was so in the moment—and, of course, he was only eight, and had probably never been in a tub like this before. (It was a pretty great tub. To him, it was a pool.) We got him dried off and into his Spiderman pajamas, and went back in to squeegee the ceiling.

One of our Christmas Eve traditions was to sit by the tree, watch "The Polar Express," and read *'Twas the Night before Christmas* at bedtime. Even though Henry and Ella had outgrown being read to, they still listened, swirling in their own nostalgic memories.

Henry was on one end of the couch, Keydell in the middle, and Ella on the other side as the movie began. My heart was full. They looked so great together.

"This movie is kind of scary," Keydell said after a bit.

"Hey, cuddle in closer," Henry invited as he pulled Keydell in for a squeeze. Ella moved over to tighten the threesome.

"Is that better?" Ella asked with a soothing tone.

Keydell shook his head yes and curled his narrow feet up to snuggle in. Before the movie ended, our little guest started to get heavy eyes, and asked to go to bed. We all carried Keydell upstairs and Henry and Ella gave him a big hug goodnight that he gladly accepted.

Jim and I sat with him on the edge of his bed.

"Will Santa know I'm here?" he asked.

As I pulled his comforter up over his shoulders I said, "Yes, we left a note at Trout that you would be here with us. When you get up, we're going to open presents from him and to each other here, and then go to my mom and dad's house so you can meet the rest of my family. Okay?"

Keydell had met my parents once before when he came for Thanksgiving, but tomorrow he was going to meet my aunt, uncle, grandfather, and fifteen year old nephew. I was concerned about him getting overwhelmed; this was a whole new family he was meeting, and on one of the most exciting days of the year. *I* got overwhelmed and I *knew* my family already.

What is going through his mind? I wondered. We all wanted his first Christmas with us to be special. The whole family was looking forward to meeting him.

Jim went back downstairs after a goodnight hug, while I stayed to give Keydell a little back scratch, gladly accepting the opportunity for some normal touching. Then, I gave him a quick tickle in his ribs to see if he would jump. He laughed and squirmed onto his back to avoid more tickling.

Then he said, "Hold my neck like this, and wiggle it." He showed me a kind of chokehold. "My mom used to do this, and it tickles," he continued.

I felt uncomfortable because it looked like I would be strangling him. I wiggled my fingers along his neck instead, and said, "I'll do it this way, okay? The other way makes me feel like I am hurting you."

"No, just do it lightly," he responded.

I gave it a try, wrapping both hands gently around his skinny neck as he laughed and laughed. Well, it might have been a strange way to tickle someone, but he really liked it. I wondered how this method had been discovered. I imagined someone trying to choke him in frustration while he laughed at them like crazy, and realized just how much I still had to learn about him. When you have a baby, everything starts from scratch. Keydell came with eight years of experience that I had no knowledge about. I still hadn't gotten to see the big file folder with his detailed records in it.

As I was leaving his room, I said, in my excited-for-Christmas voice, "I am going to go put my pajamas on and go to bed soon, too. Sleep well, and I'll see you in the morning." I also tried my first "I love you," and waited for his response.

I wasn't expecting an "I love you" back, but what he *did* say certainly took me off guard.

"Can I see you naked?" he blurted, with a wide-eyed look.

"No," I said, feeling myself back away. "Go to sleep, Keydell."

"But I want to see your boobs," he said.

When Henry and Ella were babies, I nursed them both, and even as toddlers they saw me naked sometimes, but this was different. I couldn't imagine just showing Keydell my body for the sake of showing him. I was not sure where his question was coming from, but thought maybe he had never seen his own mother's breasts—never taken a bath with her, or nursed from her. I was not sure how to proceed without making him feel ashamed of the question, but I felt like he had just reached down my shirt again.

"Keydell, I think that it would be inappropriate for you to see me naked just for the sake of seeing me. If you want to see what a woman looks like, we can look at some paintings or something sometime, okay?"

"But, why?" he asked, "I want to see your boobs!"

"It's time for bed, Keydell, Go to sleep so Christmas will come sooner."

He threw his head back down to the pillow and pulled the covers over his head. I paused in the open door waiting to see what he would do next.

"I usually leave the door open a crack and turn the light off. Are you okay with that?" I finally asked him. I had bought a nightlight for him on the suggestion of the Trout staff, but it was still dim in there.

From under the blanket, his muffled yet demanding voice answered, "Yes, that's fine. Leave a big crack."

I closed his door, leaving a gap, walked across the hall to my room and shut the door tightly as I put on my pajamas. I went back downstairs to set up the gifts under the tree with the rest of the family, and told them what had just happened.

Ella said, "That's weird Mom. What's up with that?"

"Maybe it's his way of trying to bond with me, I don't know," I replied.

"Odd way to bond," she smirked.

"Yeah, well, just be cautious when you are with him alone so he doesn't try anything on you."

I looked at Jim and he gave me a look that said, "Let's just keep an eye on that." We always could read each other's minds, and on this I was sure he heard me loud and clear. Ella was Daddy's little girl. No harm would come to her on his watch.

Keydell bounded out of bed at four a.m. on Christmas morning. Jim and I were already awake, too, excited for Christmas morning with the kids. We heard Keydell bump down the short narrow hallway from his room to the top of the stairs, shaking the horse-hair plaster walls until dust came out. His heavy heels hit the landing with a thud. I cracked my eyes open, and waited to see if he would come back to wake us up after peeking at the presents. Jim and I giggled to each other, excited for Keydell's Christmas. Edo, who always slept next to me, tried to poke his nose out the door to join the action.

Ella was an early riser, too, but four o'clock was a tad early for her. She moaned from her room as if to say, "*Really*. It's way too early."

Keydell poked his head into our room and said, loudly, "Good morning! Can I go open presents?"

"Come here, Keydell. Come say hi, and then we will get up with you," Jim replied.

Edo was dancing in circles.

Our four-poster bed, made by my grandfather for our wedding present, sat very high off the ground. Keydell was barely able to see over the top. He was on Jim's side of the bed, smiling with anticipation. Jim and I got up and followed Keydell downstairs and told him he could open his stocking, which took about ten seconds, and then asked, "Can I go wake up Henry?"

I think the deal was six a.m. at the earliest, but that was not going to stick with his current level of excitement. He knocked on Henry's door, and we heard nothing. He was out cold as usual. I opened the door slowly and went in to give Henry a rub on his back.

"Hey, Hank, Keydell is up already," I whispered. "How about we all get up and you can go back to bed for a bit after we open presents, or sleep in the car on the way to Grandma and Poppy's?"

His blonde bed head rolled my way and, through sleepy, puffy, sticky lips, he mumbled, "Ugh, okay, just give me a minute."

Keydell ran back to the living room, wiggled on the couch impatiently and shook a few presents as Henry and Ella slowly shuffled into the living room. Jim got us coffee and we all opened presents together, a little faster than normal. I think Keydell was used to ripping open his presents all at once, not doing them one at a time like we did. I liked taking it slowly, so I could see what everyone got and watch their reaction. I always knew what I would have to return by their expressions.

We were done by 5:30. It was going to be a long day.

Henry and Ella tried to sleep in the car during the hour-and-a-half-long ride to my parents' house, but Keydell had other plans. He had brought along one of his new toys, plastic army men with flimsy plastic bag type parachutes on their backs, and he wanted to open them up. By the time he got one of them out, the strings were already tangled.

"Keydell, why don't you wait until we get to Grandma's so I can help you with that?" I suggested.

"I can do it," he said loudly. It probably wasn't that loud actually, I was just very sensitive to my two tired teenagers.

The rest of the day went well, and Keydell was active but well behaved. My uncle, who was just a big kid himself, played with him for a long time, driving a remote control car around the back porch of my parents' log cabin-style house. Keydell jumped all over my linebacker-sized nephew and convinced "Poppy" (the name Henry had given my dad when he was a baby) to give him extra Christmas cookies. He was wound up most of the day, throwing his army men off the upstairs balcony, but we all had a lot of fun.

When we got home, we plopped down in the living room amongst all the Christmas morning mess. I think we all wanted to chill out and eat leftovers—all of us, except for Keydell. He got a second wind (or should I say, the wind continued), and he wanted to open all the toys he hadn't been able to bring to my parents' house. He made his handheld game beep and play songs, dumped his Legos around the room, and repeatedly threw the Nerf ball into the over-the-door basketball hoop. He was loud and bouncing off the walls. Henry, Ella, Jim and I all looked at each other; my two teens rolled their eyes.

"Oh, man. He's got energy." Henry said trying to catch a nap on the floor.

"Ya think?" Ella chirped in.

I helped him with a few more toys, and tried to keep him quiet and entertained as the rest of the group relaxed. I was already feeling concerned about the impact that bringing him into our family would have.

"The quality of our lives is directly related to the amount of uncertainty we can live with comfortably."

—*Tony Robbins*

CHAPTER 7

A NEW HOME

"The secret of change is to focus all of your energy, not on fighting the old, but on building the new."

—*Socrates*

Move-in day, January 31, 2009

I sat in meditation on that quiet Saturday morning before Keydell moved in with us. I was feeling excited to finally have him with us full-time, but also nervous about this big change for our family. I was becoming aware, after our few visits, that he had crazy energy, and perhaps some issues I didn't fully understand. I hoped I could help him. I had not known much suffering in my life, not like he had, so I wondered if I could fully relate to him. So much of understanding the Buddha Dharma is understanding suffering, and I felt I needed to experience some—or at least get more teaching around it—to fully grasp the lessons behind it. I needed to find a regular teacher.

My friend Don and I had formed a local Buddhist group so we could at least talk with one another about the teachings. Because of his extensive studies, he was a great mentor for me. He had arranged for a Rinpoche (a highly respected Lama and teacher) to come to Rhode Island to teach once and a while but after one of our meetings, I expressed my frustrations to him about finding a dharma teacher that I could be with more regularly.

"Don, you are so smart and have such great knowledge of the Dharma, but how do I find a regular teacher like Rinpoche? You've traveled the world, and studied with so many great teachers, but I'm here in little Rhode Island, feeling lost and unable to get that same experience."

"Kim, don't worry about having a teacher. One will come when you most need it. There are teachers around us all the time," he assured me. "We are blessed to have such a high Lama in our area, and we should take advantage of his teachings, but practicing Buddhism is not just sitting in meditation or listening to a teacher. It's remembering the dharma in your everyday life. It's okay. Things will happen as they should. As people come in and out of your life and challenge you or offer you something, stay present to the lessons they bring."

"Yes, I guess you're right. I'm just impatient," I said, sensing that I had just been made aware of something very important.

As I continued to sit in my meditation that Saturday, I remembered what Don had said, and thought, *I'm okay. A regular teacher will come when he or she comes. Everyone I meet can be my teacher.* This frustration I felt was a lesson in itself, actually; it was a form of suffering. It was a good thing, I thought. Maybe I just needed more of it so I could practice overcoming it.

So, I took a few deep breaths, wrapped up my sit, and sent out a prayer request: "Test me, oh great Universe, test me. Bring it on. Let me get up off this cushion and get out into the real world of suffering. Show me the path to overcoming this suffering."

I know it sounds crazy to ask for suffering, but I knew I wanted to grow spiritually and have a more direct understanding of people, like Keydell, who had suffered, so I could be of better service to them.

Lo and behold, my request was delivered. Keydell moved in. My greatest teacher had arrived, and he would bring me all the lessons I needed.

⟞╌╀╌⟝

Jim and I were excited to have a more normal life with our new child, one that did not involve a back and forth visiting schedule—and one where we could begin to help Keydell feel like he had a permanent home and family.

January 31, 2009, was a chilly evening, and it was just after dinner when we drove over to the group home to get our new son. We would still be considered his "foster family" until we got the final court date for his adoption, but for us, this was the beginning of his life as our child. We were his parents now, and Henry and Ella were his brother and sister.

"Okay, guys, let's go get him," I said.

Ella debated, "Mom, there's a big basketball game tonight. Can't you guys get him so I can go to the game?"

"Ella, I told you, this is a big day. We need to show Keydell that we are his family now, and that we are united in his adoption. I would really like you to come."

"Fine," she sighed.

When we got to Trout, the last of Keydell's things were packed in a couple of boxes, and his backpack was sitting just inside the front door, all ready to go. We had slowly been bringing his things over as he visited, and I was actually surprised at how much he still had. I guess you accumulate a few things over two years.

As we walked up the foyer stairs to the main level of the house, we saw all the boys hanging out in the living room, watching TV together. Denise must have rounded them up for Keydell's good-bye. The first thing I noticed was their fresh haircuts, including Keydell's. When I saw his tightly cropped buzz, I felt a rush of annoyance toward the counselors who had taken him for a haircut without asking me. *I* wanted to do that with him. I felt like someone did something with *my* child without asking. His hair had previously been longer and styled in a short afro; I'd had a whole day planned for him and Jim to get a haircut together while I took pictures of him in the barber's chair—you know, "Our child's first haircut." But it was already done now, closely cropped and lined up along his hairline. He did look adorable, though, so I let it go.

"Hi, Keydell," Jim greeted him. "You ready to come home?"

I thought he would be very excited to see us, but he was quite melancholy. He continued to watch the television, and barely said hello. *Odd*, I thought. *Maybe he's nervous, realizing this is for real now.* But was it really odd? He had lived with so many different people at this point that he probably didn't know who to trust. I wondered again if he fully understood what this adoption business meant.

Henry and Ella said hi to Keydell and the other boys, and commented on their cool haircuts. Denise asked the boys to say good-bye. They stopped watching TV for a second, acknowledging him briefly with quick turns of their heads and waves of their hands.

I could only imagine what they must be thinking. *Why did Kim pick him and not me? How come I'm not up for adoption?* It must be hard for the boys to see the other kids come and go to new homes or back to their own when they had to stay.

I asked Keydell again if he was ready. He finally turned his attention from the TV and said, "Wait, I have to do one thing first."

"What's that?" I asked, as he hopped up from the couch and began running through every doorway in the house. "What are you doing, buddy?" I giggled.

He replied, "I'm going through all the doorways without asking if I can come in or go out."

He was so proud of himself and it showed me that he was, in fact, happy to be coming home with us. I was glad that Keydell would now have the freedom to be in his own house, one where he didn't feel like a guest.

He grabbed one last thing from the end table and handed it to me. It was a painting he had done for an art show earlier that year. It depicted him standing in front of a house that looked like ours with a small cloud over the roof and the sun shining brightly. Underneath he had painted "I hope for a house and a family." It was like his version of a vision board and it had worked.

Ella and Henry put Keydell's things in the car. He gave big hugs to Denise and the other staff, and walked out of Trout Drive's front door for the very last time.

I walked out with a new son, and a file folder full of eight years of history.

The next morning came early, as Keydell was up at his usual time of 5:30 a.m. He had not needed to wear his Pull-Ups at Trout anymore, but last night he'd wet the bed. He slept right through it, so we found it in the morning. He woke up soaked and embarrassed.

"It's okay, Keydell," I told him. "You're just getting used to being here, and I'm glad you slept so soundly."

He was mad at himself, but changed his underwear and pajamas as I pulled the sheets off the bed. I wondered if I should go get a mattress pad or Pull-Ups, which he had probably outgrown, but I wanted to see if this would continue. After changing his clothes, Keydell bounded downstairs with his heavy-heeled steps and I reminded him not to be too loud because it was early and Ella and Henry were sleeping. It was Sunday, after all, and we normally took it easy on Sunday mornings.

Keydell was starving, so I got him some cereal while I made coffee. I needed the coffee.

Jim is an early riser, so he was up this morning, too. Jim and I loved Sunday mornings because it gave us a chance to catch up on the week. We would have our coffee in the living room where it was warm (our old farm kitchen was very cold in the winter) and watch the news together.

Not today.

I looked at Jim as Keydell made beat box sounds in between bites of food and managed to spill half his cereal across the kitchen table. "I think things are going to be a bit different in the mornings," I said in a groggy voice. He understood everything I didn't say.

Keydell was so adorable, though, sitting at the table. His chin was barely over the tabletop. He was all of fifty pounds, with the round, pudgy cheeks of youth. He had perfectly arched, thin eyebrows over his big brown eyes, and the most beautiful full lips. As a photographer, I tend to notice if someone has a symmetrical face, and he did. His skin was like mocha because his mix of black and white backgrounds. He was going to be a handsome young man. He already had six-pack abs and a muscular build, like many of the Jamaican men I had seen working on the boats in Newport; they all had lean long torsos and broad shoulders, not an ounce of fat on them.

Some people find their children across the globe; the amazing thing is, sometimes they even look like one another. We found Keydell in our own backyard. At one point, we learned, Keydell and his mom had lived in Newport, so we might have seen him around town, not knowing he would be our son one day. Weird, right?

(I love this stuff. It reminds me of how connected we all are.)

After breakfast, Jim asked Keydell if he wanted to watch the cartoon "The Clone Wars." Keydell came bounding over to the couch, leaped up to next to Jim, and almost knocked his coffee all over the front of him.

Jim said, slightly annoyed, "Easy, Keydell, settle down," and offered him a blanket to cuddle under. It was nice to see them sitting together. Keydell didn't have a father figure in his life anymore, so this was good for him.

I washed Keydell's sheets.

Ella woke up at about seven, and proceeded downstairs to the living room in her normal sleep attire, a T-shirt and underwear. She was just about to turn fourteen, and was a blossoming beauty. She has long, slender, athletic legs like my mother's; long, sandy-blonde hair with soft wavy curls—and those big eyes, green with long lashes. Her little round butt peeked out from under her T-shirt, and I saw Keydell take notice. A red flag went up right away.

I followed Ella to the bathroom and said, "Hey, I know you just got up, but maybe we should all make sure to wear some pajama pants or a robe with Keydell around." It was unusual for me to make a request like this, because our family had never been uptight about showing a little skin. I hoped to instill a positive body image in them.

"I just think we have to be careful with him until he sees you as his sister, and not just an attractive girl," I said lovingly.

"Mom, he's only eight. Do you really think he's looking at me like that?" she asked.

"Uh, yeah, I just saw him check you out, and I think he has a history of being sexually inappropriate," I replied. "It's up to you; I'm just giving you a head's up based on what I know about him. We have to give him time to get used to having a sister. He's been surrounded by boys for the last two years."

"Fine," she said. "I'll put some shorts on."

We spent the day getting Keydell settled in his room as he practiced walking around the house without asking to go through the doors. Later on, Ella and Keydell (and, of course, Edo) went outside to play in the snow. They got all bundled up and pulled out our old plastic sled from the basement. Ella showed Keydell the small frozen pond next to our house, and they spent the next few hours pulling each other around on the ice on that old sled. They were having a blast. This was cool. I'd been wondering for a while if Ella was going to feel funny not being the baby in the family anymore—but so far, so good. She was now the middle child, like Jim and I.

That evening, we all settled in for a movie before bed. Ella asked Keydell if he wanted to cuddle under the blanket. She was enjoying having a little brother, and he was so tiny and sweet, like a lot of the kids she babysat. I also thought it was good for him to get some affection. Our family was all about hugs and kisses, so Ella was just doing what she thought was natural and normal—but for Keydell, this was not natural or normal. He seemed very happy and appropriately nestled against her now, watching *Madagascar*. I sat next to them at the other end of the couch. Henry was in another chair, and Edo and Jim were lying on the floor in their favorite TV-watching spot.

As bedtime rolled around, Henry showed Keydell how to fold his blanket and put it on the shelf. As I started to walk to the kitchen to put our snack dishes away, I paused for a moment, watching how diligently Keydell folded his blanket. He wanted to do it perfectly.

After placing it on the shelf he looked right at me and said, "Did I do this right … Mom?"

Henry and Ella both looked at me, stunned. Jim smiled in surprise.

Henry asked, "Did you just call her Mom?"

"Yeah," Keydell replied. "Is that okay?"

"Yeah, it just surprised me," he replied. "Did you hear that Mom?"

Keydell had always called me Kim at the group home, so I think he was trying out "Mom" to see what it felt like. His saucer eyes looked up at me, waiting for confirmation; I said, "If you feel comfortable calling us Mom and Dad, then of course, you can call us that. We are your mom and dad now so ... By all means, Keydell."

He tilted his gaze down and smiled as he smoothed out the blanket. Ella mouthed to me "So cute, Mom."

I smiled back. This was going to be okay.

Jim and I continued into the kitchen and he squeezed my hand. "How does it feel to be a new mom again?" he asked.

"Pretty good. Pretty good."

The Monday after Keydell moved in became the first day of our new school routine. Normally I got up at 5:30 a.m. so I could beat the one-bathroom rush, while my two teenage zombies got up around six and Henry dragged himself into the shower to wake up. The start of the weekdays was usually quiet and slow as we all got dressed, made lunches and had our coffee—but howdy doody, a new cowboy was in town this morning to remind us what living with a young person was like. The dust was flying, the guns were blazing, and our new brown bean was ready to take on the day!

Keydell got up before all of us. He had wet his bed again. He got mad at himself for it, put a pout on his face, changed his clothes, and slid down the stair rail to the first floor—all in a matter of two minutes or so. Edo followed him, circling around like he does, and let out a bark; the cats went dashing off in streaks of terror, and we all convened in the kitchen. Keydell was making all kinds of noises, partnered by energetic movements of some sort, as he got out the cereal. He rammed the refrigerator door open into the back of Henry's chair as he reached up for the milk.

"Hold on, Keydell, let me help you." Henry got the milk down before that, too, landed down the back of his chair. Edo circled under my feet. Henry was annoyed. Jim yelled at the dog to sit. It was a bit chaotic and crazy for that early in the morning. We were not used to this—but I reminded Henry and Ella that they used to be that way at that age, too, even though Keydell possessed double the energy they'd had, and was twice as loud.

Being the great morning person that I am (not!) I grabbed my coffee and turned away from the chaos for a moment to look out the kitchen window above the sink. I saw the sun coming up over our back field and took a few deep breaths.

"What have we done?" I thought, "What have we done?"

Jim hugged me from behind, and whispered in my ear, "Where are his meds?"

Keydell moved in with not only his clothes and a few toys and personal items, but a few bottles of medicine as well. After we'd put Keydell to bed the night before, I had briefly looked over his files and medical records—but honestly, there was so much there, I needed more time to process it. He was on Adderall and Tenex for ADHD and Risperdal for bipolar disorder. (Risperdal apparently alters the brain's chemistry to help fight off the depression that often comes with bipolar and other mood disorders.)

I remember reading that Keydell had been hospitalized a couple of times for behavioral issues, and that his mom had depression and bipolar disorder. She had once been found on the side of the road in her car, overdosed on depression drugs and alcohol. This had been a suicide attempt, apparently. The records stated that Keydell had been very neglected due to his mother's depression, and was often left to fend for himself as a toddler with only a little help from his older brother and sister.

The documents also dated each of his moves from caregiver to caregiver; I'd had some knowledge around this before, but now I finally understood the extent of his experience. Apparently, his aunt hospitalized Keydell on several occasions and found it very hard to care for him due to his violent outbursts, swearing, and inappropriate sexual behaviors. She had enrolled him in a program at The Providence Center starting in September of 2005, and by Christmas had decided she could no longer deal with him. He was put up for adoption after she realized her niece, Keydell's mother, would never be able to take him back. He was placed into foster care early in 2006, with the aim toward adoption. A single woman, who had one adoptive daughter around the same age as Keydell, took him in. In his file was the letter she wrote to DCYF only four months after he arrived in her home. It was a long, sad statement about Keydell's behaviors and how she could no longer keep him.

He had had 200 outburst episodes within a 134-day period. She was exhausted from his violence, his profanity, his sexual aggression toward her daughter, and his aggression toward her animals. She mentioned his fascination with gore, and that he often would say things like "I wonder what would happen if I cut my finger off?" He was hyperactive and needed constant attention, and when she tried to cook, sleep or do other things besides play with him, he would get angry, throw a fit, and break things around the house. She had hoped to keep Keydell and eventually adopt him, but did not see it as a possibility at that time. She knew it would kill him to be moved again, but she was unable to "do it" any more.

This seemed to be a consistent theme in all the files I had read so far. I naively believed this was all in the past, however. Keydell had settled in very nicely at Trout, and had over 200 days of good behavior on his chart. The structure and routine must have given him a sense of security and kept his anxiety at a manageable level or something, because looking back at his history, it surely presented a very different picture than I'd seen.

In some ways, I am glad that we were not fully aware of his past before deciding to adopt him, or were just too naive to think he still might have these issues after coming into our home. What we saw and heard from Denise was that he was a sweet, kind, helpful boy. I saw this too, from the very first day. The things mentioned in the file were behaviors, they were not who he was. He was alone, innocent in so many ways—and when he smiled, he lit up the room and my heart. There was something inside him worth saving, for sure. It was like looking at a diamond encrusted in mud; our love and nurturing would chip away at the dirt, exposing a beautiful gem.

I knew very little about medications and was not necessarily against them, but I was pretty sure Keydell was on too many. For Christ's sake, his file was filled with a plethora of diagnoses, and medications to go with each. I was concerned they were masking his true issues—if there even were any. He had been given Lithium for bipolar at the age of three. I looked up bipolar and was very surprised he had been given that diagnosis so young. Most people aren't diagnosed as bipolar until their teens at the earliest. I hadn't seen anything in him resembling that. There was a brief mention of something called "reactive attachment disorder" as a diagnosis, but there were no meds mentioned specifically for that. I had never heard of attachment disorder before, but the doctors recommended a loving, stable and supportive environment as his treatment. Well, Jim and the kids and I could do that.

I told Jim I had put the meds in the cabinet and he got Keydell his morning dose. We knew we would have to keep him on everything for a while until we could consult his doctor. After fifteen minutes, the Adderall had calmed him down, and he was like a different person. He was quieter, didn't wiggle as much, and just sat on the couch after Henry and Ella left for school.

As hard as the crazy was to handle, I was not sure I liked this state any better. It was strange to see someone so young medicated. I had never directly known any kids who were on meds, but remembered dropping Ella at Girl Scout camp one summer; there were separate lines at check-in for kids with meds and those without. The "with meds" line was longer.

As I saw from the very beginning, Keydell was a smart boy, and did well in school. He loved going to school, and he loved his teachers. I think, in some ways, school was a stabilizing environment for him, just like Trout had been. There were clear guidelines during the day, he saw the same faces every morning, and he was young enough that he was given lots of recess and activity to help dispel some of his energy in a positive way. He'd had a few outbursts at school when he first started kindergarten, but that was not surprising. He was confused about his move to the group home, and everything was changing again. He must have been scared to death.

Keydell didn't mind doing his homework, either, and would sit down right when he got home from school to finish it quickly. He wanted to do well, and be a good boy, I could tell. He was also famished when he got home, because the Adderall curbed his appetite and he usually didn't eat much lunch.

We also heard, from a friend whose son took Adderall, that it could stunt a child's growth. Keydell was small in stature for his age, but already had hair under his arms at age eight, so who knew? Maybe it stunted growth, but didn't delay the onset of puberty. At this point, he was just our "little bean," as we called him, and we loved his appetite, his size, and everything else about him.

I dropped Keydell off at school that first morning at 7:40 a.m., and already missed him by the time I got to the gym.

CHAPTER 8

THE REALITY

"Where there is anger, there is always pain underneath."

Eckhart Tolle

It was mid-March, 2009. Keydell had been with us for a month and a half. During that time he'd been visited by Matt from DCYF, Angela from Adoption Rhode Island—and, to add to the mix, Chad, from an agency called Children's Friends, which provides support services for foster and newly-adopted children and their families.

Personally, I was sick of all the "support" already. We had two visits per week between the three agencies, and it took up a lot of time in the afternoons. It was hard enough for me to get work done and handle our new child without all the distractions. Each agency person was there to check on Keydell and see if he was settling in okay. *Well, let him settle in then,* I thought. With all these people continually coming, it seemed like he was still under their care and not ours.

I wanted this to end. I wanted him to feel like he could move on from that part of his life. Visits with Matt from DCYF were particularly annoying; he was our intermediary with the state, but he never had any answers for us as to when our final adoption date would be. He seemed to have his feet in the mud, and when I pushed him on the question he acted like an egotistical frat boy who had some big secret he didn't want to share with us. "Just tell us what we can expect!" I'd say. I honestly think he was overworked and hated his job—but like I said, annoying as hell.

Chad from Children's Friends was there to see how Keydell and our family were settling in. He was support for me if needed it, but he mainly tried to be like a big brother for Keydell. He worked on coping skills with him, and would play with him outside, trying to get him to talk about his feelings. Keydell was not very responsive when it came to his feelings but he enjoyed playing with Chad anyway. He loved the one-on-one attention and the constant company from another person. He'd gotten used to that at the group home.

Soft-spoken, gentle Angela brought Keydell small presents and a personal scrapbook she had worked on the whole time he had been at Trout. I didn't know she had been doing that, and I was excited to see some new photos of his earlier years. I think Keydell enjoyed her visits most because they felt friendly versus clinical.

Today, she came by with a report about his birth mom. We spoke in private before she met with Keydell.

"I've tried on several occasions to reach Sue," she told me. "But she's not answering my calls."

Sue. I finally had a name for Keydell's birth mom. I felt my heart expand, knowing her name. She was no longer just another woman who had to give up her child. I realized that, before this moment, I felt "better" than her—somehow smarter or more deserving of her child. Her name gave her life, gave her her own mother who named her and raised her and hopefully loved her. We both were women, mothers and daughters trying to find our way in the world, but she was dealt a different hand of cards that made life tougher for her.

Here was my first lesson in seeing a kind of suffering I had never experienced. I felt the need to hold her, and tell her I would take great care of her son.

"Maybe she doesn't want to have an open adoption," I replied after returning from my thoughts. "It might be too painful for her. What do you think?"

Angela told me that Matt had spoken with her and reported that she did not want to continue seeing Keydell after the adoption.

"I wanted to reach her personally to clarify this and let her know that you guys were open to Keydell seeing her, but she's not responding," Angela said. "I didn't tell you what happened though, did I?"

"No, what do you mean? What happened?"

"His mom stopped by for a visit at Trout the day after Keydell left for good. No one informed her that he had moved in with you."

"Oh my God, are you kidding?" I replied incredulously. "So that means Keydell never said goodbye to her. That breaks my heart Angela. I can only imagine how she must have felt."

"I know, it's not good."

"Who was supposed to tell her?" I asked in annoyance.

"Matt."

"Matt! Man, he bugs me. I'm sorry. This is just too much. I don't understand that at all. Has he no feelings!"

It seemed such a simple thing to tell Keydell's birth mom when he was leaving. I mean, Matt was in charge of that, wasn't he? Perhaps he tried but couldn't reach her in time. I was trying to give him the benefit of the doubt. Or maybe he was sick that day. Ugh!

Angela gave me and Keydell big hugs, and said she would see us in two weeks. As she drove away, I mourned for Keydell's birth mother, who hadn't gotten to say goodbye to her son. I wondered if Keydell realized he never said goodbye either, and perhaps that's why he hadn't seemed too anxious to leave when we picked him up to come to our house for good. There had been no closure for either of them.

⚒

Except for all the disruptive visits with case-workers, our days were going fairly smoothly with Keydell. We were beginning to see some peaked frustrations however. He was becoming more anxious, and I could tell he was trying very hard to stay in control. His energy had always been high, but it had a new sense of urgency to it. His body seemed tight and tense, like a rubber band about to snap.

Keydell continued to wet his bed every couple of nights, and that was making him very upset. Once, when I woke up in the middle of the night to change his sheets he asked, "Are you mad?" and grabbed his head around his ears and said, "I am so stupid."

I was groggy and tired, so to him it must have looked like I was annoyed. I probably was, actually. I had not done middle-of-the-night zombie feedings or wet bedding changes since the kids were babies.

I replied, "No, Del, I am just tired. Let's put this towel down on the wet spot and get the new sheets in the morning. I don't have a clean set ready."

He stood rigid next to me as I changed his PJs.

"It's okay, Keydell," I soothed. "Some kids have a little valve that helps them feel when they have to go, that develops later in life. You might have that going on, or it could be your medications making you sleep extra deeply. Not sure, but you are *not* stupid. I know you can't help it."

My words seemed to fall on deaf ears, but we put the big towel down and both went back to sleep. While I was in his room, though, I noticed some snack food and wrappers under his top sheet, stuffed between the bed and the wall. Food hoarding 101.

When Keydell woke up the next morning, he saw the towel again and got out of bed grumpy. He stomped downstairs while Henry was just getting up for school.

"How are you Del?" Henry asked as he walked sleepily to the bathroom for his shower. I loved how he called him "Del."

"Shut up," Keydell snapped.

It was the first time he had angrily lashed out directly at one of us, so I knew something was going on.

"Wow, someone's grumpy this morning," Henry whispered.

Jim and I were in the kitchen making lunches and coffee and noticed the pout on Keydell's face.

"Good morning, sweetie," I greeted him. "Do you want some breakfast?"

"Fine." He sat down heavily at the table, and crossed his arms.

Ella moseyed into the kitchen and said, "Good morning, KiKi." Keydell turned to face her head on and let out an ear-piercing screech that came from the depths of his little body. It startled all of us. I guess he didn't like the nickname.

"What the heck?" Ella glared back at Keydell in confusion.

Jim said, "Hey, what's up little guy? Let's get something to eat."

"Maybe you're hungry," I piped in. "But that is not a very nice way to respond to Ella, Keydell."

He looked around the table as if he had lost something, then reached for a permission slip that he was supposed to return to school. He slowly started to rip off one of the corners. His eyes were glazed over; I couldn't put my finger on it, but the look on his face was strange. Why would he rip that up? He seemed to need to stay angry, and have an outlet for that anger, yet ripping up that paper would be damaging something *he* needed.

"Keydell," I said. "You need that for school, sweetie, so please don't do that."

He looked up at me as if to say, "Screw you," and ripped it more. He was doing it so slowly and methodically that it looked creepy.

Jim yelled a short and sweet, "*Stop!*" and Keydell snapped out of it and put the paper down. He sat with his head in his hands for a minute as I walked over to try to talk to him. "It's okay, Keydell, are you upset about the wet bed?" I asked.

"Leave me alone," he barked. I gave him a touch on his back, but he shrugged my hand off and got up to get his cereal. I got him his meds. I figured I would ask about the food in his bed later.

He seemed to calm down as the morning continued and we drove to school, and when I picked him up at the end of the school day he seemed happy. He had a lot of energy and was talking a lot, but I was relieved that he had had a good day after our odd morning. When we got home, he jumped out of the car, ran inside, and plopped at the kitchen table with his homework like he usually did.

I got him a snack, and asked him what he'd done in school. "Did you learn anything new today?" I asked.

He told me about his math class and that they were learning some division.

"This is easy," he said. "I'll finish fast."

"Great. Let me know if you need any help."

Jim was much better at math than I, but I thought I could handle division.

Keydell happily worked for a few minutes while I looked at the mail, but when I glanced over at him again, he was breaking his pencil in half with the same frustrated look he had that morning.

"Hey, Del, what's up buddy? Can I help you with something?" I asked.

"This is stupid, I'm not doing it."

"Are you stuck on a problem?"

"I should know how to do it," he said.

"Didn't you just start this math today?"

"Yes, but I should know it!"

"Well, it's new to you, and the reason you have homework is so you can practice and see if you understood the lesson." That answer didn't satisfy him at all. "We can look up how to do it."

He thought getting help was cheating. I asked him, if he helped someone else, would he think they were cheating as well?

He just looked at me with wild, angry eyes and said nothing. He didn't want me to be right; he actually liked to find me wrong about things. It had become a bit of a game for him to point it out.

He took the lead end of the pencil and scribbled all over his math paper, ripping the center because he was pushing down so hard. Then he grabbed the whole sheet, crumpled it up, and threw it on the ground. I was shocked that he would destroy the homework that he was usually so proud of.

"Keydell, if you continue doing this, I won't be able to tape it back together, so go easy." I said as I walked over to try to get the jagged pencil from his hand.

"So what?" he said, "It's stupid anyway."

"Let's take a break and come back to it in a few minutes okay? You want to go run around in the yard with Edo for a bit, and then come back?"

He bolted outside without answering, and did just that. He liked to be timed while he ran a certain course, so I followed him out and said, "Okay, let's go around the house three times and I'll time you." He ran around once, twice, and on the third time I clocked him at fifty-eight seconds.

"Let me go again, and I'll try to do it faster this time," he frantically requested.

There was a definite undercurrent of angst to his voice, but I hoped the running would eventually calm him down.

"Okay, when you're ready, just go and I'll start timing," I told him.

Off he went as I watched the second hand tick, tick, tick on my watch. As he came around on the second lap, I saw that this time was faster than the first two. I planned on telling him it was a second faster just to help him feel better anyway, but as he came around the final corner of the house, he got cut off by Edo (who'd been following him the whole time, thinking this was the best game ever). Keydell had to slow down to avoid running over him. His fists tightened, and he threw himself to the ground, rolling, kicking, and thrashing about.

"I won't be faster *this* time," he yelled.

I tried to lighten the mood. "Oh, you would have if Edo hadn't slowed you down. Silly dog. He loves playing with you."

I was quickly learning that Keydell put a lot of pressure on himself to be good at everything. No matter what, he couldn't fail. No excuses. It started with the bed-wetting overnight, and just escalated to the math and the running. Poor guy.

I went over to sit on the grass next to him and said, "Hey, can we talk about this? It's not a big deal sweetie. We're just playing."

I tried to hug him, but he wiggled angrily away from me. He got on his hands and knees and screamed at the top of his lungs right in my face. He looked like a lion roaring at another lion as if to say, "Stay the fuck back, or I'll eat you."

I sat there as calmly as I could while the lion spit and bulged his eyes, waiting for a moment of calm. I had never been yelled at like that before. It was shocking, and got me rattled. He finally drained himself from screaming and flopped down flat on the ground, looking up at the sky with a blank stare. He looked to be in a trance.

I was confused about how to react, but thought it was my window of opportunity to be his parent and share my advice.

I was shaking but began to rub his head and offered, "Next time you're frustrated ask for help and not rip up your homework? That is only hurting you, and I am always happy to help."

Oops, not good. By saying that, I was pointing out another "flaw," which made him even angrier. He ran from me, back into the house and up the stairs to his room, where he slammed the door and flopped on his bed, crying.

I followed him upstairs, but all I got when I knocked was, "Go away!"

I stood outside with my nose about an inch from the wood, staring at the backside of the door. I wondered what to do. Since my words seemed to frustrate him, I decided to give him some space.

"I'll be downstairs if you need me," I called, but waited at the top of the landing for a few more minutes, listening.

Giving the boys space was a technique I remembered Denise telling me about. When the boys had violent outbursts at the group home, they often left them in a padded room—but I didn't have one of those.

After about two minutes of thrashing, it got very quiet, so I assumed Keydell had fallen asleep—as indeed he had. In fact, he took a very long nap. I sat quietly by myself for a while imagining him at school, holding in his anxious feelings from the morning, trying to be good—and then, when he got home, just not being able to control it anymore. Henry and Ella certainly had days when they'd come home and let it all out, too—but never with this level of anger.

When Keydell woke up, he acted as if nothing had happened. It was like he'd forgotten he had been upset. While he was sleeping, I had smoothed out his crumpled homework and taped the rip. I didn't show it to him until the next morning; I figured I would let the sleeping lion lie. He did however, finish the rest of his homework, stupid or not.

⇥⇤

The honeymoon period that DCYF had mentioned in our classes was obviously coming to an end. They told us, that the first six weeks or so when a child moves into a new home are hunky dory. The child behaves like an angel so they will be loved and accepted and then their real personality shows up. Whatever Keydell's issues were involving abandonment, self-worth, ADHD, and any other diagnoses were beginning to emerge, right on schedule. Keydell's mood was like a ticking time bomb, on edge, ready to blow at any second. He was not relaxed, and fidgeted a lot more in these past couple weeks.

In some ways, I thought his honest reactions and expressive behaviors meant he was comfortable with us, especially since he was only acting this way at home. In the same vein, I wondered *why* he was only acting this way at home. Did he not want to be here? Did he prefer school? Was he happier there? I was so confused, and it was getting worse every day.

What I could see was that, in his mind, Keydell was not smart enough, not fast enough, not the best at video games, and not strong enough—and being imperfect pissed him off. His anger was building, but I didn't understand why it was happening *now*. He had been so calm at Trout for so long; I couldn't figure out what was making him revert back to the way he'd behaved when he first arrived there. He was used to being away from his mother, but maybe being with us made him realize there was no hope of going back to her. I wondered if being with our "perfect" family triggered his feelings of unworthiness, or if he thought that he was not as "good" as his birth siblings, and that's why he got thrown out. Did he worry that, if he wasn't as "perfect" as Henry and Ella, we would eventually get rid of him too?

But Keydell *was* perfect, and he could think again. We were not giving him back. He was stuck with our perfect family, and was now a big part of it.

⚔

The next day I sat at the kitchen table, waiting for Chad to drop in for his usual visit while Keydell did his homework.

"I don't want Chad to visit," he said. "I want to get my homework done." He was so diligent.

"I know, Keydell, I'm getting kind of tired of all the visits, too, but it will only be for an hour or so, and then you can finish up."

When Chad pulled in the driveway, I walked out to give him a little heads up about Keydell's mood. "He's really into getting his homework done right away, so maybe instead of playing you can sit with him while he's doing that," I suggested.

"Sure, that's fine. How's he been doing?" he asked.

"Well, we have definitely noticed growing anger and frustration lately over what we feel is normal stuff. He's so hard on himself. Even if I work on table manners with him, or ask him to talk more softly in the house, he gets extremely upset. The way I parented Henry and Ella makes him feel attacked. He can't control his reactions to his feelings," I told him.

We walked into the kitchen and Chad sat down next to Keydell. He was a big guy, over six feet tall, so he was a real presence in our small house.

"Hey, bud, how are you? Your mom tells me you've been a little frustrated lately," he said.

"I'm fine," Keydell replied.

"What's been bothering you?" Chad asked.

"Nothing, I just want to do my homework," Keydell answered. *These visits are just one more thing out of his control*, I thought. He didn't get to choose his home, his new parents, how he ate his food, or when all these visits would happen.

They sat for a minute or two while Keydell did his math problems. Chad asked me to talk about our week and give more specifics on Keydell's behaviors. I told him about an episode during a video game with Henry, and how upset Keydell had gotten when Henry wanted to stop playing. He'd thrown a tantrum until Henry played one more game. I also told him how Keydell had ripped up his permission slip in frustration.

Keydell was still doing his math problems, but I could see his face changing. I thought, *Oh, shit. He didn't like reliving that story just now.* Maybe I could've told Chad in private what had happened, but I didn't want to talk behind Keydell's back either.

He started to get that bizarre, glazed look on his face that told me something was coming. It was like he was staring out from behind the eyes of some evil being that had taken over his body and was telling him to get mad.

"Keydell, I don't mean to tell on you, or make you feel badly about yourself, but I want Chad to know what has been going on so that he can help you out."

Chad pulled a small smooth stone out of his pocket and showed it to Keydell. "Do you know what this is?" he asked.

No reply. Keydell was staring straight ahead, stiff and lifeless. His shield was up, protecting himself from our words.

"It's a rubbing stone, or a worry stone," Chad continued, trying to hand it to Keydell. "When you start to get frustrated you can rub it to calm yourself down."

Seriously? Was he kidding? I almost burst out laughing. Did he have any idea the amount of physical energy Keydell put out during his most frustrating times? If anything, he would find that stone and hurl it at the wall during a tantrum. I almost took it from Chad myself to avoid an issue.

"I have suggested he punch his pillow," I interjected. "We've also had him run around the house or do some pull ups when he feels wound up, but sometimes it comes on as quickly, as if a switch has been flipped."

Just then, Keydell methodically reached for his homework and began to rip it up, slowly.

"Keydell, remember the last time you ripped your paper? You were not happy after you'd done it. Let's try to find another way to calm down right now. We are just talking. You haven't done anything wrong, we just want to help you find ways to stay calm when things upset you."

He didn't respond, just continued ripping up his paper and looking for more things to break. We'd gotten him upset, and he was revving up.

"This is how it starts, Chad," I said. "I'm not sure what to do when he gets like this. He goes to some other place in his head, and doesn't seem to hear us. We've tried hugging him and sometimes just giving him space, but it doesn't work that well anymore."

Chad turned to Keydell and tried to talk him down a bit. "Keydell, do you want to go outside and play? We can shoot hoops or run around?"

The switch had flipped. Keydell yelled, "No!" as he grabbed his pencil and chucked it across the kitchen.

"Please don't do that, Keydell, you could hurt someone," I said.

"Yeah, so what?" he screamed.

Then he started slapping his face really hard. Slap to the left cheek, slap to the right cheek, as if his hands hated him and were punishing him.

I walked over to him and said, "Hey, don't do that! You're going to hurt yourself. Let's sit together for a minute. I love you, buddy, and want to help you. Mommy is thinking that you never were taught coping skills around anger and frustration, and Chad and I just want to teach you how to do that. I have to tell him what's going on, or he won't know what tools to give us."

Keydell was so small but he oozed the energy and power of a full-grown bull. As I went to hug him, he threw his body into the refrigerator and bounced away from me. He screamed and screamed with the intensity of a mother who had just lost her baby. It was uncontrollable and was coming from old unhealed wounds. My arms went numb with fear and sadness, and my stomach turned to knots.

I'd seen Keydell upset before, but this time he was really freaking out.

"Del, let me hold you, sweetie. It's okay. We aren't mad at you but I don't know what you want me to do right now."

I felt myself getting upset, and took a deep breath to stay calm. The problem was, I didn't know what to do once I *was* calm.

He couldn't respond and continued to scream, looking for things to break. I tried to take things out of his hands as he grabbed them but he fought me and pulled away each time.

"What should I do, Chad?" I was starting to cry myself. Keydell was more upset than I'd ever seen him before, and it worried me.

"You're doing fine," Chad said. "Just keep reassuring him that you're here for him."

"I love you, Keydell. Help Mommy know what you are feeling. What can I do to help you?"

We went round and round for about a half hour. Edo was hiding in the den; I was crying. Keydell was screaming and thrashing, picking up everything he could while I tried to keep him from hurting himself or breaking anything. He finally ran up to his room, slammed the door and locked it. *I'll have to fix that*, I thought, standing outside his closed door.

"Keydell, please open the door, honey. I want to help you," I yelled.

Our narrow hallway seemed to be closing in on me. Chad had followed me up the stairs and was now standing next to me in what seemed like a one-foot by one-foot space. I was shaking and weak, and concerned for Keydell's safety. He had picked up what sounded like a lacrosse stick, and was beating it against the other side of the door. At least he was hitting the door and not himself.

After about ten minutes of this, Chad said something to me that was so startling, it stuck with me for a long time. "If this continues, you may have to take him back, or put him in the hospital."

"What? I'm not doing that," I said. "He just got here six weeks ago." I hoped Keydell had not heard Chad say that.

I could take more than this, and so could Jim and Henry and Ella. We had an army in place for this battle. There was no turning back.

"Keydell," I said, my voice shaking with fear. "Please, honey, I love you so much and want to help you. Tell me what I can do for you. What do you need right now?" I was spitting my words, crying, and practically yelling to get my point across. "What do you need from me? Help me help you."

Just then, the door flew open and Keydell, with his tiny, surrendering body and wet eyes, fell into my arms and grabbed hold of me in the tightest hug he could muster.

"I'm sorry," he said. "I'm so sorry. I love you, too. I love you, too. I want you to help me."

I cried even harder and held on tightly to him. I didn't want to let go. I knelt down to his level and said again, "I love you so much, Keydell, and want so much for you to be here and in our family. Let's be a team, okay?"

He hugged me again and we both just stayed like that for a few minutes. Chad quietly went downstairs and gave us our privacy. We unlocked from our hug and I put my little monster in his bed and rubbed his back until he fell asleep. I wanted to lie down right next to him, squeeze his pain out, and cover him in a blanket of safety, but Keydell had passed out cold. I went down to say goodbye to Chad.

"Wow, that was a big one," I said, my voice strained after so much crying and yelling. "He hasn't been that bad before. And by the way, what did you mean by 'give him back'? I just don't think that is a good idea, or one we would ever consider."

Chad explained that sometimes it happens. Families can't deal with a child's violence, so they give them up. I couldn't imagine us getting to that point at all, and was rather upset by the idea. We had only had him a few weeks, and *this* is what our support suggests? Giving him back, or putting him in a hospital? I would have preferred advice or insight on how to talk with our child when he was upset, or tools to use to keep it from happening in such a violent way—you know, besides a rubbing stone. Keydell needed my help, and once I let him know I was there to give it to him, he snapped out of his state, whatever state that was. Maybe he was carrying a ton of anger, fear, or confusion—or perhaps all of those—but having him leave home seemed like the worst thing to do.

When Jim got home that night I couldn't hold my tears back as I told him what had happened. I was still so shaken up. "Maybe we should do something special with him tonight," he suggested.

"I agree. I think he needs a little fun."

When Keydell woke up, we ate his favorite dinner of shepherd's pie, and played Concentration with him. He always won that card game by using his amazing memory, so he was happy and content for the rest of the evening. I think I went to bed at 8:00 that night, right after I put him back to bed. I was wiped.

⋞⊹⊹⋟

"Hey, no! Don't do that, Keydell, you can really hurt me," I said as I rushed to grab the rocks out of his hands.

"I hate you!" he yelled, picking up more rocks. They weren't rubbing stones, but they might as well have been.

That spring continued to be very challenging for all of us. Keydell's anger and frustration was escalating to giant proportions. He continually wanted someone to play with him and would get angry if you stopped. Henry tried to play video games with him peacefully, but it always ended in a meltdown. I told Keydell he would not be allowed to play with Henry if he couldn't be better at sportsmanship—but that made him mad, too.

I was out in the yard, playing with him on a very busy day. I had to do some things in the house, but he kept asking for one more toss with the ball, one more this, one more that. Finally, I said, "Sorry, bud, I have a few things to do. You can still play out here." That was when he got angry and started throwing rocks at me.

When one of the rocks almost caught the side of my head, I said, "This is hurting me. I'm going inside. You can't act like this and expect people to hang out with you." I was pissed off, sure, but mostly I wanted to get clear of those rocks.

I stomped across the yard to the door, shaking. By the time I looked out the kitchen window, he was swinging merrily on the swing set, chewing his gum. What was he thinking?

I know what I was thinking: *He is a little spoiled brat.* But how could that be? He hadn't been spoiled; in fact, the opposite.

I sat on the couch for a second to gather myself. This was getting rough. I was having a harder time staying calm, and felt on the defensive when he did things that hurt me.

After about five minutes, Keydell came bounding into the house like nothing had happened. He found me in the living room and said, "Hey, want to see how big I can blow a bubble?"

I just stared at him, stunned, as he began to blow a bubble. He had no idea what had just happened, or what I was feeling.

"Really?" I said. "You were just throwing rocks at me, and now you want me to look at your bubble? I think you owe me an apology, Keydell. Throwing rocks at someone is unacceptable."

He acted as if he remembered nothing. His face was calm; he was his happy cute self. In that moment, something clicked for me. This was more than just a behavioral problem. It was like something went on and off in his brain, a switch that, when it turned on, made him act like someone else. Was he possessed? Did he have a split personality? Was he really bipolar? It was weird. Keydell was such a sweet kid in between episodes—and then, *bam*, he was like a crazy man, an out-of-control maniac with no conscience.

I could tell Henry and Ella to go to their rooms to cool off if they did something wrong, but Keydell didn't seem to have the functioning capability to control his emotions or reactions. He *couldn't* calm himself down. I really wanted to get to the root of his issues so I could help him, but it was getting increasingly challenging to just get through a day without a two-hour tantrum. So often, the brunt of his anger was directed at me, and I wasn't sure how to handle that.

"Do you understand what you did out there?" I asked his pink, bubble-covered face.

"What?" he asked, as he peeled the gum from his nose and laughed.

"Keydell, it really hurts my feelings when you throw things at me and it makes me feel unsafe. I know you want me to play with you, but sometimes I have things to do, and you need to practice playing by yourself. I am not leaving you when I do that. I am right here."

He wasn't paying attention. He had moved on.

I sat there for a few more minutes in silence, collecting myself, and then decided to go cook dinner. That had been my original reason for leaving the yard in the first place.

⚒

Jim was in and out most days, so he didn't always know what was going on between Del and me. He would come home tired and walk right into the shit storm, or at the tail end of a meltdown. Today was one of those days.

"Just so you know, he's wound up," I warned.

"What happened? Are you okay?" he asked, immediately tensing up.

"It's okay I've got this," I said. "I'm not even sure what he's upset about today. He lost his pencil or something, and of course no matter what I said it upset him even more."

"I'll go talk to him," Jim said as he bolted up the stairs to deal with the screaming tornado flying around Keydell's bedroom.

When Jim was around, he tried to take care of things as best he could to give me a break, but his patience was wearing thin. Keydell would sometimes respond better to Jim, but sometimes it would be the same with both of us: lots of thrashing, us pinning him down so he wouldn't hurt himself or break things, and often too much yelling because we were all so frustrated and upset. Keydell would scream even if we stayed calm. Ella usually shut her door and tried to stay out of it.

Henry wanted to be as helpful as he could, because he could see how hard it was on me. Keydell was still small enough for me to hold him down when he started getting violent, but he was very strong, and would sometimes get in a good hit. When I was "handling things," Henry would often jump in and say, "Mom, let me give it a try." I felt guilty, and didn't want him to feel responsible for Keydell's behavior since *I* was the one who brought him into our home, but sometimes it was nice to have Henry there. He was almost six feet tall now, and could certainly hold Keydell firmly and safely.

Keydell was relentless in tormenting us. He would start with damaging things; when we would try to stop him, he would try harder to find things to damage. Then, once we were exhausted from holding him down, he might calm down enough for us to believe he was fine, only to start again as soon as we let him go. We would ask him to stay in his room, but he thought it was much better to ignore that request, follow us downstairs, and continue with the rage. Most times the episodes ended only because he got tired; then, the switch would flip off as fast as it had switched on. We would all be completely drained. Keydell would fall asleep, and when he woke up, he would be hungry but fine. This all would take place over an hour or two.

⊰⊱

"What the hell, Keydell? Stay out of my room and stop screaming. I have to do my homework," Ella yelled, as Keydell opened and closed her door repeatedly to get her attention. Ella had had a bonfire party that weekend in our backyard, and Keydell had been spoken to for grabbing Ella's friend's rear end. She was still upset with him. She hadn't had many kind words for him over the past few weeks anyway, and he didn't like that. He seemed to need Ella's approval more than he needed Henry's. This boy definitely had female relationship issues.

"Keydell, leave Ella alone and go play downstairs for a while," I directed him.

"No."

"Del, you know how much you like to get your homework done. Please give Ella the same courtesy."

"No."

"I am not going to ask again. If you don't leave her alone you will not have ice cream after dinner," I threatened.

He ran past me and down the stairs as fast as he could. I could hear him open the freezer in the kitchen. I let him be for a minute so I could talk to Ella.

"I hate him," she said. "He has ruined my life. I don't want him around. I don't even like coming home any more. Our house used to be peaceful, but now it's like a freakin' crazy place." She plopped down on her bed, and I sat down next to her.

"I know, Boo. I'm sorry," I said, trying to placate her. "I'm trying my best to help him and get things more stable, but he is your brother now and we have to learn to deal with him and figure things out as a family. I know it's not easy—but look at where he's coming from. He didn't have a mother who would sit with him like this, read books with him, or just go to the park like you did. He's hurting, and the more we show him love, the better he will get."

At least, I hoped so.

She turned to me with teary eyes. "Mom, he grabbed Courtney's rear end the other night, he jumps on people, and he won't stay out of my room. He's just a pure brat, and it's creepy how he is with my friends. I can't have anyone over."

"I know, but I hope your friends understand on some level what is going on and can find some patience with him—as I hope that you can too."

"I don't want to, Mom," she pleaded. "I just want him away from me."

"All we can do is try, Boo. We have to stick together. I will talk to him, and you should talk to him about your feelings, too. Okay?"

"I have tried," she replied, "but he just laughs in my face or runs away. It's like he *wants* me to be mad at him. He tried pushing me down the stairs the other day, and threw some books at me."

"Well, maybe he is mad so wants us to be mad, too. That would not surprise me. Just keep trying, even if you don't get the reaction you want. He will hear it and eventually understand. If you are feeling unsafe though, come get one of us—or protect yourself from the flying objects at least," I said with a dramatic wave of my arms. I was trying to get a smile out of her. "We need to find compassion for him, even when he's being a pain in the ass."

I gave her the best reassuring hug I could come up with, and walked out feeling so guilty. My baby girl was hurting. Keydell hadn't ruined her life, *I* had. Ella had just turned fifteen. This should be her time to be carefree and hang with her friends—but now, she was dealing with a new little brother who was out of control. We both knew we were doing something good for him ... But was it good for us?

I went downstairs and found Keydell at the table with a big bowl of ice cream in front of him. I picked it up and dumped it in the trash, bowl and all.

"Keydell, really? You were bugging Ella on purpose, so take responsibility for your actions. She asked you nicely to stop banging her door several times, but you kept pushing, and that got her more upset. Now you're eating ice cream just to upset me."

"No, I'm not. You're the one who just threw it out." He was standing now with the spoon in his hand and vanilla ice cream around the edges of his lips, looking like a rabid dog. He reached for the freezer to get the carton of ice cream out again, but I beat him to it and put the whole thing in the garbage.

"If you act like this, you will not get your way. We are done with the ice cream. Let's stop now so we don't blow this up into a big thing. Why don't you go outside and play with Edo for a bit?"

"No. It's raining," said Keydell.

"Okay, then do something inside."

"I want ice cream."

"We are done with the ice cream. It's all gone now and in the trash."

"Bitch!" He ran upstairs and opened and slammed his own door as loudly as he could. I heard Ella yell, "Oh my *God!*" She came downstairs to try and finish her homework.

Keydell's door slammed. He opened it, yelled "Bitch!" and then slammed it again. And so it went for another hour.

Henry and I would often sit at the kitchen table after an episode, talking about what had happened and what we could do differently the next time. I think he was as curious about the psychology of it all as I was, and wanted to find a solution. He knew this was hard on me, too.

"I'm doing my best, Henry, but I'm just not sure what's bothering him. He seems to be mad at me more than anyone else, so maybe he's taking his subconscious anger about his mother out on me."

"He needs more discipline." Henry said, in all of his seventeen-year-old wisdom. "Take his video games away cold turkey if he acts up."

"Henry, those games are the one thing he can control right now. I know he doesn't like to lose, but when he plays on his own I think in some ways he feels he's in control. I think we have to take it slowly. We need to start introducing new things to him—like riding his bike, going in the woods to play, or getting him on a sports team. I'm not sure he could handle being on a team with his angry outbursts, but so far he's only acted out at home, so who knows? It's basically going to take time and trial and error."

"Let's sign him up for lacrosse, Mom," Henry suggested. "He was good at it when I played with him at Trout. We have to try something."

I agreed. "That might help him redirect his crazy energy."

Maybe the sports team would help him build self-esteem. He was so athletic, I was sure he would love it. Perhaps it would help him understand teamwork and that he didn't need to know how to do everything perfectly on his own.

I was also going to look into therapy again. He hadn't been seeing a counselor since he had arrived with us.

Keydell's meltdowns tested every fiber of my patience. It was truly a test of what I was capable of—and, for that matter, what the whole family was capable of. Jim and I didn't always agree on how to handle Keydell during or after an episode, but we managed to realize that the whole thing was tough and we were each handling it in the best way we could. We were like a wrestling tag team. One tapped out and the other tapped in. I was so grateful to have Jim's help, but it was a real practice in staying calm through the storm. Sometimes, Jim and I would be so tired after an episode that we couldn't even speak. It was all too overwhelming. We needed some better strategies.

CHAPTER 9

INGREDIENTS

"We think that the point is to pass the test or to overcome the problem, but the truth is that things don't really get solved. They come together and they fall apart."

—*Pema Chodron*

"Let's take a walk to the airport Keydell," I suggested. "We both could use some fresh spring air."

It had been a rainy spring, typical for Rhode Island, but today was cloudy and dry. The light was soft, and enveloped us in calm. After months of feeling house-bound, plus all the drama of Keydell's fits, calm was surely something we needed.

I'd been wracking my brain, trying to come up with some ways to build Keydell's self-esteem. He had made comments about not being as "good" as Henry or Ella, and I wanted him to realize we are all works in progress. I'd been thinking of a way to make my explanation fun and at his level.

As we walked along and Keydell was doing his usual rock-kicking, I said, "You know what Del, growing up is kind of like baking a cake."

I didn't know where this was coming from, but I kind of liked what I came up with.

"It's a process of taking all kinds of ingredients—like your parents, your home environment, your karma and everything else—and mixing it all up in a big bowl, just like you would the flour, sugar, milk and eggs. You are like a cake in the making!" I said.

He thought about this for a minute, then turned to me and asked, "Are Henry and Ella cakes yet?"

"Well, I would say they are in the oven. They are still cooking, and so am I. I'm not sure *when* we are totally done, because just when you think you're done, someone comes along and takes a big bite out of you!"

We both laughed at that. "We're always working on ourselves, adding and taking away parts. We add what we need, and let go of what we don't need."

"How cooked am I?" Keydell asked. I loved the way he phrased that question.

"I think when you came to us you had all the ingredients you needed," I answered. "A big heart, a strong body, a smart brain, and lots of delicious charm. I believe we are all born with everything we need to be who we want to be, but sometimes the ingredients are still separated and not mixed together well yet.

"I think now you are in the bowl," I continued. "All your ingredients are together and you are stirring it all up—and I, as the chef, am helping you. It won't be long until we can put you in the oven to make you into a delicious cake, Keydell." I tickled his side. "In the meantime, we can keep working on which ingredients to keep and which ones we want to take out of the bowl, okay?"

He liked that idea. "I want to take out my anger," he said.

"Yes, I bet you do. It can't be fun to feel the way you do, and nobody wants to take a bite of angry," I said with a grin. I stopped him for a moment and looked him right in the eye. We were standing in the middle of the long road that led to the airport, and I could feel the breeze across my neck. I knelt down in front of him, holding his shoulders and said, "You know my biggest aim for you is to find happiness with us. That is my main goal as your parent; to give you the tools you need to be a happy man. I will never stop trying."

"I know," he said as he turned from me and back to the small rock, which he moved perfectly in front of his feet the rest of the way.

I asked him what flavor cake he wanted to be. Of course, he said, "Ice cream cake!"

⋇⊹⊱

I came home from a grocery run one afternoon to find all three kids playing lacrosse in the yard. Henry and Ella were passing the ball around, showing Keydell some drills and techniques since we had just signed him up for the town team earlier that week.

Ella came over, still wearing her face gear and mouth guard, to help me with the groceries, and soon, Henry and Keydell came in to see what food they could snag for their ever-hungry bodies. Keydell still had his helmet on; it was so big that he looked like a bobble head doll.

"How's it going out there, you guys?" I asked.

"Mom, Keydell is such a natural—and what is really amazing about him is that he is super coachable," said Henry. "I have never seen a kid like him before. I can show him a move and he just imitates it. It's pretty impressive."

"Yeah, Keydell, you're really good," Ella chimed in as she popped a small tomato in her mouth. Keydell grinned and soaked in her approval.

"Are you enjoying it, Keydell?" I asked.

As he nodded his head, the helmet bobbed up and down. "Do you want to watch my shot?"

"Yeah, let me get these groceries put away and I'll come out."

The kids grabbed more snacks and I put the food away before venturing out to see the big man on campus show off his stuff. Henry started off the play as he and Keydell ran back and forth a few times, across and behind the net. Then, Henry tossed the ball to Keydell, who ran around the back of the net and leaped in the air while shooting into the goal. He was so awesome and graceful, with such power behind his shot.

"Wow," I said, "that was fancy."

"See, isn't he amazing?" Henry smiled. He was so proud of his little brother.

"I think we have the next Paul Rabil here," Ella said. "You have his moves. See if you can spin before you make the shot."

So without a blink he did the same set up and added the spin. We all clapped and laughed with joy at how in-control he was. And he was having fun.

That season, Keydell was incredible to watch on the field. He had such determination to do well, and his coaches loved him for it. It also gave him something in common with Henry and Ella. Like with his homework, however, if he "messed up," he got pissed off and sometimes ran off the field mid-play. The coaches over-looked it; he was still so young that it appeared to be normal kid stuff (and really, it was; other boys did this too) and Keydell was too valuable to pull off the team anyway.

As confused and out of control as Keydell was in his mind, he was centered and in control in his body. He moved with confidence and ease. There was no hesitation in his steps, and his focus was unparal-leled for such a young boy. When he was playing, his mind seemed quiet, as if it were letting his body take over. It was beautiful to watch— like a meditation in motion. His math-minded brain gave him a quick sense of the field and what he needed to do to make the play work.

Keydell was what I call a black-and-white thinker. Actions were either right or wrong, and answers needed to be either "Yes" or "No." He didn't like gray areas. If I answered a question with "Maybe," it frustrated him to no end. He liked order, hated schedule changes, and was very organized with his things. It made getting him to do his homework and getting ready for school much easier for us than it is for many other parents. I was really grateful that at least we had some ease around that!

Keydell *wanted* to be good. He wanted to do well in school, and he wanted to be good at sports. When he had his meltdowns, I knew that, deep down in his little heart, there was a sadness about how he acted, and that he wanted to find a solution for his anger and outbursts as much as we did. He was starting to like it here with our family, and he wanted to stay.

After one outburst I asked, "Do you like being in our family Keydell? You seem mad at your situation and unhappy in general."

"I'm fine and I like it here," he answered. That's about all I got, so I took him for his word.

When he thought we disapproved of something he did, it tackled his ego. The problem was he took almost every comment we made as disapproval as opposed to the basic parenting lesson that it was. If we tried to discipline him, he perceived it as a threat and retreated or fought back like crazy. Those feelings of failure triggered him and he lost control. It took some time to realize but after seeing him on the athletic field and what triggered him there, we started to recognize that similar things triggered him at home. It was his self-hatred and fear of failing.

The spring dried out, and the sun was beginning to feel warmer on my cheeks. I knew summer was on its way. I loved summer in New England, as it always brought a more relaxed schedule for our family. We weren't running from game to game or to after-school events every day. It was impossible not to enjoy summer's more carefree feeling.

Keydell was finishing third grade at Aquidneck School, and had had very few behavioral incidents that term. He mainly got called out by teachers for being an overly active boy who liked to talk a lot, but we could deal with that. He hadn't had a meltdown for a few weeks, and I felt like we were turning a corner. Maybe we had successfully redirected some of his negative energy toward sports. We still worked on his inappropriate touching in social situations—like using Henry's friends as climbing poles and Ella's as objects of tight hugging—but thankfully, our community was starting to know Keydell and understood what was going on. They saw how athletic and cute he was, and not how upset and violent he could be.

Until the summer of 2009, that is.

We had been members of our local YMCA for many years. Henry and Ella had attended their pre-school, and we used their athletic facilities to work out. They ran a great summer sports camp so we decided to register Keydell for a few weeks to continue his love of sports while the local town teams were on a break. The idea was to keep him active and give him the opportunity to try a variety of sports. The camp hosted hundreds of kids in various activities, but this first week Keydell's group would focus on football.

I packed his lunch box that first morning, and off we went. It was a warm summer day and Keydell seemed happy to be going. After I left him with the camp counselor, I headed back to my studio to do some editing.

About an hour later, my phone rang.

"Hey Kim, you might want to come down and pick up Keydell," said Mike, the YMCA's second-in-command, and a friend of ours. He was great with kids, since he acted like a big kid himself. He didn't sound playful in that moment however.

"Oh man. What's up?" I asked.

"Well, we've tried to calm Keydell down but he is throwing everyone's lunch box into the street, he hit another camper, and is screaming like crazy," Mike answered.

"I'll be right there."

I drove the endless ten minutes to the Y's backfield, where the campers played football, and parked my car. I took a few deep breaths before getting out. I noticed Keydell sitting alone under the small pavilion while the other kids were playing football. Mike was watching him from about twenty feet away. As I walked over, I could see that he'd been crying, so I guessed he'd come out of his anger state and was now in the phase of his meltdown where he was exhausted and somewhat stable again. Mike came over to me and explained again in front of Keydell what had happened.

"A bunch of the kids were playing toss," Mike explained. "Keydell wanted Dan, the camp counselor, to pass the football to him every time, and got upset when he didn't. When he did get the ball and one of the kids teased him about how he caught it, he beaned it right at his head, hard. Then, when he was spoken to, he got very mad, and started throwing the lunch boxes into the street."

The campers stowed their backpacks and lunch boxes on the picnic tables under the pavilion, so Keydell had easy access to their things. I couldn't help but imagine the scene. On the one hand, I figured the Y staff had seen it all before, but watching a kid totally loose it can be pretty shocking.

I looked at Keydell and he was getting that contorted face again. His brow was furrowed, his eyes were on fire, and I could tell he didn't like what he was hearing. He stood up quickly, looking for something to throw. I grabbed him and knelt down in front of him holding his shoulders firmly. I wanted eye contact.

"Hey, let me hear your side of the story, Del," I said soothingly. "What was bothering you enough to throw other people's stuff?"

This was the first time he had had an outburst where it really affected others.

"I hate it here," he said. "The game is so unfair. Every time Dan or one of the other kids threw the ball to me it was a bad pass so I wanted them to do it over but they wouldn't do it." His body was stiff and planted in place.

"Well, sweetie, I don't think they would throw you a bad pass on purpose. Everyone is trying to learn to play, and it's okay if someone can't throw or catch well. You have to be patient. There are a lot of kids at this camp, and you have to take turns. It's not kind behavior to damage other people's things because you are upset, Keydell. You can be upset, but you can't throw their things."

I tried to remind him to take deep breaths to calm down. Where was Chad's freakin' rubbing stone when you needed it? Actually, he probably would have thrown that too.

"Look," I said, "Mommy and Daddy have to work so we can have food, our house, and be able to do fun things sometimes. If you behave like this at camp we have to stop everything and come get you, which means we can't work. Your behavior affects that, okay? Do you understand that when you get upset like that it affects everyone?"

He started to cry again and I gave him a big hug. As Keydell got in the car, Mike said, "Wow, what you said to him was so clear and calm. I think he understood, don't you?"

"Mike," I said, "I wish he understood and could actually do something about it. He hears me, and I hope that someday he will be able to control what he's feeling. He's not mean; he is frustrated, and it comes out as anger. Maybe it changes from frustration to anger, but I really think he is a sweet person down deep. Sorry about him hitting the other boy."

Mike explained that Keydell would have to stay home a day for doing so.

"I understand," I nodded. "Thank you, and sorry again about all this."

Knowing I would now have an upset child on my hands, I prepared myself for chaos for the rest of the day, and possibly tomorrow when he woke up and realized he was not going to camp. I was annoyed, and I could feel my blood boiling. I could hear the tension in my voice as I spoke to Keydell, and knew I needed to take it down a notch. I took a few deep breaths, told myself to be calm and patient, and tried to put aside my own frustrations and anger. I knew fire only fueled fire.

"Are you okay?" I asked after I got in the car.

"That counselor sucks," said Keydell.

"That is not very nice," I warned. "Can you find a better way to say that, please?"

"He kept throwing the ball too high" he replied. "He never gave me a good throw."

We talked again about sharing and taking turns and I realized that, again, the incident was about him feeling like he didn't hit perfection at what he was doing. He wasn't really mad at the counselor; he was disappointed with himself.

"I'm really sorry you didn't get what you wanted, Keydell, but you cannot hurt other people. Ever. It's *never* okay to hit someone unless your life is in danger. The boy that laughed at you was not kind, but you should always try to be kind no matter what. Niceness first! I promise it will always pay off in the long run," I coached. Keydell was quiet the rest of the way home.

The next morning when Keydell came downstairs he was okay. Maybe he was relieved he didn't have to go back to camp. Perhaps he was embarrassed about what had happened.

"How are you this morning, sweetie?" I asked.

"Good," he replied.

"I have to do some work today, but maybe later we can do something together," I suggested. "But since you're not going to camp, I want you to clean your room and I have a few other chores for you."

Keydell turned on his heels, marched back upstairs, and slammed his door. "I'm going back to bed," he yelled. "I hate you."

Well, I guess I jumped into that too soon. My thinking was that his behavior caused us all to have to adjust, so he was going to have to do some chores to make up for it. I didn't think it was that bad, but he sure did. He was already banging on the wall repeatedly, his heel tapping like a mantra: "Not doing it, not doing it, not doing it."

Jim was out in the office barn already that morning, and was coming back in for a second cup of coffee when he heard the noise.

"How's Del doing?" he asked.

"Peachy." I answered. "He's already revved up. I told him he had to clean his room today and do a few chores, and he didn't like that."

Jim gave me a frustrated look that took me off guard. I thought he believed I was wrong to ask that of Keydell and get things going with him.

"I just wanted him to know that his behavior wasn't going to get him a day off," I explained.

Jim stormed past me to the bottom of the stairs, and yelled up to Keydell. "Stop kicking the wall."

Keydell did not listen at all. In fact, I think he kicked harder and with more frequency. Jim stomped to the top of the stairs, signaling he was coming, opened Keydell's door—and, with a glaring look said, "CUT. IT. OUT! Your mom asked you to clean your room today, that's it."

Whew, he was on my side; he wasn't upset with me. He was just tired of all the fits like I was. I went upstairs to play backup.

Keydell just looked right back at Jim and said, "I'm not doing it."

"Yes, you are," Jim told him.

"Not doing it, not doing it, not doing it, not doing it."

He could be so defiant, and we would be so forceful. We never had to do this with Henry and Ella because they usually had remorse for what they had done wrong. They knew they had to suck it up and make up for it. Keydell always refused what we asked. It was as if he felt entitled to do only what he wanted. He needed to understand the consequences for his actions, but putting them into place was basically setting ourselves up for a two-hour battle. It was exhausting. It seemed his aim was to wear us down.

"Keydell," I said. "You're going to have to do the chores at some point, so you can either do them now and get it over with and have the day to play, or you can continue with this drama, wear yourself out and still do the chores later. I have to get to work, and so does Dad, so please try to calm down and start cleaning your room."

I looked at Jim and said, "Let's just leave him alone for a bit and you can go to work. I have this."

We started to head downstairs to give Keydell space and have that second cup of coffee. As we were walking down the stairs, we heard something hit the wall in the hallway. Then something else hit, then something else. I could feel my shoulders tightening, and I knew Keydell was winding up for a meltdown.

"Keydell, if you throw your things like that, we keep them. Please just take some deep breaths and try to relax for a few minutes," I said.

Something else was thrown against the wall in his room, and he again repeated over and over, "I'm not doing it, I'm not doing it."

Jim turned to go back upstairs. "Stay here, I'll talk to him." I knew he was pissed. Jim opened Keydell's door with a jolt. It startled him and made him jump. I could hear his feet hitting the ground from downstairs.

"Cut it out," Jim yelled. "All we asked you to do was clean up your room. You want to keep going like this? Just try me. Keep going and there will be more problems."

Jim's voice was strained and intense, so I went up to the room, even though he'd told me to stay put. Keydell was on his back on the bed. Jim was standing over him, holding him down.

"Stop throwing things and kicking the wall," Jim said to Keydell. "Just calm down and try to relax."

"Jim, try to just hold him in a hug like Denise suggested," I whispered in his ear as Keydell screamed. "Tell him you love him and want to help him."

Jim picked a protesting Keydell up off the bed and held him tightly in his arms and just kept saying, "We love you, buddy, it's going to be okay. Just take some deep breaths." Jim began calming down as much as Keydell. I think the tight hugging was good for both of them. "Mom and I just want you to know we love you, but you can't act like this over chores. Just keep relaxing."

I'm not sure why the tight hugs worked sometimes, and sometimes not—but in this moment, Jim's big, loving arms were slowly melting Keydell's tiny body into putty. His 230 pounds next to Keydell's fifty made him look like a big bear next to its cub. Jim always had that way of calming babies, too. Ella had been a colicky baby, and he would hold her against his chest and rock her for hours to calm her down. It usually worked. He was working his magic again with Keydell.

They sat like that for five minutes or so as both of them started to breathe more normally again. I could see Keydell was coming out of his state. Jim eased Keydell back in front as he stayed seated on the bed. Keydell had big crocodile tears in his eyes as he looked at Jim.

"It's okay, Del, you're okay now," Jim said.

"Can I have something to eat?" Keydell asked.

We both smiled and followed him downstairs to get some breakfast. I touched Jim's arm as a way to say, "Great job." Then, he headed off to work while I sat with Keydell for a bit. Later on, Del and I did the chores together.

CHAPTER 10

ADOPTION

"I'm full. I'm Fuller."

—Comment my family always made at dinner when guests said they were full.

It was August 23, 2009—the end of a crazy summer filled with emotional ups and downs. Keydell had been with us for eight months. The big day had finally arrived when he would officially become our son. We let him choose which last name he would take; Fuller, my maiden name, which I had kept, or Miller like my husband and our kids. He chose Fuller. He thought it was cool to have the same initials as me: KF. Maybe he did love me. I was flattered he wanted to be a Fuller, especially since my parents had all girls, and no one to carry on the Fuller name from our side.

My good friend Cris, who was one of the Adopt-a-Home Moms, was our lawyer for the adoption. It was nice to have someone we knew, since this was such a personal event. My whole family came to Providence for the big day. Angela from Adoption Rhode Island and

Chad from Children's Friends came as well, and Matt from DCYF even made an appearance. He had come through for us in the end.

It was a very hot August day, but I think I was sweating more from nerves and anticipation than from the heat. We all went upstairs to the courtroom waiting area and sat near two other families who were there for the same reason. It was heartwarming to watch all of our families interacting. It supported my belief that, no matter who your family is made up of, they are still your family. Keydell was being introspective but hyper, so I had him count the checkered floor tiles in the long hallway we were sitting in. He looked so handsome in a little polo shirt and plaid shorts, so much better than the silky sports attire he normally wore. I didn't want to move from my seat in case the judge called us in. I was wringing my hands trying to keep from crying.

"Cris, what should we expect in there?" I asked, trying to talk through the lump in my throat.

"It will be simple," she explained. "The judge will have me present the case, he will ask Keydell if he wants to be in your family, and ask you if you are ready to have him in yours. Then, he will rule on the case, and we will sign the papers. You'll get sent a new birth certificate with your names on it listing you as his parents."

"His birth mom's name won't be on there?" I asked.

"Nope, you get a whole new one."

Interesting. We wanted us to be his official parents, but didn't want to remove his birth mom from the certificate, either. Somehow I thought that would be unfair to Keydell since he knew who she was. I didn't think he would ever forget her name, but I wanted to make sure he always knew where he came from.

We sat in the waiting area, watching the other families go in nervous and come back out smiling. We congratulated them. Then, finally, it was our turn.

Jim and I sat at a big courtroom table with Cris and Keydell between us, and the rest of our family sat in the seats behind us. I was so emotional; I knew I was going to lose it. Henry and Ella sat directly behind us, and as I looked back at them I had an overwhelming sense of pride. They were amazing, and I was such a lucky mom to have all these babies. The judge was an older man with a great sense of humor, and began by saying hello to all of us and exclaiming about what a great day this was. He looked at Keydell and said, "You are a very lucky young man."

I sure hoped Keydell felt that way, too. Our chairs swiveled, and Keydell was taking full advantage of it. He was swinging side to side, dangling his feet above the floor. He used the table to propel himself with each turn. I think his mind was elsewhere, but his body was in the present moment. He looked so vulnerable in that giant chair.

Cris presented our case, and the judge asked Jim and I to stand and answer some questions. "Do you pledge to keep Keydell safe in your home? Do you understand that you are going from being a foster parent to an adoptive parent?"

I could barely answer because tears were running down my face and my throat was closing up. Even though things had been tough with Keydell, I could not talk about him with friends or family without tearing up with love. He was a part of us all now, and we loved him and admired his strength and courage.

"Yes, yes, yes, all of the above, yes," we answered. Then, the judge asked Keydell if he understood what was happening and that he was going to become a Fuller.

Keydell answered, "Yes." I think this was the first time he realized he was staying with us forever. He had found the home he wanted— the home he had painted while still living at Trout Drive. He would never go to a foster home again; he would not go back to a group home. He would not go back to living with his mother. We wanted him in all his perfection, and it was important that he understood that. He had been given away by everyone he had lived with so far, and thought of himself as a "bad" boy and not worth keeping.

I wondered what his little eight-year-old mind was thinking as he listened to the official proceedings. I really hoped this was what he wanted, and that he would be happy with us. I loved him so much, and so did Jim. I knew that Henry and Ella did as well, even as hard as it had been thus far.

The judge hit the gavel to the wood—and we were a family. Just like that. Everyone clapped as I bawled my eyes out and hugged Jim, Keydell, and my big kids. We presented Keydell with a sports jersey we had made with the name Fuller on the back, and asked Cris to take our first new family group photo together. It felt awesome. We went home and had a big party that included his friends, our whole family, and some of the Adopt-a-Home Moms. We had a Slip-n-Slide and an ice cream cake to celebrate what we called "Keydell's new birthday." He gets two birthdays each year now, one on the day of his adoption, and one on his actual day of birth. (He asked me if he could get presents on both days, too; I said, "First things first. It's really just an excuse for us to eat more ice cream.")

CHAPTER 11

RELEASE

"Don't let the behavior of others destroy your inner peace."

—*Dalai Lama*

I am so fucking sick of this. He is so rude and awful to me. Holy crap. Sometimes I just want to throw my hands in the air and say "screw it." You want to act that way, go ahead. See what happens on your own. I will stop trying to help you since you don't want my help anyway, you little shit.

This is what went on in my head sometimes. Nice, huh? Sometimes I actually said it out loud, and I hated myself for it. I never wanted Keydell to feel like I would give up on him—because I wouldn't—but some days, he got me. He got me so good, and I would lose my shit just like he did.

He started throwing things out the car window—like the new watch I had just gotten him. He threw things at me, broke things, banged up his walls and floors, and called me a bitch. I was seeing a side of myself I didn't know existed. I was not a yeller—well, I *hadn't* been a yeller, but I guess I was now—and it drained me to be angry. I could only imagine how Keydell must have felt. I wanted to run. I wanted to scream. But mostly, I wanted to find some help.

Someone fucking help me! Fuckity fuck fuck fuck.

I was so tired, and felt so guilty for causing my family all this drama. Even Edo had figured out how to open the back door and run to the field when Keydell started heating up. Fucking Christ, I'd even traumatized the dog. I was trying to be a good person. I was trying to stay calm and understand. I was trying to be compassionate—but holy shit; it was *hard* sometimes.

When things reached the breaking point, I would usually go sit on my back steps or in my office barn and cry my eyes out, trying to breathe slowly. My body felt like it was filled to bursting with tiny bugs, all squirming around and pushing at my skin to get out.

Someone said once that your emotions change every fifteen seconds. Mine were going from anger, to rage, to frustration, to annoyance, to frustration, to sadness. Not good, not good at all. It was the first time in my life that I'd felt helpless.

Yet ... I still had so much empathy for what my son was going through. It was bad, but I knew I could hold on for just a little bit more.

CHAPTER 12

THERAPY

"It is wiser to find out than to suppose."

—*Mark Twain*

Henry was starting his senior year of high school, and Ella was a freshman. It was a big year for them both, with one high school career ending, and another beginning. It seemed crazy that we would be looking at colleges this year for Hank.

He and Ella took off for school that first day in the white Jeep Henry had bought for himself with his acting money. He and Ella had both gotten roles in a movie called "Dan in Real Life," that was filmed in Rhode Island a few years back. Keydell and I prepared to walk to Forest Elementary School, which was just down the street from us. We had moved him from Aquidneck School for third grade so we wouldn't have to drive him daily, and he was trying to be brave. He put on his new backpack, and was wearing his favorite silky sports outfit as we headed out the door with Edo leading the way.

"Are you nervous, Del?" I asked after a few minutes of silent walking.

"I won't know anyone," he replied. His pace had slowed down a bit.

"But, just think: you'll make new friends in no time. Then, when you move to the middle school next year, you will know kids from both elementary schools combined."

"Yeah, that is pretty cool."

Keydell didn't love change like I did. Moving from place to place felt interesting and exciting to me; for him, it was scary and challenging. He'd wanted to stay at Aquidneck School, but Forest was so much closer and more convenient.

"You will be amazing today, Keydell. Just be kind to everyone and introduce yourself. Many of these kids won't know each other either, so enjoy and have a great day."

He accepted a sideways hug from me and walked the rest of the way down the path to the school doors on his own. He did not look back or wave goodbye.

⊶⊷

For our family, fall also meant soccer season.

I had sponsored a recreational team for several years now, and had coached a team when Henry and Ella were little (even though I had no idea what I was doing—I ran track in school). Both of my big kids now played for the high school. Since Keydell had done so well with lacrosse and it seemed to help him, we signed him up for the Kim Fuller Photography-sponsored soccer team. Ella was the assistant coach so she could fulfill her community service hours.

The past lacrosse season showed us that Keydell was more than just a good athlete; he was the whole package. Along with his athleticism, he had drive, determination, and a passion for sports.

He, Henry and Ella had participated in a short road race this past summer, and even though he had not originally planned to race, Keydell jumped in at the starting line at the last minute, wearing his blue jeans and worn-out sneakers, and ended up finishing just after Henry in seventh place. He had beaten most of the high school girls' cross country team, not to mention two hundred other runners. It was a local charity run, so there were no competitive runners involved, but we were still impressed. He finished with only two tiny beads of sweat on his brow and got his first medal. We knew he would do well in any sport that involved lots of running, so off we went for our first soccer game.

We set up the folding chairs that lived in the back of my car along with a stadium blanket, and watched the game.

"Jim, look at him go," I said excitedly. "He's so fast, even with a ball at his feet."

Keydell was a natural. This was his very first game of soccer and it looked like he'd been playing for years. All the kids were so little that the soccer ball practically came up to their knees, but Keydell moved with the ease of a cat playing with a jingle bell. He had a natural sense of the game, knowing where to be on the field and how to get the ball in the net. I was so impressed.

"I think he is Pelé reincarnated," I said to Jim.

"Yeah, he's something. He was good at lacrosse, but I think he's even better at this."

Saturdays at the soccer fields had been our social time since Henry and Ella started playing recreational soccer. No more clubs or bars for us. There were seven fields at our local park, so the place was hopping—and, to us, as fun as the club scene, minus the dancing—and I did love dancing.

I first met "The Rays" dancing. We all took a Latino dance class at the YMCA every Tuesday morning, imagining ourselves as music video stars, or like the Fly Girls on "In Living Color." Though the dance class was just a memory now, my kids scoring goals was a great excuse for some happy dancing. We had a lot of family dance parties in our living room, too, so I got my jollies out when I could.

After the game, Keydell came running over, full of chatter and replays of the game.

"Did you see that first goal? It went right through that boy's legs. My second goal was cool, too, wasn't it?"

Keydell's coach came up to us and commented on his play.

"He's really good," he exclaimed. "Glad to have him on the team."

"Thanks, we just adopted Keydell and when he lived at the group home down the street, they couldn't let the kids do team sports. It was too hard to get them to practice and games."

"Well, he's made up for lost time. Sorry I had to pull him out after the first few goals. We were running the other team into the ground," his coach apologized.

Jim and I laughed and thanked him for his coaching. I think from that day forward Keydell has had a soccer ball at his feet every single day. He had found his passion. He only played one more season of lacrosse after that, and mainly because he thought we wanted him to. He dove into soccer and it became a year-round activity.

It made me feel hopeful to see him so sure of himself out on the field, surer of himself than anywhere else in his life, and completely focused. He would sometimes act completely silly before a game, but as soon as the whistle blew he was all business. It centered him. It was encouraging that all these sports could be just the thing he needed to find some ease and happiness in his life. It was a start. It was a start.

At the end of the fall season, he was invited to try out for Middletown's travel team. He made the A team, the top tier, easily.

November 17, 2009

Keydell's medications and health care were covered through the Neighborhood Health Plan of R.I., thank goodness. We were also given a small check each month (which we hadn't known we were getting before the adoption) to help cover some of his special needs. It wasn't much, but it helped. With the economy in a slump, our businesses had slowed down. When I think back on that, though, it was a blessing in disguise because it gave us the time we needed to take care of Keydell. We might have been a bit broke, but caring for him was important.

We'd been seeing Keydell's pediatrician on a regular basis so that his medications could be maintained, but she recommended we find a new therapist. He needed someone to talk to and to monitor his meds more carefully. She was happy to keep him on his current medications for the time being, but we told her we had concerns that he was on too many things for what seemed to be the wrong reasons. He seemed depressed and still was having a lot of violent outbursts. We would get a break from them for a few days or weeks but they always returned. We found a social worker, Dr. Sonya, through our health insurance provider, and began looking for a psychiatrist to help with his medications. We scheduled an appointment with Sonya early in November, just before Keydell turned nine.

Her office was in the back of a small office park in Portsmouth, just one town over from us. When we pulled into the parking lot and got out of the car, Keydell delayed going in by picking up some rocks and kicking them toward a field at the edge of the lot.

"Nice kick, buddy, but let's do that where there are no cars, okay?"

"I was kicking away from the cars, though," he pointed out.

"Yes, but if you slipped it could break a window so let's go inside and meet Dr. Sonya."

"But I didn't slip," he argued.

"Keydell, please, let's go in." The boy needed to be right. He couldn't understand the possibilities of what might happen. He only understood facts so, in this moment, there was no reason he shouldn't have been able to kick rocks in the parking lot full of glass windows. Exasperating.

The waiting room was shared by two therapists. When we walked in, we saw a teenager sitting in one of the chairs waiting for her appointment. She was alone. Eventually, someone who might have been her mother came in and sat next to her. They looked nothing alike, so I thought maybe she was adopted, too. The first thing I thought was "Oh shit! She's a teenager, and still coming to therapy."

I wanted to "fix" Keydell and return to a more peaceful life again. I had high hopes we would do that sooner rather than later. One could dream.

The waiting room had good window light, and some kids' drawings hung on the walls along with posters and marine art. It seemed like Rhode Island office décor mandates the use of marine art—either sailboats on the bay, or images of the Newport Bridge.

There was a toy computer on a small children's table, so Keydell and I played with that while we waited. It had some games on it that challenged his mathematical skills. Perfect for him. I wondered how the therapy would go. I certainly couldn't imagine Keydell lying down on a long leather sofa and talking about his feelings.

Sonya poked her head out the door and called for Keydell. She was an athletic young woman of about thirty-five with a friendly smile.

Keydell, still focused on the computer math game, said, "One minute, I want to finish this problem." (This delay tactic would become a regular thing, and a test for my patience every time we came here.) The game kept buzzing as he got the answer wrong over and over again; finally, after the third attempt, he got frustrated, shut it off, and walked toward Sonya.

"Hi, Keydell, I'm Sonya," the doctor said in introduction. "Come on into my office and pick a chair."

He walked right over to a nice leather chair that swiveled and rocked. *Oh no,* I thought. *That chair is asking for trouble.*

I was so cynical all the time. I didn't like it. Normally, I was a positive, fun person, but lately I had lost my mojo. I was too tired to be fun. I was walking on pins and needles most of the time trying to avoid a bad scenario. I had a whole lineup of events in my mind that *could* happen just because of a freakin' chair. Sadly, my assumptions were often right.

"So, Kim, I want to get a general sense of why you are here," Sonya began. "Then, I will ask Keydell some questions. Okay?"

"I guess I just want to have someone who Keydell can talk to if needed," I replied. "He seems to have a lot of anger and frustration, and it's often directed at me, so I thought it best to find someone else he could talk to. I would also like some tools to help us help him at home because Jim and I are finding that what we did with our older two doesn't work with Keydell. He is out of control."

The word "control" made me cringe. I did not want to sound like some kind of control Nazi who wanted ways to keep my child in check. I hated to see parents who wouldn't let their kids be kids—who kept them from playfully stomping in puddles because they might get dirty. It was self-control that I wanted for Keydell; I was hoping he would find ways to do it himself with the help of any tools I could give him. Taking deep breaths wasn't working.

She asked me basic questions, like how long we had had Keydell in our home, who else lived with us, did we have pets, etc. Then, she asked about his past.

"Well, his mother had a lot of issues of her own," I explained hesitantly, not wanting Keydell to get upset hearing me talk about her. "She could not manage or care for Keydell."

I went on to explain his frequent moves and how we met him at the group home.

She looked at Keydell and said, "Boy, that is a lot of moving around, huh?"

Keydell was looking at a toy on her desk. "Can I play with this? Who set up the Legos down there? Can I play with them?"

"In a minute you can, but let's talk first," said Sonya. "Or, how about this, you can play as long as we can still talk together, you and me."

I thought that was a good idea. It seemed less formal, which would probably work much better with Keydell. Play a game, get him to relax, and perhaps she would get some good intel at the same time. I, too, learned things when Keydell and I played games—so why not the therapist?

"Why do you think you're here, Keydell?" Sonya probed.

"I don't know," he answered. "What my mom said I guess."

"Do you understand why your mom wants you to come see me? She says you have some anger and violence at home. Can we talk about that a little bit?"

"Sure," Keydell said as he focused on the Lego pieces.

"Do you understand that your mom and dad love you and want you to be happy in your forever home?"

"Yes."

"We do really love you, Keydell," I interjected, "and want you to know that no matter what you are staying with us, okay?" Hopefully, the official adoption and the million times I said we were keeping him, no matter what, gave him confidence around that concern.

He just nodded his head and continued playing.

Sonya asked me what kinds of things triggered Keydell and what kinds of things we would do when he got upset.

"He seems to have a low opinion of himself, so even if he does something small and I ask him not to, or to do it a different way because it is safer or keeps things flowing better for our household, he gets very mad," I explained. "It seems like he doesn't want to follow the rules, but I actually think he's mad at himself for breaking one of them. I don't know. It's hard to tell sometimes."

"Then what happens?" she asked.

"Well, he gets frustrated and breaks or throws something to release his tension. When we try to stop him, he gets more defiant and it escalates into a major thing when it could have just been a very simple teaching moment. It's so frustrating parenting him. It's like he just wants to do what he wants, when he wants, and not be told what to do *ever!*"

"Okay, so what do you do when he's throwing things and having a tantrum?" she questioned.

"Jim and I try to talk him down," I went on with a quiver in my voice, "to make sure he doesn't hurt himself, which often means holding him down. And for me, I'm often trying to dodge flying objects." Every time I talked about it I was right back in an episode. I could feel the physical sensations in my chest. It got tight, and my stomach hurt.

"So, Keydell, can you hear in your mom's voice how this upsets her?"

"Can I take this apart and make my own thing?" he asked, instead of answering the question.

"Can you answer me and then you can do that?" Sonya asked again.

"No, I can make my own thing and *not* answer the questions," he replied.

I looked as Sonya as if to say, see this is how he can be defiant.

"Maybe for the first few sessions I can spend time with Keydell and we can work on some ways to calm his anger and frustrations," she said. "And then, if Keydell is okay with it, we can have you in here sometimes, too, and all talk together."

"I want her in here all the time," he said.

"Okay, well, let's play it by ear and see how it goes. Our time is up for today so let's pick up the Legos and say our goodbyes," Sonya suggested.

"They were already all messed up down here. Why should I pick them up?" Keydell asked.

"True," Sonya said, "but now they are not put together, they're just scattered around. So it would be helpful for you to pick them up and put them in the bin for the next person. I'll help you."

"Or, I can stay and build something and leave it here." As I'd seen so many times before, he wanted to control the situation. He wanted to leave the Legos *his* way, and not the way Sonya had asked. It seemed so petty to me to feel the need for that kind of control, but for him it was not petty at all. Letting go of control is hard for most people; it makes them feel vulnerable. I guessed that, for Keydell, vulnerability was not a good feeling *at all.*

"That's a good idea, but we don't have time for that, Keydell," I said, reaching down to get the process started. "Let's just pick up and head home. I'm getting hungry."

He stared at me in defiance as I put the Legos away and closed out our session. Sonya joked with Keydell for a minute and said that next time he came they would play a game together. I wondered if she would offer a rubbing stone to help him too.

See, so cynical.

We continued with Sonya over the next few months. The more I had to report on his behaviors, however, the more upset he would get. I felt like a tattle-tale, and had the sense that this was making things worse. I decided to call Sonya before our appointments and give her the weekly report to avoid doing it in front of him. Some sessions were smooth but seemed unproductive; some were tense, and ended in us leaving while Keydell was melting down. I had to navigate the hallway with a screaming child and hope that I could get him into the car. This therapy was going to take a while, if it even helped at all.

I sometimes suggested an outing, like some pizza or an ice cream, after the sessions, but only if he ended the session without a fuss. Of course, if he hadn't earned the special treat after the session, I had to listen to the screaming and name-calling the whole way home. Fortunately, it was a short ride, but still long enough for me to get lost in my worry.

Okay, wow, that's loud. Just breathe, Kim, and drive safely. Is his seat belt on? Are the child safety locks on? Lock the windows so he doesn't throw something out. I don't know if this is helping.

More screaming from the back seat.

Breathe and keep calm. What is bothering him? Is it my tattling? I think there is something wrong with his brain wiring, honestly. Should we stop? He always acts up a bit after each visit, so maybe it's too much. Maybe he needs more time with us first.

"It's okay, Del, we will be home shortly. Hang in there," I yelled over his screams.

Breathe, Kim, breathe.

CHAPTER 13

THE GOOD, THE BAD AND THE UGLY

*"Most people fail to see reality because of wanting. They
are attached; they cling to material objects, to pleasures,
to the things of this world. This very clinging is the
source of suffering."*

—*Majjhima Nikaya*

Winter, 2010

Soccer, therapy, the Christmas from Hell, more therapy, screaming, chaos, broken toys, crying, more screaming, door slamming—and, in between, rays of light.

"Guess what, Del?" I began. "Your coach for the spring travel
team just sent an e-mail and wants to do some winter practices in
his basement. He has a cool mini soccer field that he made himself, and has it set up down there! Sounds awesome, right?"

It was after school on a raw January day. Keydell, head down,
was focused on his homework at the kitchen table. The winter

sun was already low in the sky, shining through the window into my eyes and bathing the room in a cool blue light as I sat across from Keydell, awaiting his answer. I tended to get blue this time of year, just like the light, but today the sun felt good on my face and Keydell was in a good mood.

My photography work gets slow in the winter months, but Rachel and I had gotten a few jobs for Wabi Sabi Way, a business we started together leading workshops on how to find peace in the workplace. That day, I was preparing my materials for one of the sessions, which always lifted my spirits. I had to laugh at the irony of switching from my household of anger management to teaching others how to find peace, but Keydell's behaviors gave me many opportunities to practice patience, compassion, empathy, and awareness around his suffering and my own. It helped me relate to any struggles the workshop participants might be having, too.

"That's cool," Keydell responded. "When are we doing that?" As he looked up from his books, the light caught his face like a Hollywood spotlight. I paused before answering to take in his glowing angelic face and see him just as he was in this moment, erasing all my thoughts of his previous disturbing actions and behaviors. He really was a beautiful child, and I wanted to take in this goodness. I needed to practice this: taking in the good more often, so that my own actions reflected my love for him and not how I was affected by him. Yes, he tested me, and yes, I got upset, but I was in love with this boy and I wanted that to shine through all the pain.

I held that good thought for one more minute, locking it into my brain, and clued back into his question.

"It's tonight, for about an hour, so I'll take you."

Jim Teeters, his new coach, had not met Keydell yet, so I thought it would be good if I arrived a little early to talk with him and hang out for the practice in case something happened. Keydell had been pretty good at most of his lacrosse and fall soccer practices, but since his summer meltdown at the YMCA camp he'd been behaving badly more frequently around others outside of our immediate family.

It seemed like the closer Keydell got to people, the worse he treated them. Over Christmas, my brother-in-law Rob and sister Amy were visiting, and Rob played games with Keydell for hours. Amy called up the stairs to Keydell's room to let Rob know she was packed and ready to go, so he told Keydell he had to leave.

"But the game isn't over!" Keydell screamed.

"Sorry, Keydell, but I've been up here a while and I can't make Amy wait any longer. It's getting late. We'll play again when I come back."

As they were walking out the kitchen door, right under the roof line of his bedroom, Keydell opened his window wide and chucked a metal car at their heads.

"What the hell?" Amy yelled up to him. She had heard me talk about his behaviors, but hadn't seen much of them yet. "He threw this car and almost hit me!"

I ran up to his room and caught him getting ready to throw another one. I grabbed it from his hands and yelled down, "Sorry, Ames, he only does this to people he loves, so try to take it as a compliment."

I shut his window and gave him the evil eye. I couldn't get into it at the moment. I still had company.

We got to Coach Teeter's house before the other kids, and were escorted down to the basement by the coach's son, a tall, gentle young man of about fifteen whose energy was sweet and calming. He walked slowly and gracefully as he led us past their large, barking dog (which made us jump) and down to the basement.

As we got to the bottom of the open stairs, we saw the mini field. It was really cool. It was made from plywood and fake turf, and was about twelve by fifteen feet, with walls at each end that had soccer ball-sized holes cut out for target shooting. The sides were made of netting, and the ceiling was fairly low, which forced good ball control. It was a fun and creative use of the basement space.

Coach Teeters was setting up the mini field but looked up to greet us as we walked over to introduce ourselves.

"Hi, Coach Teeters, I'm Kim, and this is Keydell."

He reached over to shake Del's hand. We had been practicing handshakes, so I was proud to see Keydell take his hand firmly.

"Hello, Keydell, I'm Coach Teeters. You can come in the field area and warm up if you want."

"I hope you don't mind if I stay," I said. "I'll sit off to the side so I don't bother you guys."

Coach was fine with that, even though the other boys would most likely be dropped off by their parents. If this practice had been for Henry or Ella I would have left them, too, but I felt like I needed to lay some groundwork for the coach.

"Sometimes Keydell can get a little excitable around new experiences or with his friends, so I thought I might just stay for the first practice," I whispered to him. I didn't want to embarrass Keydell.

"I understand. We're only here for an hour or so to get the boys touching the ball as much as possible before the spring. He can do some of this at home, too," he replied.

I could only imagine how *that* would go. He'd kick the ball in anger, and break a window. Man, I was negative.

I quickly noticed where the coach's son got his calm demeanor; Coach Teeters was just the same. His voice was deep and soothing, and he spoke his words calmly and carefully. You could tell he was passionate about the game of soccer, and was happy to be coaching. I mean, who else would put this kind of setup in their house?

Keydell, Charlie, Tyler, and Michael (his soccer posse) started to dribble around, practicing some drills to warm up. Keydell was having a great time, but I could hear in his loud voice that he was winding up. After a few times kicking the ball harder than needed and whacking it in behind one of the walls, Coach asked him to settle it down a bit and stay in control with the ball. He had the boys play a two-on-two soccer/tennis game that required them to chip the ball back and forth over a low net. It was going along well until Keydell got too aggressive and Coach asked him to sit down to the side for a minute.

In the gentlest of voices, he said, "Take a short break, Keydell, and when you're ready, you can join us again."

He was so calm. I remembered when I used to be calm like that.

I was really hoping things would not escalate, but Keydell was in a mood. After a few minutes Coach asked if he wanted to come back in the game. He stood up from his "break" spot and kicked his ball hard, straight upwards; it ended up smashing the overhead light bulb. Glass flew everywhere.

I jumped up from my seat to help clean up. "Sorry, Coach Teeters," I said. "I'll get you a new bulb."

The coach turned to Keydell and calmly said, "I'm happy to have you down here for practice but you're going to have to follow the rules. This is a small space and you need to respect it, as well as the other boys."

Damn, his voice was smooth. It was calming me down as well.

Keydell was getting that look in his eyes, glaring at Coach Teeters, so I thought maybe I should take him home before he got any worse. Normally, if I managed to stay calm when Del was upset, he tried harder to upset me, and I could see his little mind thinking about doing that now as the coach remained cool. I really wanted to let his coach deal with this and stay out of it, but I was feeling responsible for Keydell's actions.

"Maybe we should go home and call it a day, Keydell." I said. "Practice is almost over anyway and I know you're tired from school."

Coach Teeters then suggested, "Why doesn't he just sit for one more minute and he can come back in when he's ready? There's no hurry."

"Your call, Coach." I sat back down in the chair where I was supposed to be staying out of the way. I think *I* was the one with control issues right now.

Keydell actually cooperated and sat back down, too. He loved soccer so much that I think it was making him want to behave; not to mention the magic spell Coach Teeters had put on him with his charm and patience.

After practice, we were able to get out of there and to the car before anything else happened, so I took the opportunity to chat with Keydell about the light bulb and practice. I looked over my shoulder to the back seat, thinking about his sunlit face from earlier that day. He certainly didn't look like that now.

"Keydell, I really want you to hear me," I began, trying to embody Coach Teeters' demeanor. "You have got to try to listen to rules and follow them if you want to do things like this. You can't just do what you want and think that there won't be any consequences for your actions. Mr. Teeters is your coach, and he's trying to help you get ready for the season and get to know you better. Do you want to show him how good you are at soccer, or how mad you get?"

"Leave me alone," he replied. "I just want to go home."

"We have to replace that light bulb, so we are going to the store first, then home."

I called Coach Teeters later that evening. "I am sorry about the light. I got a bulb for you."

"Oh, it's fine. It's not the first time that's happened. How is Keydell?" he asked.

"He's okay, but I thought I'd just give you a heads up about him. He's an incredible athlete and, as you can see, a good soccer player. This is his new favorite thing for sure."

"Yes, he's got some good skills but lots of energy."

"Ah, yeah, he's newly adopted," I explained, "and we've been having a lot of issues at home with him. I thought I should give you some insight and some things that might help you with him, if he needs it, at practice or on the field."

"Alright, sounds good," he said. I felt in that moment, remembering how calm he had been with Keydell, that this man could teach me a few things.

I explained what tended to upset Keydell, his need for perfection, and how he either lashed out or shut down if spoken to about his behaviors. "He doesn't seem to realize how he affects others," I said.

He paused before he spoke back. "Well, we'll just play it by ear and see how he does. I've coached many boys who get upset at a game and walk off the field, for example, but he'll have to learn that he has to behave at practice so I can run it safely. It's good that he has that passion and fire in him. We'll just have to direct it in a positive way toward the game."

Now I was in love with this man. He obviously had worked with kids, was very patient, and was willing to guide and support Keydell in a positive way. If he'd been one of those coaches who screamed and yelled at the players, I don't think it would have worked; Keydell would have shut down with someone like that. But Coach Teeters, even today, is one of many angels who was sent to us to help Keydell.

Keydell continued to train once a week with his travel team and behaved most days, with a few exceptions like disruptive talking or acting overly hyper compared to the rest of the active boys. Coach patiently worked with him, and loved his dedication and focus toward the game. We would often talk after practices just to check in with each other. He was so willing to listen to what was going on at home, as it helped him understand Keydell's behaviors at practice. Coach Teeters was interested in all of his other players in the same way, and would support each one with the same enthusiasm, but with our circumstances, we were particularly grateful for his patience and support. If Keydell had gotten kicked off the team, I think it would have ruined what little self-esteem he had built up around his talent in the sport. He came home excited after practices; it kept his endorphins up, and high endorphins meant a happier, calmer boy (most of the time).

To keep a good thing going, we signed him up for the YMCA basketball team that Jim and Henry had decided to coach. They could keep an eye on him there. There was only one practice and a game each week, so it complemented the once-a-week indoor soccer practice. Keydell wasn't so good at basketball, however. He had a hard time controlling the ball while dribbling, and even though they lowered the hoop for the age group, he had a terrible time getting the ball in the net.

We saw the first glimpses of his sense of humor though, when he said, "I am the whitest black guy I know. I stink at basketball, and I've never eaten Kentucky Fried Chicken!" We all laughed so hard when he announced that. To me, it was another glimpse of the light I knew was in him.

Biologically, he was one quarter white, but I don't think Keydell identified with one race over another since he had been raised by both white and black family members. His aunt was white, his birth mother was half white and half black (and supposedly part Eskimo, too), and his siblings' father was black. Most of the staff members at Trout group home were white, as were ninety percent of the kids at school, so he had influences from both races equally. He was his own person for sure—but one stereotype he did fit was how he moved. The boy could *dance*.

Whenever we had our family dance parties in the living room, Ella would play DJ and pop on a variety of tunes from all genres. Then, she and I would move around the room with abandon. At first, Keydell would just watch as Ella lifted and twirled like a ballerina. I could tell he was dying to get up and move around, too, but was waiting for inspiration to strike.

Once he stopped ogling Ella's body and heard a song with a good beat, he got up his courage and joined us on our living room rug. He was fluid and expressive. His movements were low and grounded, like a tribal boy dancing around a bonfire to the beat of drums. He was happy and at home in his body. He closed his eyes and moved with ease. Having watched him play sports—and now, seeing him dance—I thought that tuning into his body might be a way for him to access his feelings. Maybe he could learn to calm himself by moving and breathing through his pain.

I often sat in meditation, focusing on my body's sensations because it kept me in the present moment. When I am in the moment, I worry less, and don't fret about the future. Perhaps Keydell could learn to focus on the sensations that came up in his body versus all the thoughts that were negative and upsetting. His mind was at peace when he moved. If it was a stereotype for him to be a good dancer or a good athlete, so be it. Moving was obviously the important thing; being white or black was just on the outside.

Keydell gave us a break from his tantrums for the rest of that winter, and it felt like a deep exhale. I had heard from other parents who have children who suffer from anxiety or depression that the spring and fall are the worst times of year for their child's moods, and we were seeing that, too. So for now, I was soaking in the peace. It was so nice to enjoy each other again and see Keydell relax. Sadly, it didn't last very long.

Spring was in the air. The trees were budding and the crocuses were poking their heads out in the yard. It made *me* happy. I was being drawn out of my winter-weather funk as I anticipated the next exciting months for our family. Our firstborn was graduating from high school, and his lacrosse team had made the state play-offs. Henry's college acceptance letters had all come in, and he was leaning toward a school in Orange, California called Chapman University. It had a business school, an acting program, and club lacrosse: it was everything he wanted.

He was excited about going off to California, and so were we, but I was surely going to miss him. I wanted my kids to travel, though. Jim and I tried to take our two on trips as often as we could, but this was different. This meant Henry would be away from us, on his own journey, and although I knew he would be fine, I was choking down tears.

Henry's and Ella's lacrosse games were a big part of our lives, and a total blast. The parents of the boys' Middletown High School lacrosse team were a rowdy bunch, so we had a lot of fun at the games. Jim led the fanfare with his bugle at every game, and whenever Middletown scored, one dad blew a conch shell as the rest of us stomped our feet on the metal bleachers. We were loud and crazy—but, overall, positive.

Most of Henry's friends, whom he'd known since elementary school, were either on the team or came to watch, so it was always a town-family affair. We were trying our best to focus on Henry as he moved through all these great events of his senior year; we managed to be at most of his games, and, of course, to celebrate his college acceptance letters. We were proud parents—but the yang to that yin was Mr. Delly.

I called him Delly a lot now. We all used nicknames, but the list had grown. Henry called him Brosef, Delsif or Del-broski; Ella still called him Ki-Ki, which he hated, or Little Delly. Jim and I called him Del or Delly. I had nicknames for Henry and Ella, too (Spanky and Boo-Boo), so I think hearing us call him something other than "Keydell" made him feel connected to all of us more.

Spring brought more upsets, though, as spring tended to do.

We kept Delly going with the soccer, took him on nature hikes and swimming at the YMCA pool, and sent him out into our back woods to explore, all in hopes of keeping him happy. He loved putting on a pair of Ella's old rubber boots and trekking back to the creek deep in the trees, coming back muddy and with his short afro full of sticks. It made me smile to see how nature pulled him away from his video games and out into its calming grasp. He loved being outside, but when it was cold his hands got painfully frozen—so he, too, was happy for spring, even when his tantrums didn't seem to reflect that mood.

When we brought him to Henry's or Ella's lacrosse games—or anywhere with lots of activity and a crowd, for that matter—he lost his shit. He'd climb on everyone, pull at people's feet from under the bleachers, and scream or throw things at Henry's friends if they wouldn't play with him. He was just a pain in the ass. We had to watch him every second, which made it hard to relax. I'd be damned, though, if I missed Henry's or Ella's games because Keydell was in a hyperactive mood or didn't feel like coming. Believe me, we'd had to stay home from things on many occasions due to his behaviors, but the outdoor games were manageable. We tried babysitters, but how could we even begin to explain how to handle Keydell to someone who didn't know him? We hadn't even figured this out ourselves yet! *Oh, just pin him down if he's upset and don't be bothered if he calls you a "fucking bitch." It's all good.* Yeah, right.

Once, we left Keydell with Henry and Ella to go to a school meeting, and he ended up chasing them around the yard with scissors. Henry finally tackled him to the ground and called us home. We didn't do that again for a very long time. We made it work in other ways, most of the time, but since we never knew how Keydell was going to behave, we were always on edge, even when cheering at a game.

His behaviors were getting more intense, and he obsessed over the craziest things. He was obsessed with mechanical pencils for one, and the lead refills. If he misplaced the pencil he was using at school, he would lose his mind. He would sit on the floor, digging through his backpack—and then, when he couldn't find it, hit himself in the head, screaming and yelling and calling himself stupid. It was hard to change his thoughts once he believed he had lost the pencil. If I tried to talk to him about it, he would stare off with a blank, dazed look, and ignore me.

I would say something like, "Del, why don't you look for it tomorrow in class? If you can't find it, we can get a new one."

That was not good enough. He had created a whole story already about what had happened to his pencil. "It will be gone. Someone stole it, and I will never find it."

My "help" would just make him angrier. He wanted things settled immediately. He didn't want a plan, or something to think about for the future. He wanted to fix it then and there. As strong and fluid as his body was, his mind was weaker, and stuck.

I tried to get him moving when he was upset, and suggested he take deep breaths or run around to calm down, but my ideas were often rejected with a scream. He would only run if *he* chose to, not on my suggestion.

Of course, these types of upsets would happen just as it was time to go to a game or event, making the situation even more stressful. If I asked Keydell to sit with me at a game so he wouldn't go crazy and start bothering everyone, he would become defiant and kick the bleachers repeatedly, or bounce his ball loudly. I would go off and kick the ball with him for a bit, even though I really wanted to watch the games. It became harder and harder to pay attention to Henry and Ella, since Keydell needed so much supervision. Jim and I ended up taking turns.

His travel soccer practices moved outside, and Keydell started his second season of lacrosse. I decided to help out with the team, to keep an eye on him. He was happier doing his own thing and being active, but even here we were seeing escalated behaviors. He was becoming more and more sensitive and frustrated with himself. He just couldn't seem to find balance. I was worried about his medications being wrong, but still hadn't found time to see a psychiatrist so he could be re-evaluated. I began to believe he was battling depression.

By June, Keydell was a full-on mess. Every afternoon for a month straight, he began physically and mentally bashing me the moment he stepped into the house. I did my best to get prepared and keep his schedule smooth and predictable, but nothing helped. He had snapped, and was spiraling down. One afternoon, he threw rocks at me while I was just sitting in the yard waiting for him to get home; we hadn't even spoken to each other yet, and he was already upset. He groped at Ella and me more frequently, and wouldn't stay out of Ella's room; he couldn't play any games with Henry without completely losing control. We were all stressed to the max. And this was all on top of college visits, exams, games, work, and tight finances.

It was time to get more help.

⚔️

I called Sonya for an emergency appointment. I really wanted to talk to her about some other kinds of help we might be able to get for Keydell. I was sure that something was wrong with his brain. He was not just a poorly behaved child; he had no control over or connection to his feelings, and thus his actions. I tried doing breathing and body awareness meditations with him, and asked him to draw what his anger felt like, but both exercises were complete failures. The latter usually ended in ripped up paper and thrown markers and crayons. I was running out of ideas, and so was Jim.

I had called Hasbro Children's Hospital because I was told about a program they ran for kids with behavioral problems. To get in, Keydell would have to have a full brain evaluation, which I thought would be great considering I thought his brain function was the issue, but there was a three-month wait just for the evaluation. Once in the program, I would have to make the for-ty-five-minute drive to Providence every day after school and stay there for four hours before driving home again. Honestly, we were not going to live long enough to do all that with the violence Del was exhibiting.

I was in tears every night for a month. When someone comes at you with nasty words or threats of hurting you every day, it gets scary. I felt like I better understood people who were abused by their spouses or by a parent. My body felt numb, and some days I just wanted to sit and stare at the wall. I had lost my sense of hu-mor, and wanted laughter back. It was so weird to be out of ideas for helping Keydell, too, because normally I was full of them.

After another day of violence, I had to drag Keydell into the car so we could get to the appointment with Sonya. He had gotten upset and thrown things in Sonya's office before, but I wanted her to see the full-blown version of his temper.

"Keydell, we are either going to see Sonya or I am calling 9-1-1," I warned him. "I cannot take this anymore, and I need to get you more help. You cannot keep threatening me, breaking everything, and hurting yourself."

"Why don't you just give me back?" he yelled. "Your life would be so much better!"

"I don't want to give you back. I want you to stop hurting us and yourself! I love you."

I attempted to put his seatbelt on as he thrashed around.

"You have to calm down Keydell. If you don't, I am going to call the police and it will not be good." I threatened to call the cops be-fore, too, which was probably the wrong thing to do. It most likely reinforced his unworthiness.

"Fine! Let them take me to juvie," he retorted. "That's where I belong anyway."

"No, you don't," I said with exasperation, "but this needs to stop before you get any older or stronger, or something bad will happen, and I can't help you at that point—so please, let's go see Sonya and see what we can do."

"We go there all the time. What can she do?" he demanded.

"I don't know, but she needs to see you like this to fully understand what's happening. We need to ask what more we can do besides talking in her office and having you wig out. It would really help if you talked to her more and tried to get to the root of what upsets you so much."

"Fine." And he settled in so I could buckle him.

I was not proud of threatening him with the police or 9-1-1, but I was going for shock value to see if I could get him to stop. I was really hoping I would never have to call the cops on him.

I was shaking as I drove to our appointment, and felt like a knotted 130-pound ball of flesh. I was no longer five-feet-six; I was a shrinking flower. When we got to the waiting room, I was relieved that Sonya came right out to get us. I was hoping to avoid him running off, which he had done once before. Sonya saw that I was very upset and sat us right down. Keydell immediately began spinning in his chair, knowing I was going to tattle on him; he just looked like he wanted to get something started. He saw the toys on the shelf and went right for them.

"You guys okay, Kim?" Sonya asked.

"Not really," I said. Keeping my eye on Keydell, I continued. "Since we saw you last, things have continued to get worse and worse. Keydell has been coming home every day and going into a violent meltdown. I just don't know what to do. For a while I thought things were getting better but it's really escalated out of control. We can't seem to get back to a balanced place. I swear he feeds off my energy so he might be feeling the tension in me when he gets home and just picks up where he left off from the day before. We've been trying so hard to stay calm but I know we're not doing a very good job lately. I've come very close to hitting him and so has Jim. That's not like us."

Keydell was starting to throw the toys across the room, one at a time, in a slow, taunting fashion. I asked him to please stop, but he picked up more and continued. Sonya then asked the same, and got the same result. We tried to change his thinking by asking him about soccer or school, but he was already in that other place—that place he went to and returned as someone else. His face had changed; he was locked and loaded. He started ripping drawings off the wall that other kids had made for Sonya. He knew just how to get to people's hearts; he pulled all the games off the shelves so that the pieces flew everywhere, and ignored anything we said or did.

"Oh, my God, Sonya, I need some help," I begged. "What should I do? He's been acting like this for so long now. I really like you, but I don't think this talk therapy is what he needs right now. His brain is fucked up."

"Kim, I'm not really equipped for what I think he has going on," said Sonya. "I believe he has attachment disorder. My brother works with this so I know a little bit about it, but am definitely not able to help you out. Sadly my brother lives in Virginia."

Her tone was filled with fear for us, but the words "attachment disorder" stuck with me. Was this the brain functioning disorder that my gut was hinting at? He didn't seem to care if he hurt us, and he didn't seem to have any remorse for his actions. Was he not "attached" to us? He would say "sorry" after an episode sometimes, but then do it again the next day. It made no sense.

We were flailing around the office as we talked. Keydell screamed and thrashed about. It was like a scene from "A Perfect Storm."

"So what do we do about attachment disorder? Is it something that can be cured?" I yelled over the screaming. The patients in the lobby must have thought the devil was in here.

"It depends on how badly he has it. You need to get him into a facility before he hurts you or himself."

"But where?" I lunged for Keydell's arm before he could pull the bookshelves over. "I've tried Hasbro, and they have a huge waiting list. Where else is there for kids? I don't know what to do," I said in a panic as I tried to hold Keydell down.

We both had our hands on him, holding his arms as he kicked and screamed on the floor.

"Go to the emergency room and admit him. Sometimes that moves things along quicker. They will look for placement for him."

Placement? *Placement?* Oh God. I was going to puke.

As I dragged Keydell out of the office, my heart was racing, but it felt like it was crying. Could a heart cry? I was so scared about admitting him to a hospital. I felt like it would be the beginning of an end. I was really freaking out, but at the same time knew we had to do something. I called Jim on the way home from the appointment as Keydell was throwing his watch and shoes out the window and screaming, and told him what we had to do. We had to get him to a hospital to see if we could get some help. I told him what Sonya had said, and he agreed. I was crying helplessly. Keydell was my baby, and he was not okay.

CHAPTER 14

LESSONS

"When the student is ready, the teacher will appear."

—*Buddhist proverb*

June, 2010

"Keydell, I am so sorry, but we have to do this. Mommy just doesn't know what else to do. I'm really hoping this will get you some help quickly." I was pleading for him to calm down as we drove down East Main Road to our house.

Jim had called 9-1-1 while we were driving home. Shortly after we pulled into the driveway, Jim ran out to help me as an ambulance arrived. When the paramedic jumped out to see what was happening, Keydell had already calmed down but looked terrified. He couldn't believe what he was seeing. I think the reality was hitting him that he was going away because of his behavior. I felt sick thinking of his fears, and tried to reassure him. I bent down in front of him to get his full attention and looked directly into those saucer eyes, which were glazed over with uncertainty.

"We're going to visit you every day, Del, and we're not leaving you there," I assured him. "This is just so we can get the help we need more quickly. I know you don't want to feel this way anymore, so hopefully this will be a good thing in the long run. We love you so much so please know we are going to be with you the whole way, okay?"

Blah, blah, blah was probably what he heard. Little did I know at the time that sending a child with attachment disorder away from the home is one of the worst things you can do. In that moment, I thought I was doing the best thing for him.

Keydell was taken to Newport Hospital. I rode with him in the back of the ambulance while Jim followed in the car. Keydell was silent, as was I. Our fears hung in the space between us like fog. As soon as he was admitted, we briefed the doctor about what had been happening. The hospital called in their on-duty mental health worker, who would be in charge of placing Keydell in a facility better suited to helping him. I was still hoping our emergency route would help fast-track him into the Hasbro program. I hadn't realized how many children suffered from mental health issues until I tried to get help for Keydell. I certainly didn't want to institutionalize him, but I was sure there were better therapies than what we were doing—at least, I hoped there were. Maybe the doctors at Hasbro would better diagnose him, and adjust his medications at least.

Henry and Ella were sad to see Keydell this way, but understood what Jim and I were trying to do. We all went to visit the following night. We walked into his room—and there he was, lying in the bed with the television on, playing cards with a nurse. He was as happy as a clam.

That little stinker, I thought. *He's getting everything he wants, and everyone's focused attention, so he's happy.*

That was certainly the way it looked. I glanced over at Jim and said, "Can you believe this? He's back in the system and working it."

"I think he likes it here," Jim replied. "It must feel orderly, and he knows what to expect."

"Yeah, he's got his food on the little menu to pick out, the TV when he wants, and a nurse to play with him," I noted sarcastically.

I couldn't help but wonder whether this reminded him of the structure of the group home he'd become so comfortable with. Maybe our home life was too chaotic for his busy mind.

He really didn't seem to care what was happening next, or if he was home or not. He was definitely putting on a good face. He was all smiles as he showed us his bed and how it worked, the TV remote, and his hospital socks with the rubber bits on the bottom. While the kids stayed in the room to visit, Jim and I went out in the hallway to talk to the caseworker. She was a kind and thoughtful person who spoke with a soothing, reassuring tone.

"There are no beds available anywhere in Rhode Island," she said. "We can keep him here for a week, but after that the insurance coverage will no longer cover a regular hospital stay. I'll keep him and maybe something will come up in the meantime—but if not, you'll have to take him home."

It felt like it was getting darker in the hallway as I took in this news.

"We were really hoping to get him into the program at Hasbro," I explained. "They supposedly have a great after-school program where they can work with us together. Is that not available?"

"Well, first he'd have to be admitted to the mental health ward of Hasbro, where there's no room right now, and then he'd have to be evaluated to see if he could get a spot in that program. It's quite a process," she informed us. She waited patiently while I thought about it.

"So we may have to wait to get in there anyway, even though we've taken this emergency route? Is that correct?"

"Yes, it's all based on who they have room for. But there may be other places he can go, so let's see what we can find."

Jim and I were confused, but succumbed for the moment. I didn't really know what else to ask anyway; this process still seemed like the best chance to get him started at Hasbro. We sat with Keydell for about an hour and then said our goodnights. His tiny frame looked so small in the single bed, but we left him smiling. The nurses thought he was the cutest thing ever, of course. He just has another side to him. Don't we all?

The next night, I had a Buddhist group meeting at Don's house. He lived across the street from the hospital so I thought I'd go to the meeting and then over to say goodnight to Keydell.

"How are you Kim?" Don asked as we walked to his living room. He had a huge Buddha statue, which was very settling, in the bay window seat. There were lots of plants and great color in the room so I loved coming to our meetings here. His partner Michael joined us, too. He always gave me big bear hugs, which I loved, and also made me feel calm.

"Not so good," I answered. "Keydell is across the street in the hospital. His violence was getting out of control and we had to admit him."

"Well, sit down and let's talk if you want. You're doing the right thing," he assured me. "You don't want him, or you, to get hurt. It might be good to get some space and see where this goes. We can only do our best and then stay present to what is happening. Just love him and understand that he is who he is. Remember all things are impermanent, as is this. It will change."

"I know, you're right," I replied. "I am trying so hard to just be with him and not expect him to be someone he's not, but I need to find a way to help him so he can stay with us, Don. I'm afraid that, when he gets older, he'll be too much for me to handle if Jim and Henry aren't around, and that he'll have to live somewhere else. I want to try to help him before he gets to that point. He's such a sweet boy with a huge heart. I know it's in there, dying to come out and be more prominent than his dark side—the side that is controlling him right now."

An image of Darth Vader inviting Luke Skywalker to "come to the dark side" popped into my head. I believe Vader chose the dark side because it felt powerful. Maybe Keydell felt powerful and somehow in control when he was in his "dark side," too. Anger can feel good sometimes, and since Keydell had very little control in his life, maybe when he was angry and raging he felt good! *Oh, help me, somebody!* I thought. How could I help him feel in control without the anger?

I connected back to Don. "I really think there's something wrong with his brain, and wonder what can be done for him."

"Mental illness is tough, Kim, and sometimes it's about getting the right medications, too."

"I think he's been misdiagnosed, so maybe we can at least get to a proper diagnosis while he's in the hospital or at some other mental health facility." I replied. "All that we've been going through is really putting my practice to good use, though. I work on patience, understanding the impermanence of things, and watching my attachments. I look at what I'm holding onto so tightly that is causing me this personal suffering."

I was holding onto perfection, I thought. I wanted to be—grasped at being—the perfect mom. My good track record for raising kids was being broken, but I was determined to keep going.

Then, Don said something that blew me away.

"You do realize, Kim, that Keydell is the teacher you have been looking for? You put it out there that you needed one, and look who showed up?"

He was right. Keydell was presenting lessons to me that I had not been tested on before in my privileged life. Listening to and reading the Dharma from great teachers was one thing—but Keydell made me put my practice into action. I had found my most important teacher, and he certainly wasn't who I expected he would be.

Again, me with the expectations.

"I knew you guys would help me find the upside to all of this." I said.

Michael leaned over and gave me another hug. I needed it. Even though I had my family, I felt alone sometimes in my struggles; that big hug made me feel like I was okay.

We sat in meditation for a bit together. I decided to do a *Metta* or loving-kindness meditation, and send out loving kindness to Keydell and my family for all they had helped me with. I imagined them in front of me, and imagined breathing white, loving light toward them.

I said in my head, "May they be happy, may they be healthy, may they be free from danger, may they live with ease." I truly wanted all of that for my youngest son, and for us as a family. Then I sent a little loving kindness to myself.

Toward the end of that week, the social worker called us to say that she had found a spot for Keydell at Westwood Lodge. The name made it sound like a ski resort, but it was a facility for kids in Westwood, Massachusetts. He had to be taken there in the ambulance right from Newport Hospital, so Jim and I followed in the car. It was almost two hours away, and we arrived around 8:00 that evening. As we pulled in, our headlights illuminated on an old, cracked road edged by a dusty, crappy lawn that barely qualified as such, and a few trees scattered here and there. It looked like something out of the "Twilight Zone." We pulled into the parking lot, which sat about two hundred feet from the entrance where the ambulance had pulled up. The skinny EMT, who looked about seventeen, was getting Keydell out of the ambulance as we walked over; he told us all to wait outside. The fire alarm was going off, and they needed to make sure nothing was wrong.

"Sometimes one of the kids pulls the alarm, so it could just be that," he said with a hint of a Boston accent.

This place was really creepy. I wanted to grab Keydell and run. He only had the pajama pants we'd brought to the hospital for him, a little T-shirt, and sneakers on, and the night air was damp and chilly. The building was slightly run down and very drab looking.

"Jim, what do you think? This place gives me the creeps," I said, leaning into him for comfort.

He grabbed my shoulders and pulled me in for hug. "Let's just check in and see what they say."

Keydell was just standing there like a scared puppy, tail between his legs, shoulders slumped. He looked so sad. I *felt* so sad as I bent down to talk to him and tried to give him a hug. He flinched as I touched him. I was wracked with guilt about bringing him here, but at the same time was ready to surrender to my deficient abilities. What else *was* there to do? After standing there for about half an hour in the nippy early-summer air, the alarm stopped screaming and we were finally escorted to the office inside. The fluorescent lighting made everyone look sickly, but we sat in the bucket chairs in the lobby and waited for someone to check us in.

"Keydell Fuller?" a nurse called out. At least, I think she was a nurse.

"Right here," we said.

"Please fill out this paperwork and then we'll take Keydell to his room."

We did that, and proceeded through a series of locked doors that needed a code or swipe card to get through, down a long hallway, and down another long hallway. We passed the cafeteria, which was basically an open room with a few tables in the middle and a kitchen at one end. Keydell's eyes were darting all over the place, taking it all in. He had lived in lots of places, but I don't think he had ever been in a place like this. He was very quiet— and, I'm sure, scared. *I* was scared.

We entered one last door that led to the sleeping wing. As we followed the staff worker, we passed other rooms along the hall, and could hear various noises and activities going on. Some kids were screaming, some were in the hallway wrestling angrily with staff members, and some seemed to have their parents with them. Oh my God, this was so crazy.

I was quickly becoming aware of the fact that Keydell was not an unusual case. We were not alone, at all, in our situation. Not that I had actually thought we were—but we had never known anyone else who dealt with his kind of behavior at such an extreme. I was not sure why or how any of the other kids had ended up here, but they all seemed to have control issues of some sort.

We went into what would be Keydell's room, and looked around. It was spacious, with only a closet and two beds inside. The walls were blank except for a couple of kids' drawings hanging over one of the beds, and there was no carpet or throw rug. The nurse showed Keydell to his bed near the window and asked him to take out the drawstring from his pajama pants. His pants literally fell down from his skinny waist without the string. A young boy came bounding in the room just then and said he was Keydell's roommate. He was excitable and anxious for attention, showing us his drawings. I was actually glad Keydell had a roommate because I knew he got scared at night alone. Jim and I asked the staff worker what we could bring for Keydell, besides some elastic-waist pants, and what was going to happen now that he was here.

She stood in front of us with her check-in clipboard and looked at it for guidance.

"Let's see, you can visit during the visiting hours tomorrow and bring more clothes. Make sure he has some slip-on shoes and pants with no belts or buckles. It's all for safety." She pulled the checklist off her clipboard and hung it just inside the closet door on Keydell's side of the room.

Based on some of the behaviors we had seen from Keydell, I totally understood. We certainly didn't want him to hurt himself. Still, it was hard to think of what a child could do with a shoestring.

"When will we meet with a doctor and schedule some time to work together?" I asked.

"The doctor will be in on Monday morning to evaluate Keydell, and then he'll most likely call you."

It was only Friday. "So he'll go the whole weekend without seeing anyone? How long do you normally keep kids here?"

"Normally it's about ten days or so."

"Ten days? What will you do for him in those ten days?"

"Let's wait until the doctor can talk to you, okay?" she instructed. "I'm just the intake nurse here, and I don't have the specifics yet. We need to evaluate him first." She left the room as we said our goodbyes to Keydell. I just cried.

"We love you so much Del. Be strong and helpful so we can get you home soon."

He looked exhausted. Thankfully, it was bedtime for the kids, so I hoped he would pass out the minute we left. I reminded him that I would be back tomorrow with some clothes. We left his meds with the Westwood Lodge staff; along with the T-shirt on his back, that was all he had.

On the ride home, Jim and I calculated when ten days would be up. Henry was graduating high school in eight days, Keydell only had twelve days until his third grade year was over, and we had a family vacation planned to Utah in two weeks. The most important things in that mix were getting Keydell healthy and celebrating one of the biggest events in our oldest son's life. We didn't want his graduation to be overshadowed by what was happening with Keydell.

When we got home from Westwood that night, we filled Henry and Ella in.

"Can we go see him?" Ella asked, still in her lacrosse gear.

"No, only parents are allowed to go," Jim explained. "We can bring him notes from you guys, or pictures if you want. He can't really have anything in his room."

"Poor little guy," said Henry. "He must be so sad."

Ella was teary with agreement.

Boy, I was feeling like all of this was my fault. "Yeah, he looked pretty sad. There were also a bunch of other kids in there who were screaming, or had the same look as the kids in the group home used to have," I said. "You know, that look like, 'I've got this figured out, but get me the hell out of here.'"

The place seemed to be run like a group home, too, with rewards for good behavior and a tightly scheduled routine for television time or video-gaming, and, of course, eating. I thought that Keydell, in some ways, felt at home with that kind of structure—but that didn't mean that he wanted to be back in it.

I hated to say it, but maybe he'd realize now that he had to shape up. Even though I knew in my heart there was more to his healing than just him deciding to be good, I hoped that this place would freak him out enough to try harder than he already was.

Ugh, I was so confused.

⋇

The next day, Jim and I took some clothes to Keydell, and brought lunch so we could eat and hang out together. We'd gotten a call from the head social worker earlier that morning and had set up a time to talk while we were there. After getting buzzed in, we went to Keydell's room.

"Hey, buddy, how are you?" Jim asked.

"Good," Keydell quietly responded. He was standing on his bed, trying to see out the high window.

"We brought you some clothes and slip-on shoes."

"Finally. I can go outside now!" He turned toward us with glee. "I couldn't go to the playground this morning because I only had socks on. My sneakers fell off without the laces."

"Well, here you go sweetie," I chimed in. "We can go out now and play a bit before lunch if you want. How did you sleep last night?"

"Can you bring my blanket when you come next time?"

He was settling right in.

I had asked the staff earlier if we could take him outside, knowing how much he needed to burn off energy, so they showed us the back door to the playground area.

"What did you bring for lunch?" Keydell asked as we walked out. "They're having ice cream for dessert today and I really want some. Oh, and can you please tell them I don't have a chocolate allergy. They think I have a chocolate allergy and I couldn't have cake last night."

He was already working the system. He was talking like he used to talk at the group home. It was those little things—like looking forward to a piece of cake—that kept him going. He was making sure everything was all set for his stay.

It was an unusually warm day in early June, and the sun was blazing, so we only stayed in the playground area for a short time. Keydell was happy to be outside, and with us, so we decided to take a walk around the property and into the shady area of the front "lawn." (The willowy trees gave *some* shade, at least.) We threw around a small rubber ball that Keydell had found on the ground, and then went in to have our bag lunch. It was hard for Jim and me to be there and not be doing something more productive. This visit was really no different than visiting the hospital. They were just keeping him here until the next step, whatever the hell that was.

As we were eating in the cafeteria at one of the big oval tables, the social worker appeared and introduced herself.

"Hi, I'm Jean. I'll be Keydell's case worker while he's here," she said. She was about fifty-five or so, with short dark hair, and stocky, like an aging field hockey player. She seemed seasoned to the job.

"I'm Kim and this is Jim," I said, standing up to shake hands. Politeness first!

She sat down across from us to explain what was next. "On Monday when the doctor checks him out, he'll most likely take him off his meds so we can better evaluate him," Jean explained. "In the meantime, we'll do small group activities where the kids talk about self-esteem issues and being kind to others, and work on writing down what they value in their lives. Things like that."

"Is it all group activities, or is there individual counseling?" I asked.

"Mostly group work," she replied.

"So when will we be asked to come in and work with him as a family?"

"Well, you can come at any time during visiting hours and stay with him. Someone is always around to answer any questions you might have."

"But aren't we going to do any therapy together, or work on any strategies for when he comes home?" I asked.

"This is more of a respite facility," she explained. "It gives families a break from whatever's been going on, and gives the kids a chance to calm down before going home again. We do evaluate them, but we don't do therapy sessions with the families."

I looked at Jim with a quizzical, "what the hell?" face, and said to Jean, "We need tools to help him, not a respite."

We did need a rest, actually, but that wasn't what we thought we were bringing him here for. I got it, but now I was really confused and disappointed.

"How long do you need to evaluate him?" Jim asked.

"We'll observe him to see how he does with adjusted meds, so that will take most of the week at least," she answered.

"So, are you trying to diagnose him or what?" I asked.

"The doctor will try to do that, yes," Jean replied.

Ten days did not seem to be enough time to get him off meds, watch him in a setting outside of the home, and see what behaviors he exhibited, I thought. How could they tell what was going on in so short a time? Jim and I explained to Jean the kinds of things he did, and she assured us that she'd update the doctor.

Walking to the car, I said to Jim, "What's he doing here? I feel like we should just take him home. This is not what I thought it was going to be. I really thought they were going to work with all of us together, but it seems like they're just evaluating him and giving us their feedback. When he comes home, we'll be back where we left off, trying to figure out what to do on our own. It's no different than the therapy we've been doing, except he stays here instead of coming home."

"He looks so sad in there," Jim said.

I didn't always know what Jim wanted to do in situations like these. His body clearly told me he had empathy for Keydell—but did he think we should keep him here, or not?.

He often left parenting decisions up to me, and for the most part agreed with my choices—but this wasn't like deciding whether our son or daughter could go to the movies if they hadn't done their chores. This was uncharted territory.

We were like lost ships, tossed around in a storm with no island to land on. It was hard to see or understand how this might play out. I suppose that, with all things in life, you don't really know what could happen, but we often have a pretty good idea, especially if we have some experience around the situation. With this, we didn't. We would just have to keep riding the waves and hope that the wind would take us where we needed to go.

Jim continued, "Let's wait and see what the doctor says tomorrow, keep visiting him in shifts, and go from there. We have this respite time, so let's make the best of it and go have some dinner together in Newport."

"Sounds good," I agreed. And it really did sound good. It had been a long time since Jim and I had gone on a date.

We ended up going to our favorite place on the wharf, and then to a party that one of "The Rays" invited us to. I talked with friends who knew our situation well and were sympathetic to our woes. I always felt better when I could vent to an unbiased ear. Not too many people knew what we were going through at home, but the ones who did were totally there for us.

I was feeling numb thinking about Keydell and what must be going through his mind. Was it that he had to be "good" to get the reward of some ice cream, or was he wondering whether he would ever get to come home again?

Jim and I had one too many drinks that night, and some good sex when we got home—two things we had not done in a very long time.

⛛

During that week of commuting back and forth to Westwood, we also fit in an awards night for Henry and continued to plan his huge graduation party. Ella was in the midst of exams and winding down her freshman year. With all of this going on, Jim and I were tag-teaming our visits to see Keydell. Jim went to see him early in the week because I had a photo shoot. (Oh, yeah, we were still trying to work, too. Sheesh.)

He came back telling me Keydell had been great on the visit. They played cards and hung out for about an hour. "He was a bit hyper because he's off his Adderall," Jim said, "but I think they want to keep him on the Risperdal for his moods. I want to check that drug out more, however. I haven't heard great things about it."

I trusted Jim to do the research. He had been in the health care sales industry for a while now and read everything; he was an information sponge. We believed Keydell was on Risperdal for bipolar disorder, which, based on what I had read, I did not think he had. Risperdal is prescribed for other mood disorders too—which might be why the doctor thought it would be a good idea to keep him on it—but although Keydell had taken the drug since coming to us, we'd seen no help from it either way. It didn't seem to matter if he took his Adderall or not, either; he might get a bit more hyper without it, but his outbursts were just as frequent.

I went to see Keydell that Friday, one week after he'd arrived at Westwood and the day before Henry's graduation. It was such a bummer that he was going to miss the graduation but, at the same time, it would give us space to enjoy the event without worrying about him. He had never expressed a desire to go anyway.

I followed the long hallway down to Keydell's room and found him sitting on his bed, bouncing. I asked one of the staff if Jean or the doctor was there so I could talk with them. As I waited for someone to come by, I tried to connect with Keydell and gauge how he was doing.

He was now jumping on the bed. He wouldn't answer any of my questions, just blabbed out nonsense and told me to watch how he could jump up and bounce off the wall. I tried to keep my cool, but it was challenging.

"Keydell, how about we play cards or something instead of jumping on the bed?" I tried to distract him. "I'm pretty sure you shouldn't be doing that in here. Plus, I only have an hour with you so it would be nice if you could settle down a bit."

Ugh. I sounded like the parent who wouldn't let her child jump in the puddle.

His hyperactivity was more manic than usual. He took out his deck of cards from a little table next to his bed and said, "How about 52 Pick Up?" He threw the cards around on the floor. "Get it? Now you have fifty-two cards to pick up."

"Oh, very funny," I said, trying to find my sense of humor, which had packed up and moved to another state months ago. "Let's pick those up and play Concentration or something."

He was a ball of energy. He joined me in picking up the cards, but as I was bent over, he squatted down in front of me, put his hand down my shirt and grabbed at my bra.

"Del, come on," I said as calmly as I could. "You have to stop doing that kind of thing, sweetie. You know that it makes me and Ella feel very uncomfortable." I think he did know that, and was trying to push my buttons.

He just looked at me with that dead-eye look as I sat all the way down on the linoleum floor to get at his level. As I faced him with legs crossed, Indian-style, we started to pick up the cards again. Then he reached over, grabbed my crotch and said, "That's what I am going to do to Ella when I get home."

I tried hard not to react, but I felt so discouraged in that moment. "Keydell, that is not cool, and you know it." I could barely speak from the aching in my soul. "I really want to bring you home soon, but this kind of behavior is not helping. You cannot touch Ella or me that way. It is crossing a line. Ella needs to feel safe in her home, just like you do."

He jumped up, ignoring me, and did a headstand on his bed. His feet were high in the air and he kicked his heels against the window. I picked up the rest of the cards just as Jean walked in.

"Hi Kim, how's your visit going?"

I stood up and faced Jean with my arms crossed and shoulders squared. I was obviously pissed off.

"Well, as you can see, Keydell is really wound up and bouncy, so it's hard to talk to him. We tried to play cards, but that was a bust."

"Why, what happened?" she asked.

I shifted legs for emphasis, "Look, I don't know what the doctor thinks, or how you all think he's doing here, but it's been a full week and we've gotten no tools or advice regarding what to do when he comes home," I began. "He just grabbed my chest and crotch and said he was going to do the same thing to his sister. What is that all about? I don't understand where that comes from, or how to handle it. Can you recommend someone who works with adopted kids or children with mental issues, or do we just live with this and get respite care every now and then?" My hands were now waving in the air, like I was batting away that last idea.

"Kim, I understand your frustration," Jean soothed. "Finding mental health care for children is difficult. I was part of a children's hospital for years, and worked with these kids a lot, but there are so many who have issues, and so few social workers available to give the help that is really needed."

"So what, after the weekend we just take him back home and hope that he hated it enough here—no offense—that he won't want to come back?"

I was being snippy, but what a waste of time! I knew Jean was doing the best she could, but I had totally misunderstood that this was just a respite facility, and was partially mad at myself. *There's my anger at feeling out of control*, I noticed.

It was nice to have a break from the meltdowns, sure, but we still had to drive two hours each way for an hour-long visit every day, and nothing had really changed. Maybe some parents didn't visit and just took the break; I didn't know. All I knew was that I'd had grand expectations, and they were not being met.

Wah, wah, wah.

"When can we take him home?" I asked, before Jean could comment.

She took a deep calming breath (which I'm sure she had to do often), and slowly replied, "The doctor will give him one more physical on Monday morning, and you can take him home after that. Hopefully, the doctor can recommend what to do about his medications if he feels a change is needed. It will only be a recommendation, so you'll need to follow up with your own doctors, of course, to get the meds in place and monitored."

Well, at least I knew I had a task: I had to find a psychiatrist. Tasks were good: they made me feel useful ... and in control.

I went over to Keydell in a bit of a huff and said, "I'm leaving now, Del. I'm sorry we didn't have a better visit. Henry's graduating tomorrow, and we have his party afterwards, so I probably won't see you until Monday, when we can hopefully take you home."

I could tell he understood how I was feeling and was trying to calm down. "Do I get to go back to school before the year ends?" he asked.

"I really hope so, Del, I really hope so." I gave him a quick touch on his head, said goodbye, and left.

Feeling numb from the whole visit, I walked away from The Twilight Zone and drove home in silence. I don't even think my thoughts were working. I just felt so deflated and sad. I was sad that Keydell had to go through all this, I was sad that it didn't seem to be making a difference, and I was sad that I was sad.

Buck up Kim, your oldest son is graduating tomorrow, I told myself. *Switch gears and get in happy mode. It was time to celebrate all the successes of Henry's life so far and be there for him on his big day.*

My thoughts were working again. They were telling me to stay in the moment. There was nothing to do but enjoy the weekend and let Keydell be. He was safe and, come Monday, I could get back to that compartment in my head. I turned the radio on and called Jim to tell him I was on my way home.

⇥⇤

Jim and I got up early the next morning and went to set up some of the decorations for the graduation party, which was being held at the home of one of Henry's friends. The celebration would include ten families, so we each had only one or two small tasks to do. Jim and I were responsible for the tent and table decorations, chipped in for food and drinks, and brought our grill to help with the burgers and hot dogs. When we got back to the house, Henry was just waking up.

"Hey Hank, big day! We are so proud of you." Jim and I hugged him. I had my happy face on.

"Hi Momma and Dad," he yawned. "I'm going to get a shower and then I have to head over to the school to get ready."

"Okay, sweetie," I said. "We're going to wait here for Grandma and Poppy and Amy and Lisa, and then head over." My whole family was coming, and Jim's sister Patti, the one remaining relative he was still in touch with, would be joining us, too. We had a light lunch planned at our house after the morning's graduation ceremony, and then we'd head off to the big cookout around 5:00 p.m. It was going to be a full and fun day.

My parents arrived, along with my sisters and their husbands, and we piled into as few cars as we could to go over to the high school. I was doing my best to keep the lump in my throat at bay. Sometimes, when I'm around my parents and sisters, my emotions rise to the top. I guess it's because they know me best, and I feel like I can let it all hang out.

"How are you feeling today Kim? Are you just so proud of Henry?" Lisa asked. Her son Nick was graduating next year, so this must have felt very sentimental to her, too.

"So proud," I said. "He's fifth in his class."

"How are you doing with Keydell and all?"

"Can't really talk without crying, but it's not easy," I told her. "I'm trying to focus on Henry today and be up and happy. I don't want to ruin it for him."

The graduation was great. The weather was warm and sunny, the valedictorian's speech was fantastic, and all the kids looked so happy. High school graduation can be such an exciting time for kids. They often go off to college with some newfound freedom, but still have that security of home.

Henry had settled on Chapman University, so he had some very exciting changes coming his way. We took lots of pictures after the procession (even though Henry was anxious to get to some of the other graduation parties before his own began), and then headed back to our house for lunch. I was already exhausted, but had a nice cold beer in the backyard with my family to relax before the cookout. I was on a roller coaster ride of emotions, for sure.

I was feeling particularly sentimental about Henry leaving the nest, and would miss his constant support, but I also knew that this past year had been hard on him. It was time for him to go and find himself, and not worry about me. I really was happy for him. On the down side of the emotional ride, of course, was my concern about Keydell's return home.

We all lingered in the warm June sun that afternoon, and then headed over to the big shindig under the tent. I really loved all of the boys in Henry's group (and the one lovely gal who tolerated them and hung out, too). They'd been friends since elementary school, and some as far back as pre-school. There must have been over a hundred people at the party, and we all had a great time. We sat at the "Henry" table that we'd decorated with his senior photo and some memorabilia from his high school years. Each of the boys' tables was similarly decked out. I'd taken most of these kids' senior photos, so it was nice to see their young smiles again, eager and ready to take on the world. There was so much hope under that tent.

Jim and I played volleyball and chatted with all the parents. The grill was cranking along with the music, and everyone was having a great time. I went back to our table to chat with my parents and noticed my cell phone had a missed call on it. I recognized the number; it was from Westwood. They had never called me unless I called first.

I left the tent with a nervous stomach and dialed Westwood. "Hi, this is Kim Fuller. I got a message that you called. Is everything okay with Keydell Fuller?"

"Hold on, let me connect you to his hall," said the nurse before putting me on hold. I could hear the party music pumping under the tent and people laughing and carrying on. My sister Amy was looking at me from the edge of the tent with the quizzical look of

"Is everything okay?" I gave her the thumbs up and the signal to hold on a second and turned my back to her as I was connected to someone on the other end of my phone.

"Hi, Mrs. Fuller?"

"Yes, that's me."

"We called because Keydell wanted to talk to you. He's been having a tough day and I really think he needs to hear your voice."

"Okay, can we talk now?" I asked.

"Sure, I'll put him on."

All of a sudden and with no greeting, Keydell's raspy little voice came through the line and said, "Hi, Mom. When can I come home?"

My heart burst out of my chest and the floodgates opened. I tried so hard to keep it together, but I just lost it. He sounded so sad, and I wanted to reach through the phone and pull him as close as I could to me. I'd never felt so desperate in all my life.

"Oh, honey, I am so sorry you aren't here with us. I'm going to come get you on Monday and we're going to bring you home. Can you hang on until then?"

"Yes, but I don't like it here. I want to come home." He was crying, too, and I could just picture him standing at the pay phone with the giant receiver held to his ear.

"I want you to come home, too, buddy," I assured him. "I don't like it there, either. I love you so much and want you to know that you will always be able to come home to us."

"Okay, bye." He hung up. Just like that, the conversation was over. I stood in the street, with the cell phone still to my ear, not remembering how to move, looking back at the party. No one knew what had just happened but me and Keydell. I put my secret back in my heart and off my sleeve, and put one foot in front of the other to walk back to the happy tent.

I was glad it was dark, because I was still all splotchy from crying. I went straight back to the table, set my phone down, and danced like a maniac for the rest of the night. I still, to this day, think that was one of the craziest highs and lows of emotion I have ever been on. I was the happiest and the most heartbroken I've ever been, all in the same day, with not much in-between.

CHAPTER 15

VACATION

"Coming together is a beginning; keeping together is progress; working together is success." Henry Ford

Monday, June 22, 2010

Jim and I drove to Westwood to get Keydell and bring him home. Ella had exams, and Henry was enjoying his first weekday morning after graduation by sleeping in. As long as everything went well, Keydell would be able to go to the last two days of third grade, and say goodbye to his friends and teachers before we left for Utah. He loved school, and hated to miss a day, so it was important for him to have that closure at the end of the school year.

Keydell was sitting on the edge of his bed when we arrived, looking fragile and tired, but he was all packed up and ready to go. He'd been off his Adderall since he'd gotten to Westwood, but his zoned-out look and still body made me think they'd given him his dose this morning. I needed to check in with the doctor before checkout to see where we stood with his medications.

"Hi sweetie," I said as I entered his room. "How're you doing?"

"Good. Can we go now?" Keydell answered, bouncing up off the mattress.

I walked to the bed and rubbed his back for a second. He lifted his shoulders to protect his ticklish neck.

"In a minute," I chuckled. "We just have to check in with the doctor first. Did he come to see you this morning yet?"

"No."

Just then, a bald, low-slung, heavy-set man with glasses came into the room. He wore the typical white coat with a pocket protector and some pens sticking out of it, so I assumed he was the doctor. Like I said, this was the first contact we'd had with him.

"Good morning," he said with an outstretched hand. "Keydell is all set to go. He's still on the Risperdal for his mood swings, and he's back on his Adderall for the ADHD." He got right to it, and seemed anxious to move on. We were not his only case.

"Does he have a psychiatrist who can monitor his meds?" he asked us.

"No, we've been getting his medications refilled through his pediatrician," I told him. "Is that okay for now? I've been looking for a psychiatrist this week, actually, but I don't have an appointment yet or anything."

Jim was standing next to me, gazing out the window. He looked annoyed and ready to get out of there.

"Our recommendation for Keydell is that he stay on Risperdal and the Adderall for now, but if something changes, it's good to have a psychiatrist who knows him and can make any adjustments."

He hadn't once sat with Keydell that we knew of, or asked us about him personally. He didn't know him outside of the ten days he'd been there. I appreciated the information, but we'd learned nothing new since Keydell had come here. He was on the same medications, and we had no new tools in our arsenal.

"Well, thank you for taking care of Keydell." I managed to say. "Is there anything else you can suggest for us moving forward?" The question was my last attempt to see the upside of this whole experience.

The doctor said no, and goodbye. I imagined his last words being, *"Thanks for coming to the Westwood Lodge, we hope you enjoyed your son's stay. Please come back and see us sometime."*

Our respite was over.

Jean joined us in the room just then and said, "Hi, Fullers! (Jim loved being called a Fuller.) I want you to know I think Keydell is a great kid. I know it's hard sometimes, but just keep doing what you are doing."

What, managing our little monster? Keeping scissors and knives up high, and windows and car doors locked so he won't jump out? Got it.

I knew that so many kids came and went, with such varying degrees of mental illness or behavioral needs, that Westwood was not designed to include family therapy. Basically, after the child's stay, they wish you good luck and send you on your way, knowing that they may or may not see you again for another respite. Keydell *definitely* would not be coming back. I had to stay strong and keep him with us.

I sat in thought, staring out the front window as Jim drove us down Westwood Lodge's long driveway. I felt so uncertain as to what would come next, but realized the best thing for all of us was to be together. I thought about all of Keydell's behaviors, and wondered what he really needed to heal. Was it just going to take time, love, and reassurance? Could we keep him safe until that time went by? We were most concerned about him hurting himself, especially when we weren't around. He had often said he wanted to kill himself, but had never made any serious attempts.

"I want to die," he would say. "Your lives would be so much better without me."

He believed all of our problems were because of him. I loved this little guy so much, and was so proud of him for trying so hard, yet I knew that there was more to understand and do. I was not giving up. The past ten days had made us all realize that being apart was not the way to go; we needed Keydell with us. I needed to stay open to the way his mind worked, and try to help him reframe his thinking to more positive thoughts, just as I was practicing in my meditation. He was locked into being a bad boy, being stupid and worthless, which of course made him very unhappy. I was going to figure this out. We were still in for a long road ahead—but for now we were together with our little bean.

I was happy to tuck him into bed that night and give him a nice back scratch. I sang some bedtime songs, read him a book or two, and quietly settled him in for a much-needed sleep in his own bed. I told him he could go to school the next day, and that I was excited for our trip to Utah.

"Me too," Keydell said, looking lovingly into my eyes for one of the first times. "I'm sorry, Mom."

Oh, my heart was breaking. He was such a sweet child, deep down inside.

As tears welled in my eyes, I said, "I'm sorry, too, buddy. I feel like I made a mistake with Westwood. I didn't understand what that place was about. I love you and will always love you, and just want to help you find the peace and happiness you deserve. You know you deserve that, right? You have been so amazing this past week, and we are proud of you."

He nodded his head as he rolled stomach-down into his sleeping position. I pulled the covers up over his shoulders, and turned on his lava lamp. He switched on the little fan that he kept next to his bed, which blew right on his face as he slept.

Jim came in, too, and gave him a big hug and kiss goodnight before we shut out the light.

⇒╬⇐

Keydell had never been on a plane before—or, for that matter, left Rhode Island at all, except for one weekend trip to Maine with us. He was excited. He'd been very happy being home the past two days, so we were hopeful that this would be a good vacation for all of us. We helped him pack his own little suitcase on wheels and headed to the airport. I carried his birth certificate with me for the security check, just in case there was a question as to how we were connected to this boy who didn't look like us. As it turned out, there was little to be concerned about. They just asked Keydell if we were his parents and sent us through to the gate. I wondered if it would have been that easy if we were black parents with an adopted white child.

It was a four-and-a-half hour-flight, so we'd loaded the iPad with some games. Each seat had a personal television, too, so Keydell was happy as a clam sitting between Jim and me. He fell asleep after eating his snack and charming all the flight attendants. I smiled at his relaxed, sleeping face, and at how curious he'd been about every detail of the plane. He wanted to know how everything worked, wanted to push any button he could, loved watching the flight pattern on the TV monitor, and thought incessantly about what kept this thing in the air. He had talked with my navy pilot dad a lot about planes, and they would sit and make paper airplanes together while my dad went over the aeronautics. They would fold the wings differently to see if it changed the way the paper glided through the air. Keydell took it all in and was very focused on the topic. I was grateful for the somewhat relaxing flight.

We were staying with friends who had recently moved to Utah from Rhode Island. They had seven kids ranging in age from two to twenty one, and had a beautiful home in the hills of Park City with a guest house for us to stay in. It had an amazing view overlooking the hills and a golf course from the back patio.

The first morning we were there, I got up early and sat on the patio wall for my meditation. I wanted to check in with my state of mind and just sit, noticing my body's sensations as I tried to de-stress a bit. So much had happened over the past few weeks, and I wanted to get grounded again.

I tried to just feel the sun on my face and not let my emotions direct my thinking. I visualized Keydell as if for the first time—with fresh eyes, and not with the past feelings around his abusive behaviors toward me. I saw his face in all of its innocence, wearing the smile I had seen a few times, especially when he was on a soccer field, and prayed for him to find peace. I focused on staying present to what he needed, and what he was telling me in his own unique way. I needed to remember to enjoy the good—and there was so much good. I knew I was growing and learning from all of this. I mean, I had asked for suffering, and now I was getting it.

The word "wanting" popped into my mind. I *wanted* Keydell to have a nice trip. I *wanted* to find out what the heck was going on with him, and I *wanted* to feel happy again. I understood from my Buddhist teachings that grasping too tightly to expectations or ideas can cause a lot of suffering, so I knew I had to practice just being present to my reality and not just what I wanted things to be like. I didn't know if Keydell would ever be calmer and more controlled, or if he would ever feel truly happy with us; all I could do was keep responding to his needs with an open heart, and let his life be whatever it was going to be. Either way, worrying about an outcome did me no good.

At the end of my sit, our friends' cat jumped up on the wall and rubbed against my arm as if to say, "Everything is cool. Just keep breathing—and if you can find it in your heart, please pet me." I met his immediate need and gave him a good rubdown.

Henry and Ella found lots to do with our friends' older kids, and Keydell was happy with the younger bunch. We went to a theme park where Keydell rode all the crazy rides, and even bungee-jumped with our friend. He had no fear of thrill rides, but still didn't like the dark.

Four days into our six-day visit, we all went over a neighbor's house for a cookout. It was one of the first times all the kids would be together at one time. The neighbors had a great outdoor patio with a hot tub that everyone wanted to go in before dinner. Keydell loved swimming and hot tubs, but he tended to use hot tubs like he would a pool, swimming around, diving, and splashing under the water.

At one point, the hot tub was filled with the older kids, including Henry and Ella. Keydell wanted to join the party.

"Del," I whispered, pulling him aside to talk for a second, "I just want to remind you that you can't splash and kick or swim around underwater when all the big kids are in the hot tub. You have to wait until they get out to do that, okay? If you want to just sit in there, I'm sure they'll be fine—but you have to sit still."

"Fine," he replied, as he jumped in the tub full of teenagers.

I went about socializing and getting some food when I heard Ella say, "Keydell, please stop. You just kicked me."

I turned toward the hot tub and, sure enough, Keydell was swimming around with his feet up in the air. It was a big hot tub, but not big enough for that.

I walked over and Henry said, "Mom he's being pretty annoying. I don't want him to have a problem."

"Hey Del, I don't want to have to ask you get out."

He lasted only a few minutes without doing it again. He seemed completely unaware of his effect on the others in the tub.

"Come on out for a while, Del, and maybe get some food with me. We can play cards or something," I said.

"I'm not doing anything," he screamed. "I was just going under to check out the bubbles."

"Out, now please. You can go back in later and blow all the bubbles you want."

"I hate you, Ella," he yelled. He splashed her in the face as he climbed out of the hot tub, not caring who he stepped on.

As he sat with me, I could see that he was upset, but was also doing his best to hold it together. He'd been doing so well, and I didn't want him to feel like he'd messed up; I just needed him to understand that he had to take a break.

"Del, it's okay," I told him as we started a card game. "You didn't do anything wrong; it was just the wrong time. I'm not mad at you. You've been so awesome on this trip and I am proud of you." He started to pick at his burger and rip his napkin. I looked at Jim, who was walking over to help and I whispered, "I think we may have a problem in a minute. Maybe I should take him back to the house for a little while, or for a walk."

Jim nodded in agreement, "I'll come with you."

As we got up, his drink spilled all over the table. I grabbed some napkins to wipe it up before it got on someone's lap, but Keydell saw the frustrated look on my face and started marching toward the exit gate.

"It's okay, bud, let's just clean it up quickly and then we'll go see the sunset."

He was starting to hit himself in the head.

"I am so stupid," he said.

I was frantically wiping up and keeping an eye on him at the same time. Jim caught up with him just before he opened the gate to the front of the house. The neighbors' VW bus was sitting in the driveway; Keydell plopped down next to it and leaned against the tire. He was screaming and crying from the depths of his tiny body, but this felt different than previous meltdowns. It was as if all the tension he'd held inside through the week at Westwood, and the stress of trying to be happy and well behaved for our trip, was oozing out from every pore in his body. He was wailing from the pain of defeat, rather than the power of anger. I think he felt he had let us down.

Jim and I just sat next to him while he worked it out. I was able to pull him onto my lap without resistance, and the three of us just sat there as the sun went down over the hills.

The rest of the week was incident-free. As we packed our bags to head home, I watched Keydell carefully put his things in his little suitcase. When he was sure all of his things were packed, he helped me with mine. He was trying so hard to be a good boy. I knew he hated Westwood and never wanted to go back there, or to any other place like it, and I hoped he understood that our dedication to helping him was why we put him there. His actions seemed to be saying he did understand.

When we landed at the airport after the red-eye flight, Keydell was hyper and bouncing off the walls. At the baggage claim, he dashed in between the other passengers from our flight and attempted to grab our suitcases from the carousel. I asked him to please just let Dad and me do it. He got pissed off and ran away from us. I assumed he wouldn't go far because we were his ride home. I realized only later that he'd wanted to show us his good side again, and I had missed it.

⊰⊱

It didn't take long after our trip from Utah for Keydell to start feeling and acting the same way he had before his time at Westwood. As hard as he tried to stay in control, his frustrations, violence, and dangerous behaviors won out, with only a few moments of peace in between.

I was exhausted, frustrated, and, frankly, not doing very well. I could feel the stress in my body, and was often on the edge of tears. I showed up at my sister Lisa's house one day, crying and shaking after an episode with Keydell. She was so surprised to see me this way and had no idea how bad things were. In her mind, I was the strong one in our sister trio; I was the one who had it all together. Well, sister, not today.

I tried so hard to enjoy the good times in between meltdowns, but I was always on edge. Our life was a constant stream of ups and downs, and we never knew when Keydell would go crazy. He'd started going to a new camp that was a little less crowded than the

YMCA camp, but he nevertheless had problems, and we got many calls. One day I got a call that he'd run all the way across the field next to the school where the camp was held, and none of the teen camp counselors could catch him. I told them not to chase him, just to keep their eyes on him and I would come get him.

Jim and I started arguing more about how to best handle Keydell, and even calm Henry was losing it. He got so sick of Keydell's behaviors toward me one day that he slammed the door to his room and broke the full-length mirror that hung on the back into a million pieces. Ella was rarely home if she could help it.

I had begun looking for a psychiatrist, but did not go back to Sonya again. She'd told me she didn't feel equipped to work with Keydell so, even though we liked her, we moved on. We still had our evaluation appointment at Hasbro in a few months, but we needed something more immediate. I called Child and Family Services here in Middletown but their doctors use the same basic talk therapy we'd already been doing. They had in-home care staff that could work with us, which I thought would be great, but they were very short-handed, and no one was available.

It was unbelievable how hard it was to get help for a child with mental illness. We just hung on, cherished the times that were normal, and kept reassuring Keydell that we loved him.

Did I love him? Would he accept my love for him? When our birth children were born, Jim and I loved them like no other kind of love we'd ever felt. It was instant. Here, in front of us, were babies we created from our own love for each other, and they were perfect. It was an egotistical experience, and we thought everything they did was magical and beautiful.

Several people have asked me, over the years, if my love for Keydell is the same as for Henry and Ella. Of course it's different. I loved Keydell like I loved Jim at first, minus the sexual attraction. I was drawn to him; I saw something in him that was special, and knew we needed to be a part of each other's lives. It's the kind of love that grows as we experience things together, and begin to understand and trust each other. In one way, though, it is the same kind of love I feel for Henry and Ella: a love that almost hurts, it's so deep.

Keydell was an innocent child that I couldn't help but feel compassion for. I admired him and respected his strength and resilience. So my answer was always yes, I love Keydell. Even if he couldn't fully love me back, or love me the way I was used to from my birth children, it didn't matter. I had to accept his way of showing his love, no matter how I "wanted" it to look. I had to learn to expect only what he was capable of giving, even though I wasn't even sure what that was. We hadn't adopted Keydell because we wanted a child to love us; we adopted him because he needed someone to love *him*. He needed someone to trust, someone who would fight to the death for him.

Deep down, I knew he was grateful for his adoption but he still felt separate from us. His needs were focused on being safe, going to school, and playing sports and video games, and maybe not so much about being "connected" to us as deeply as a birth child might. While that sounded harsh, it nevertheless felt that way to me sometimes; it was something that would have to slowly evolve. I've always loved deeply and quickly because I believe in love. I trusted the source of love, my parents and sisters. How could I expect that of Keydell, who had never had that trust in others? Trusting in a mother figure, especially, hadn't gotten him too far. For him, a birth mother meant neglect and distance, not caring and closeness. I would have to continue to earn his trust, and show him that I was in this for the long haul.

These were the thoughts that gave me strength to keep going. Even when Jim and I were at our wits' end, we would regroup and remind each other to keep going—to keep loving him, and to keep loving each other.

CHAPTER 16

MY BREAKING POINT

"We must accept finite disappointment, but we must never lose infinite hope."

—*Martin Luther King*

E arly in July, just after we got back from our trip, I ran into a woman at Frosty Freeze who I knew was a child psychologist—as was her husband, Dr. Martin. I told her about Keydell, and asked if she might work with him.

"My husband would be a better choice for you guys because he works with a lot of boys with behavioral issues," she said. "But keep in mind, Kim, from my experience, it takes as long for a child to adjust to a new home as the time he or she was in the system."

No way, I thought. That would mean about five years for us. I wouldn't make it. It had only been a year and a half so far and I was dying. I brushed off her words but called her husband the next day and made the appointment.

"We're going to try a new doctor, Keydell," I told him one morning at breakfast. "I know you liked Sonya, but this guy may be better for you. He might have better tools for helping you control your anger, okay?"

"I don't want to go," he replied. "It's a waste of time."

"How about we get an ice cream after the session?" The bribe worked, and he agreed.

We drove to Dr. Martin's office in Newport and entered the waiting room. It had an old New England-house smell of horsehair plaster and wallpaper, and a lot of mauve and pink decor. He didn't have anything in there for Keydell to play with except for a big tank full of colorful fish. Naturally, Del wanted to stick his hand in the tank, mess with the filter, and put things in the water. When was the doctor going to call him in so I could sit there by myself for fifteen minutes?

"Hi, Keydell. Would you like to come into the office?" asked Dr. Martin as he appeared in the waiting room. He was about sixty years old, with little round glasses and white hair. I wondered if this frail-looking man could handle Keydell. "You can come, too, Kim, for a few minutes so we can check in. Then, Keydell and I can talk alone." I thought that was a good idea.

We followed him past an old staircase in the dimly-lit hallway, and into a small office that had probably once been a bedroom. There was a couch along the window wall that Keydell and I sat on as Dr. Martin sat across from us in his chair. He had a yellow legal pad on his lap, and no computer in sight. Very old school.

In his quiet, calm tone, he said, "Tell me a little bit about Keydell and what's been going on."

Keydell had already found some kind of decorative knick-knack to play with on the end table. I turned to him and asked, "Do you want to start, Keydell, or should I?"

"You go," he replied, fondling the snow globe.

"You sure?"

"Yep. What does this do?" He was playing with this thing and bouncing it between his legs on the couch cushion. He was already uncomfortable.

"It's just for decoration," Dr. Martin replied.

I took a deep breath and started in on the dreadful tattling. "So Keydell has been with us for about a year and a half now and he's been having a lot of angry outbursts. He will not follow the rules of the house, and has some inappropriate behaviors toward his sister and her friends that we would love to get some help with."

I told him about Keydell's history of behaviors and living situations and how he'd been removed from a foster home for similar behaviors. I told him his birth mom and aunt had shared custody on and off when he was very young and explained that his anger was often directed toward me.

I could see Keydell's eyes becoming angry, thin slits, and felt badly that I had to say all these things in front of him again. I tried to balance with some positive input.

"Keydell is very smart, does his homework, and is a great athlete as well. I think maybe we just need some tools to help him manage his anger."

Dr. Martin then asked me about my parenting style.

"I'm pretty straightforward and fair, I think." I felt defensive around his question. I totally did not think this had anything to do with my parenting style, even though I also felt I had no idea what I was doing with him. I had already raised two great kids.

"Jim and I set the rules for our tiny household so we can all live in it with a peaceful flow. Henry and Ella have always understood consequences for their actions so we've rarely had to put them on restriction or take away privileges. Keydell doesn't take his consequences or responsibility for his actions. He just gets more and more angry and violent when we enforce a rule or tell him he will lose a privilege if he continues the behavior. He gets defiant and tells us to 'shut up' or says, 'I don't care, go ahead and take things away,' and sometimes he just breaks whatever it is we say we will take away as a kind of self-sabotaging act."

Dr. Martin looked at Keydell and asked, "Do you think what your mom is saying is accurate?"

"I don't want to talk about it," Keydell whispered with his head down and body slumped into the couch. I was concerned he would break that knick-knack—but, in a way, I wanted Dr. Martin to witness firsthand Keydell's behaviors.

Dr. Martin asked if I would step into the waiting room. Keydell said, "NO, I want her to stay."

I looked at Dr. Martin for my next move.

"Sure, but, let's you and I play a game together, Keydell, okay?"

God, more games. We'd gone this route. I knew this method helped open the child up but, damn it, I wanted something Keydell and I could do together.

He pointed Keydell to a shelf with some games on it and asked him which one he might like to play. I took the glass snow globe from him before he left the couch and carefully placed it back on the side table. After a few minutes, things were going well so I signaled to Keydell that I was going to go outside now and give him time with Dr. Martin. Maybe he would open up with him because he was a male. I wanted time alone anyway.

I got up from the couch and looked back at Keydell as I slowly shut the office door behind me. He was on the floor playing, but still looked agitated. I left the door open a crack, hoping I might be able to hear some of what they talked about, or how Dr. Martin might keep Keydell cool. I didn't want to spy, but thought I might get some new insights. I had only been sitting down with my Vogue magazine for about two minutes when all of a sudden I heard screaming, Keydell was upset.

That didn't last long, I thought.

He came storming out of the office and said, "We're leaving."

"Does Dr. Martin need to see me before we go?"

"I don't care. I'm leaving," Keydell barked.

"Okay, let's go, I can call him later if need be."

Dr. Martin poked his head out the office door just as we were dashing out. I yelled over my shoulder, as I chased after Keydell, that I would call later for another appointment.

We got in the car and, as promised, I headed to the store for some ice cream. As I pulled onto the main street, Keydell rolled his window up and down, up and down.

"Honey, please don't do that, okay?" I asked. "Just leave it down. It's hot in the car." He kept doing it anyway.

"Keydell, that is very distracting while I'm driving, sweetie. Can you please not do that? What kind of ice cream do you want anyway?" I asked, trying to distract him.

"I want the kind I can cut myself with," he said.

"Oh Del, let's try to have some fun now," I pleaded. "I'm just trying to help you."

"I don't want your help."

"Okay then, help yourself. But I get the sense you don't know how. With Dr. Martin's help you should try to get at what's upsetting you so we, or you, can work on healing your pain around it. If you don't talk to him or us, we won't know what to work on."

"I don't like going to the therapist, it takes up too much time and I don't get to do my homework or play video games or soccer," he complained.

"I know, hang in there and just keep trying, please." In the back of my mind I thought, *Is this even worth it?* We'd tried talk therapy before, and the sessions almost always ended badly. Maybe he needed a break to just play and be a kid. Maybe the therapy was a big fat reminder that he was "damaged" and needed fixing.

He didn't want to hang in there. He was still messing with the window when I heard something fall out of the car. It scared the crap out of me because at first it sounded like something hit my car. "What was that?"

"It was my shoe," he said.

"You threw your shoe out the window?"

"Yep."

"Keydell, that could have hit another car and caused an accident. You can't do that, even if you're mad."

"I just did," he snickered.

"Well, you're out a shoe, again, and we are definitely not getting ice cream now. That is unacceptable and you know it and I asked you several times nicely to stop and you chose not to. If you're upset, you need to try to keep it in the car or at home. You cannot put other peoples' lives in danger because *you* are upset," I explained in an obviously tense tone.

Then he opened the car door right as we were driving along. My emergency light flashed and beeped on the dashboard and I nearly shit my pants I was so scared. He had never taken it this far before. Thankfully, he had his seat belt on, and closed the door as quickly as he'd opened it. We were only going about twenty-five miles per hour, so I pulled over quickly and stopped on the side of the road.

My heart was racing, and I could barely hold the steering wheel my hands were shaking so much. I looked back at him and said, "Holy cow, Keydell. You scared me to death. What are you thinking, buddy? You could have fallen out of the car. Being upset is not worth hurting yourself over, okay? My God!"

I was still rattled but turned back around to collect myself before driving again. Keydell was sitting in silence. I think he'd shocked himself out of his state when he saw the road whizzing by below him. I didn't think he'd ever do *that* again. We were both quiet as we sat there for a few more seconds before driving the rest of the way home. The ride was only five minutes, but it felt like an hour. I just wanted to get him home safely.

⇥⊹⇤

August 2010

Psychologists do the talk therapy and psychiatrists prescribe medications. For the longest time I thought any therapist could do both. That took me a while to understand, but after a very long search and talking to many people about psychiatrists, I finally found a woman in Bristol, Rhode Island, about forty-five minutes from us, whose specialty was working with children.

Dr. Lillia Romero-Bosch had a beautiful, modern waiting room designed in soft greens and blues. I wondered if she had decorated it herself; if so, my artistic eye was appreciating her sense of style. It felt soothing to walk into that waiting room compared to others we'd been in, which made a huge difference for me. I was immediately calmer and more relaxed. She had a coffee and hot chocolate machine set up on an end table in the lobby that drew Keydell's eye. As we waited to be called to our appointment, he asked if he could make a cup of hot chocolate. All I could imagine was him spilling on the beautiful furniture in the lobby. Thankfully, we got called in just before we had time to make a cup.

"We can get one for the ride home," I said as I nudged him toward her office door and away from the machine.

Her interior office had a red, grey, and white color palette that was as pretty as the waiting room. Keydell even commented on it because he loves red. I sat in a dark red leather chair near her desk and Keydell found some block puzzles on the floor to play with. Dr. Bosch watched Keydell while looking over her notes about his history. We had discussed his issues over the phone before I made the appointment, so I was happy not to have to rehash it in front of Keydell again. Our appointment was for only thirty minutes, so she was efficient and to the point. I explained how we thought Keydell was not on helpful medications. She noticed he had dark circles under his eyes, and asked about his moods other than during the meltdowns. I told her I thought he had a hard time being joyful or feeling happy, that the few times he did smile, it looked forced or fake. "I've wondered if he might be depressed." I said.

"I think Keydell might have some depression based on what you're telling me and by what I can see on his face," she began. "I would suggest slowly taking him off the Risperdal, which has to be done very carefully so you don't risk spikes in blood pressure, and once off that, start him on some Zoloft. That would be around early September. Zoloft is an anti-depressant. Are you okay with that?"

"I think I am," I said, smiling as I watched Keydell and wondered what he was thinking. He had already put the whole puzzle together and was almost done with a second one. I was excited for the possibility of Keydell being happy for a change. I knew Jim would be happy to take him off Risperdal, too. It obviously was not helping any of Keydell's symptoms. The side effects included restlessness, nervousness, and bladder control issues, all of which he experienced, so good riddance.

"I can see that Keydell is very bright," she said to me, noticing the puzzle. She turned to him and asked him to explain how he was feeling about his life with us.

"Do you sometimes feel sad, Keydell, or that it's hard to feel happy?"

"I guess," he said without looking up from the floor.

"Well, we want to change that for you, so we're going to try something new."

"Okay," he said, looking up this time.

"I'm not even sure he needs Adderall," I said. "He's plenty focused, and I can deal with a little extra energy, but let's start with ending the Risperdal and go from there."

"Yes, one step at a time," she agreed. "We can better gauge our results if we change the medications slowly. And, you can take him off the Adderall at any time without a weaning process and see how he does; it doesn't linger in the body. Follow the directions carefully for the Risperdal withdrawal, and we'll meet again in two weeks to see how he's doing."

I really liked her. She was very engaged with Keydell, and very good at reading his body language and facial expressions. Even though she prescribed medications, she seemed to have a holistic approach to his well-being, and I appreciated that. I liked that she didn't push drugs on him but wanted to find the right ones for him. We had a plan.

We left her office, got the cup of hot chocolate and headed back to Middletown. When we got home, I told Jim about the appointment. He was happy to hear Keydell was getting off the Risperdal.

"I think he should stay on Adderall, personally," he said a bit agitated by my suggestion to take him off.

"Well, what do you think about trying a few days off while it's still summer and see how it goes? I mean, it's not like he needs to focus on school right now."

"I think it helps more than just for focus," he said turning away from me to do something else.

"He's so small still, and maybe he'll grow if he goes off of it," I reasoned. I was following him out of the room now.

"We can try if you want, but I think he needs it." He was being agreeable, but I knew he was concerned. I thought sometimes that when Jim saw Keydell frustrated, he could relate. Jim lost things frequently, and had some organizational and focus issues that frustrated him, too, so maybe he was more sympathetic to Keydell.

He was leaving it up to me. I decided we would give it to him on camp days but try not using it on weekends and see how it went. That was agreeable to all three of us, even Keydell. He wanted to be good and feel good, so I think he was nervous going off the Adderall and thought he might have more meltdowns. At this point, though, what was one more meltdown? We began the slow process of taking him off Risperdal.

⚒

Around that same time, a wonderful young man came to stay with us. He was a twenty-year-old English lacrosse player who'd stayed with us two years prior while his team was in the U.S. for an exchange program with Henry's summer lacrosse team. He was a dark-skinned, small-framed athlete from India who ended up being a great companion and role model for Keydell. His name was Krishna, which in the Hindu tradition, is the name of a supreme deity worshipped by many and adored for his mischievous pranks. Krishna lived up to his name and was a very happy, animated young man who brought a much-needed bit of fun into our home. Keydell especially liked Krishna because he was from England, the home of his favorite soccer team, Manchester United.

Krishna arrived in early August, about three weeks before Henry was supposed to take off for college. We'd warned him about Keydell, and that things could get a little tense in the house sometimes. What was interesting is that, because Krishna had no previous experience with Keydell's behaviors, he could see him from an objective perspective. He saw his amazing soccer talent and his sense of humor, and was able to navigate the upsets over video games. He showed Keydell new techniques on the real-life soccer field as well as the video game soccer field. He didn't have to deal with all the upsets directly (and there were many that month), so could just enjoy the good parts. Looking at Krishna was like looking at a possible grown-up version of Keydell. I imagined him laughing and being joyous like Krishna, and even being built like him, and it gave me such hope hanging out with the both of them together.

As the summer rolled on, it was time to say good-bye to Henry. We gave him a going-away party, and took a family photo together afterwards. We even included Krishna in the picture.

"Call me any time Mom, if you need to talk about Del," invited Henry. We were standing together at the edge of the party having a private moment. "I want to hear all about his soccer games, too. He's going to be amazing."

"I will, Hen, thank you for all you've done. I wish you could have spent more time with him as just a brother, and not always as my security guard. Maybe when you come back for Christmas, things will have settled down a bit."

"I know, I feel like we bonded some, but I wish I could be closer as he grows up."

"We'll have the summers," I assured him pulling him in for a big hug.

I cried my eyes out as my first child left for college. This was not going to be easy, but I knew Henry was going to have an amazing experience in California. He was born for that laid-back, carefree life style.

After Henry left, Ella continued bussing tables at a popular Newport restaurant, so Krishna, Keydell and I would often do things together. We went to different tourist and favorite locals' spots, and up to Providence to see our city and RISD. I think his favorite trip was our hike at Beavertail Park in Jamestown, so I decided to take him to one more beautiful spot: Sachuest Point, a beautiful strip of land in Newport surrounded by water and a rocky shoreline on three sides. Keydell had been having a tough day, so I thought it would be good to do something active and fun. Nature could work its magic on him.

Sachuest Point has a walking trail about two miles long that circles the strip of land. You can veer off the path to climb on the big rocks at the edge of the shoreline, and the three of us happily started out to do just that. Keydell sprinted ahead, then back again, and then back out. He was having a blast, and Krishna and I chatted as we walked along. We climbed, sat in the warm sun, and watched as Keydell navigated the giant rocks like a billy goat. He had great balance and confidence in his step.

After sitting for a bit we climbed further along and got to a section of beach. We started skimming rocks into the water and making sculptures by stacking rocks. At one point, Keydell was right at the water's edge, trying to stack his set of rocks, and the water rolled in just enough to get his shoes wet. We giggled a bit as he backed up as fast as he could. His sculpture kept falling down and he was starting to get frustrated. He was so focused on getting this one big rock to balance on another that he didn't see the next wave of water coming in again. This time, it rolled in stronger and farther, and got him really wet. Krishna and I started laughing harder, because of the way it startled him and made him jump.

Wrong thing to do.

"Sorry, Keydell but you jumped so high and let out the funniest little screech," I said. "I didn't mean to embarrass you."

He walked over to the rocks I was stacking and knocked them down with his foot.

"Hey, it's okay, Del, it was funny," I smiled. "It's important to be able to laugh at yourself sometimes. I've had that same thing happen to me before, too."

"It's not funny. I want to go." He marched up to the trailhead and disappeared for a minute.

"Should we go get him?" Krishna asked.

"Just let him cool off first and see if he comes back," I replied. "Sometimes it makes things worse if I go after him and keep bugging him."

Honestly, I'd been enjoying our day, and wanted to stay right where I was and pretend nothing was going wrong. Living in denial would have been so much easier than my practice of looking at reality.

About a minute later he marched back down the hill path that led from the trail to the shore, tripping over the rocks and heading right down to the water again. He was like an angry little man and it was hard to contain our laughter because he was so determined.

He took off his watch, one we'd just given him (to replace the one he'd thrown out the window), and threw it in the water.

"Hey, Del, don't do that," I scolded. "We just got that for you and now you'll be without one *again*! I'm not buying a third watch. We're done."

"Who cares?" he barked back, glaring at me.

"I do," I answered. "I work hard for my money and I want you to learn how to take care of your things. This hurts you, too, you know."

"Oh well, I guess I just won't have a watch then," he said with a sassy swagger back toward us.

Keydell was obsessed with watches. He always had to have one on to know what time it was. I think it was a way for him to feel in control of his day, so I was happy to supply him with one if it helped. I was not, however, going to be the endless supplier if he was just going to keep throwing them away.

"You're right, you won't have a watch now but I want you to understand that this was your choice. You didn't have to do that to make your point. You made it worse for yourself, it's no skin off my back, Del, but you're out a watch."

He started running back toward the trail. I looked at Krishna as if to say we'd better get going.

"Keydell, please wait for us," I yelled. "It's a long way back, and I want to walk together." I scurried up the cliff's edge to the trail. It was really hot outside, and the last thing I wanted to do was try to find him if he bolted through the trails and got lost.

When we got off the beach we caught up with him. He was sitting on the trail off to the side and would not get up to walk. He was trying to get me upset and it was working. It had been a long summer of this behavior, and I had run out of patience.

"Keydell, please get up. Let's go back to the car, go get a snack, and start over," I pleaded. I was trying not to lose my shit in front of Krishna.

He stood up, took off one of his sneakers and threw it right into a huge bramble bush. It landed in the middle where there was no chance of recovering it without getting completely scratched up.

"Well, now you're going to have to walk all the way back with one shoe on," I said. "Again, you're only hurting yourself, not anyone else, Del."

"Do you want a piggyback ride Keydell?" Krishna asked.

"You know what, Krishna, thank you, but he needs to understand what he's done. He can walk with one shoe." Oh, yes, I was getting stubborn, too.

Keydell then started to take off his other shoe but I grabbed him and made him stop.

"Guess what, Del, you want to take your things off and throw them? Well then, take everything off and you can walk back in your underwear."

I stripped him of his T-shirt, shorts and other shoe as he flailed around screaming and yelling. The straw had broken on this camel's back. I was not able to handle this anymore. He was a mess and only getting worse. He screamed and cried all the way back until Krishna finally did carry him the rest of the way to the car.

"I don't want to go back to Westwood," he yelled out.

"You're not going there, Keydell, but I need to take you to a hospital," I told him. "I don't know what sets you off like this and I am one hundred percent out of ideas." I was going to go straight to Hasbro this time and just walk into the emergency room there. Fuck it. I wanted in on that program *now*, and this seemed to be the only way.

By the time we got in the car, he was soup. He was limp, crying out, and scared. I had a pit in my stomach. Just two months after he'd gotten home from Westwood, and we were back to this. I was thinking back to when Chad from Children's Friends said, "If this continues, you may need to take him to the hospital." I was quick to judge then, but understood now how parents could feel hopeless. I certainly was not giving Keydell back, but I thought if we got him to the emergency room directly at Hasbro, then maybe, just maybe, we could get him into that program faster. Hasbro specialized in this stuff. They must have a better way to figure out what was triggering him, or if something deeper was going on.

When we got home, I called Hasbro and told them I was on my way. Jim and I got Keydell dressed again and hopped into the car. We drove the forty minutes to the hospital while Keydell slept in the back seat. He had already calmed down and was probably in shock. I noted to Jim that he had been on his Adderall today yet all this still happened.

It was about 7:30 that evening when we arrived at the hospital. We walked into the emergency area, which was a very large waiting room with checkered floors, a play area for kids, and an open, inviting layout. Jim, Keydell and I all maneuvered in silence and found a seat near a window. I checked in at the desk, gave them Keydell's Neighborhood Health Care card, and sat back down.

"They said they would take his vitals but it might be a while before they could get a room for him," I told Jim.

Keydell was slumped in his chair, still a bit sleepy from the ride. I lifted him up a bit and held him around the shoulders next to me.

"You doing okay, Keydell?" I asked.

"Yes."

"Do you want to walk around over near the play area?"

"No, I'm fine."

After about thirty minutes, they called us into a small room. They took Keydell's blood pressure and his weight, and gave him a quick once-over. The nurse was very kind, and asked if Keydell needed anything. *How about me?* I thought to myself. *I could use a drink!*

She told us to wait in the waiting room again, and someone would call us when they had a room.

After about two hours, I looked at Jim and said, "This may be a while longer, you know—like, all night. Maybe you should go home and get some rest; I'll call you in the morning. If, by some miracle, we get done early, we'll just wait."

"Are you sure?" Jim asked in sympathy. "Keydell, are you okay with that?"

He nodded, so Jim took off. I was glad to relieve him of this situation. I was very protective of Jim for some reason. He was very strong and a great father, but I think this was wearing on him even more than me. He looked older, and tired—as I'm sure I did, too.

Keydell and I found a vending machine and got some crackers. By about one or two in the morning, we were called to the desk and put in a room. As the nurse walked us through the quiet hospital, I felt like I was in a dream—or should I say, a nightmare. The walls seemed to be made of shiny, cold metal, and all the lights were flickering fluorescents. It felt sterile—but not in the way that other hospitals feel sterile. More like sterile of life. It seemed bare and empty, like it had been abandoned.

The nurse led Keydell and me through a locked set of doors (the loony bin, I thought) and into a small room with a single bed on one side and a chair on the other. That was it. The room was overly bright, the sheets were bright white, and the overhead light was way too strong for this time of night. The nurse told us to rest here, and the doctor would be in later.

"How much later?" I asked.

"I don't know. It could be a while," she said. "Try to sleep if you can."

Oh, like *that* kind of later. Like, in the morning! What did she expect me to sleep on, the hard, plastic chair?

Keydell got up on the bed, all excited to play on it. I let him bounce around for a bit as he finished his crackers, then he just fell asleep. Dead asleep.

Well, at least he's *at peace right now. Little bugger.*

As I stared at him, I wondered if he truly lived in the moment. When he was mad he was mad, when it was over it was over, when he was tired he slept. Sadly, his moments were so often filled with pain. I tended to mull over every detail of a meltdown to try to figure out what had happened, what I had missed, and what I could do better the next time. I worried about when the next episode would commence. In other words, I had a tough time letting go of what had happened and staying present. The emotional pain from his behaviors toward me clung to my body for days, and sometimes, before it could dissipate, new pain would jump on top. He could be so mean, and I didn't have time to recover. I had to learn not to take his actions and comments personally, but it was really difficult.

Keydell was doing what he needed to do: sleep. He felt no need to rehash the day at the shore, or worry about what was going to happen later, but I certainly did. I felt it was important for him to look at his past actions and reflect on a better way to behave—but in those moments of reflection, he would just get upset again.

Now was the time for sleeping. We could practice reflecting later. This was taking too much out of me. I only had so much energy in a day, and at that moment I was wasted.

I sat in the chair and tried to relax. It was so bright in the room and I couldn't find a light switch anywhere. Seriously, it was like a prison room. After bobbing my sleepy head back and forth for about an hour in the chair, I tried to climb on the bed with Keydell to get some sleep, but it was too narrow to really work. After lying there for a bit with eyes wide open, I decided to give up on the notion of sleep.

Around 5:00 a.m., I heard some activity in the hallway. I hoped it was the doctor.

Instead, I saw a teenage girl and her crying mother walk past our door and into the room next door. I could hear the nurse begin to talk with them.

"Do you know why you are here?" the nurse asked.

"Yes, I guess," the teen responded.

"Do you remember that you tried to kill yourself?"

I could hear the mother start to cry again. *Oh, man*, I thought. *That must be horrible.* It was hard to imagine wanting to kill myself, or Keydell really wanting to kill himself. You'd have to be pretty depressed to do that. The few times Keydell said out loud that he wanted to die, it felt more like a jab at us than a real threat. I'm not even sure he would know *how* to kill himself. Hearing this somehow made his past words seem more real, though. This *really* happens. Kids get depressed enough to want to die.

Hopefully, the Zoloft would help with Keydell's depressed feelings, and help him gain some control there. We still had a week to go before we could start that medication. He looked so innocent in the little bed, peacefully sleeping away—and right next door was a possible future for him.

"Stop it, Kim," I said to myself. "Live in the freakin' moment. Live in the moment. Worrying does no good, remember?"

As the nurse wrapped things up in the next room I could hear her coming toward our room. I was beyond tired at this point, but felt invigorated that a solution, or at least a next step, was on its way.

I got up from the chair as she came in and walked toward the bed to wake Keydell.

"How's he doing?" she asked.

"Thankfully, he slept all night and is calm now. We brought him in because we had a really rough day yesterday. He has been having really rough days throughout the summer—and, if I'm honest, the past year and a half."

"Tell me a little about what's going on," she invited.

I sat back down in my chair and leaned against the back. I had to find some energy to talk about all of this again.

I explained our whole story, his symptoms of behavior, how we had him in lots of sports and some therapy. I explained about our

Westwood experience and how I thought it was going to be a place for help but turned out to be only a respite facility.

"I'm really hoping we can get some help from you here." The tears were rolling down my face now and I could barely speak. I was like a dead battery holding on with the last of its juice to keep the guiding light alive.

"I know you have a great program, but a long waiting list for the evaluation. I do have him scheduled for one, but it's months from now. We're really hoping to start things sooner. He's just been so crazy, and we're out of ideas and energy."

Then, the nurse replied with the most deflating statement I'd ever heard in my life.

"You guys are really doing everything you can for Keydell, and it's all the right things," she began. "We really don't have room in that program, so it's best to stay on the list. Except for getting full-time help at the house, you really are doing everything that is best for him."

I burst into tears again and tried hard to stay clear and on point. "But, you don't realize, we can't take it anymore."

"What do you want to do, Mrs. Fuller?" She asked me.

That hit me like a brick wall. What did I want to do if they couldn't admit him to the program? Was I that woman whom I'd judged so heavily—the woman who would give a child back when things got tough? My head was spinning. Based on what she'd just told me, my only options were to give him back to DCYF, or take him home and keep on keepin' on.

I'd said I couldn't take it anymore—but could I? I sat there crying, staring at her, waiting for an answer to come out of my mouth.

She looked back at me with great sympathy and said, "I know this is really hard, but you are doing all that you can, and you are doing a good job at it."

There it was: acknowledgement. We *were* doing a good job and we *were* doing what we could—and it wasn't fucking working, but I was never going to give Keydell back to the system and I knew that. I could do this. I *had* to do this. I would never forgive myself if I didn't find the strength to make this work. I might have felt helpless, but Keydell was feeling more helpless, and he needed us. We were his last chance.

I looked though my wet, blurry eyes at the nurse and said, "Thank you for your help." Then, we walked out to call Jim to pick us up.

CHAPTER 17

BIRTH MOM

"When we meet real tragedy in life, we can react in two ways - either by losing hope and falling into self-destructive habits, or by using the challenge to find our inner strength. Thanks to the teachings of Buddha, I have been able to take this second way."

—Dalai Lama

Jim arrived at Hasbro around 7:00 a.m. I could barely walk I was so tired. I entertained Keydell out in front of the hospital while we waited and thought, "I have to remember to keep my sense of humor. He responds well to that. Now, where did I put it again?"

When I used to visit him at the group home, we would play endlessly with balloons in the living room, bouncing them back and forth in the air as we counted how many taps we could get without the balloon touching the ground. He loved to count. He loved to play. I think because his outbursts were so large, I forgot he was just a little kid who needed simple play in his life.

We climbed along the front wall and counted the bricks as he stepped on each one. He was happy to be going home. Our car ride was quiet, but I briefly explained to Jim what the nurse had told us. I was feeling numb, and a bit like I imagined a blank canvas might feel just before the artist lays down the first brush stroke: empty, vast, ready for some color and life. *Please let the most creative artist come by and paint a beautiful picture for me,* I thought. *One of hope—and, perhaps, a scene with a path leading me to something else to try for our boy.*

When we got home, I slept for a while and Jim took over hanging out with Keydell. It was two days before our son's first day of fourth grade.

⇌⇋

Twelve hours later, I stood at the bottom of the stairs looking up at the Tasmanian Devil in angel wings.

Keydell was sitting on the first landing. His silky sports shorts showed off his muscular but youthful body that was now held tightly and in a ball of anxiety. He looked so defeated, holding his knees tightly to his chest and rocking back and forth as he tried to hold it all in. He looked like a bomb about to blow, with skin that could no longer hold in its nuclear power.

And blow he did. I don't even remember what set him off in that moment. In hindsight, I think his emotions were finally coming to the surface, and he was becoming aware of something very important.

I had nothing; I really had nothing. All I could do was stare at him and watch him go. I didn't even know what to feel. Was I angry that we'd just gotten home from the hospital and he couldn't even give us a day of peace? Was I sad for him? I seriously just looked at him with *nothing.* I couldn't even find that sense of humor I hoped to tap in to. Jim flew past me and grabbed Keydell by the arm, dragging him into his room. I was too weak to stop him, even though I wanted to.

I could hear Keydell screaming, "I hate myself, I hate myself," and heard him slapping himself in the face and body. Jim was speaking loudly, too—not quite a yell yet, but a growl. I walked like a zombie to the top of the stairs peered in the door. Jim had Keydell pinned to the bed, holding him down so he wouldn't hit himself. Keydell kept freeing his hand from Jim's hold and continued to smack at his own face.

"I want to kill myyseeellllff," Keydell screamed.

I was shaking and weak, and could feel the tension in the air. No one was calming down; we were all yelling. I was yelling at Jim to calm down, Keydell was yelling in pain, and Jim was yelling to be heard. It was not helping, but the yelling was a release for us, too, sometimes.

Then, Jim did something that I will always admire. He turned the situation around by grabbing Keydell's hands and slapping his own face with them. Jim was right in Keydell's face, holding our son's tiny brown hand against his own red face and slapping away.

Jim yelled out, "You want to kill someone? Kill me, kill me, Keydell. How would that feel?" as he continued to slap. Jim trusted that Keydell cared about us, and that this would snap him out of what he was thinking.

It worked. Keydell turned his thoughts away from himself and toward Jim, whom he did really care about. Jim stopped, breathing heavily, still holding his face inches from Keydell's, who looked back at him with terrified eyes. Something was bubbling up from within, and when it surfaced, it shifted everything.

Keydell closed his eyes, opened his mouth wide and yelled at the top of his lungs, "I want my mommy! I want my *mommy!*" I think the words even surprised him.

I went over to the bed, and knelt down, knowing that he didn't mean me. "Is that what this is all about? You want to see your mom?"

Jim slowly let go of his grip on Keydell and began to relax. My heart was aching, and not because I was jealous that he wanted his mom. I felt that we just had a breakthrough, and I could feel his pain so deeply. He never had closure with his mom. He never got to say goodbye to her when he found he was moving out of the group home. He slowly softened each muscle in his body, and began to sob.

It was a release from the depths of his body. I could almost feel as if the demon that had taken over his body in the last year and a half had flown out of Keydell's gut and released him from the horror he'd been living with. Jim slowly sat down next to Keydell as he wept. He and I connected eyes as I mouthed, "Wow."

I knew right away what Jim was thinking. He was going to find Keydell's birth mom. I was thinking the same thing. We knew her name, and with Facebook and Google searches we were sure to find her. I watched Keydell as his tears flowed freely, and gave him a big hug. I think Jim and I felt we had finally gotten to something. The artist had arrived, and a new color had appeared on my blank canvas. Here was my sign from the Universe: maybe, finding his mother was just the thing to start the process of healing for Keydell. Maybe we could at least know if she was still around, and give him some insight to what she was up to if she wouldn't talk to us.

"Keydell, we love you so much. If we can find your mom we will talk to her and see if she'd be willing to see you," I told him. "Come here and sit with me, sweetie. When we were going through the adoption, Angela tried to talk to your mom about an open adoption that would allow her to see you, but she stopped returning her calls. We think it was too painful for her to see you, but we're not certain. She loves you very much, I'm sure, but she had a lot of problems of her own. You know that, right?"

Keydell shook his head yes.

"She could not get you the help you needed, and was very brave to put you up for adoption so you could get parents who could help you. But I have an idea: maybe while we're looking for her you could write her a note telling her all the things you'd like to say to her. If she can't see us, maybe we can at least send her the note." Keydell hated to write, but thought it was a good idea. "I'll help you if you want me to," I offered.

The memory I have of that moment has stayed with me since. We'd felt so empty of ideas, drained by what was going on, and helpless in our lack of knowledge around mental illness and why Keydell acted the way he did. Jim used to get upset with me when I pushed Keydell to examine his feelings and get to the root of his problems—but this was why I did it. Things come out eventually, if you dig deep. Maybe this was just the tip we needed to move things forward for him and get some answers to our questions about his very early years.

It was getting late and we were all exhausted from the afternoon, so we had some dinner and put Keydell to bed early. We filled Ella and Krishna in on what happened when they got home, and Jim and I chatted about how to find Sue, Keydell's birth mother.

The next day, we located her on Facebook. Jim sent her a message and she got right back to us. She was over-the-top excited that we'd contacted her—as were we.

⚒

September/October 2010
Jim and I had a few back-and-forth interactions with Sue through e-mail and one phone conversation. We were taking it slowly, and continued to check in with Keydell about how he felt about seeing her again. There had been a lot of changes lately, including Henry leaving for college, Krishna heading back to England, and the drama of the summer, so we waited until November to set up our first visit at a Chuck E. Cheese.

Keydell had been on Zoloft since September, and hadn't had a meltdown since he screamed for his mom. He was in a good place.

His first year at the middle school had begun, too. He rode the bus for the first time and, of course, was always fifteen minutes early to the bus stop each morning. Middletown's fall recreational soccer had started, and he was playing on the Kim Fuller Photography team again. Things were going well, and we wanted to keep it that way.

We had no idea how a visit with Sue might go, but by November it seemed like he was ready. Sue asked if she could bring his siblings as a surprise, and we thought that would be great for Del. Henry was home for the Thanksgiving holiday, so we all packed in the car and drove to the meeting spot.

"Are you excited to see your birth mom, Delski?" Henry asked.

"I guess," Keydell meekly replied. I could tell he was nervous because he barely spoke and stayed awake for the whole ride. Ella held his hand as we all rode in silence. I remembered what Sue looked like from seeing her at the group home, but when we got to the Chuck E. Cheese and I saw her sitting inside the window, I remembered how much Keydell looked like her. She was still very large, and Keydell so small, but their faces were strikingly alike.

I felt guilty for having him all of a sudden. What was that about? I'm not sure I would have been happy seeing my children with another mother—but, at the same time, I knew it had been her choice, so I was conflicted. Sue saw us and walked with her two kids, Patrick and Kamaria, to the front door. When they saw Keydell, they smiled with excitement. Patrick walked over and gave him an awkward hug, then looked at Sue and said, "I wondered why you brought us here, Mom." He looked at me and said, "We didn't know he was coming." Patrick, who looked to be about thirteen, was very friendly and open, and seemed like a normal, happy young man.

We all said hello and introduced ourselves. Keydell's sister, Kamaria was only eleven or twelve, and big like her mom. She had a lovely smile, but was very shy. Ella tried to engage with her by complimenting her on her outfit and hairdo, which made Kamaria smile even more. We found a table but it was a very tight squeeze for all of us so Henry and Patrick decided to stand. Sue sat on one side, Keydell quickly slipped in next to her, and Kamaria sat down next to him. He looked like a tiny pea between two large, cozy pillows. He certainly wasn't built like any of them. I was directly across the table from Sue, with Jim and Ella next to me. The place was loud and full of kids running around, playing on the indoor playground equipment and in the bin of colorful plastic balls. Normally, an environment like this would overstimulate Keydell, but as I looked over at him he kept glancing between Sue and me with the most peaceful and natural smile I had ever seen on his face. I was so relieved. I thought this was just what he needed. I was happy to have an open adoption if it was good for Del. I knew he was part of our family now and that we were to care for him. I also knew that Sue could not take him away from me. He was my baby now, but he remembered her, and she had been a big part of his life before he came to us. She sounded quite sane on the phone, and was presenting herself that way again. She was a quiet soul and spoke softly to Keydell.

"How are you doing Keydell?"

"Good," he answered.

"What have you been up to?"

"I started to play soccer," he said. "I'm really good."

"He is," I piped in. "He has amazing athletic ability in general."

"That doesn't come from me," Sue said with a grin.

Oh man, I had to bite my tongue. I had a million questions for her, but I didn't want to ask with Keydell sitting there. I wanted to know about his father, about his birth and Sue's pregnancy. Had she been drinking or on drugs during that time? "Why was Keydell so difficult?" I wanted to scream. I was looking for someone or something to blame, but I knew deep down that Sue had done the best she could for him. She seemed kind and sad, and I had to give her a lot of credit for coming to see Keydell with us. It couldn't have been easy.

They didn't say much more to each other, so we ordered some pizza while the boys left the table to play some arcade games. Ella stayed with me and talked with Kamaria while Sue and I discussed Keydell.

"I was so excited when you guys contacted me," she said. "I thought I would never see him again."

"We thought you didn't want to see him," I replied. "That's what Matt from DCYF told us, and Angela said you stopped answering her calls, so we left you alone about it."

"I was told you wanted a closed adoption," she explained. That surprised me, and I wondered if she really had been told that or just couldn't handle it at the time. Either way, I was shocked.

"What? Really? Well that explains a lot. And, by the way, I'm really sorry that you showed up at Trout without knowing Keydell was already gone. It must have killed you not to be able to say goodbye."

"Yes, I had Patrick and Kamaria with me too."

"Well, here we are, and we can meet anytime Keydell would like to," I said.

I filled her in on how he'd been behaving, and she admitted that was why she had given him up.

"It was very hard to care for him because I was battling depression," she explained.

She didn't always have Patrick and Kamaria with her, either, depending on how bad she would get. They were back and forth with their father, and Keydell stayed with her aunt. She told me her aunt was very upset when she put Keydell up for adoption—but, at the time, neither of them felt capable of taking care of him. We'd heard the same information from DCYF so I knew that was the truth.

The pizza arrived a few moments later and everyone came back to the table to eat. I kept noticing how much Keydell looked like his mother, and that he shared some of his siblings' traits. There is no denying your birth family. Maybe looking at her familiar face gave him the sense of belonging that he so craved. Maybe seeing her here gave him confirmation that he was not just a bag of garbage that had been tossed out, but the wonderful, lovable guy we'd been telling him he was. I'd said over and over that he was not given up by her because he did something wrong, he was given up out of love. Maybe that felt clearer now. She did love him and wanted to see him, he at least could see that.

After our pizza we ordered a birthday cake for Keydell so we could all celebrate his life together.

⇒⊱⊰⇐

So many thoughts went through my head after that first visit. I went from wondering if Sue thought I was doing a good job with her son to thinking, "Wait, why should I care? She got all the good times with him during her visits, and we took him home for the hell on wheels."

I started to compare my life to hers, and make note of what enabled us to keep Keydell when she couldn't.

One, I could hang in there because I wasn't struggling with depression. Two, I could hang in there because I have help from a great husband and kids.

Who knows where each person's inner strength comes from? I was blessed with a stable and supportive family, and I myself was healthy. Sometimes I felt like I was going crazy, but I knew that was only stress. Sue lived a different life, one filled with many mental and physical challenges; I was baffled how we ended up being a part of each other's lives. Circumstances brought us together— she, by birthing a boy she couldn't care for and, me, by taking him in because I could. It was beautiful, and we were now connected as two moms trying to do the best for their children.

At the end of our visit no one seemed that interested in giving hugs or kisses goodbye, something I almost always do. I expected Keydell to run to his mom for a long goodbye, but it took some prompting to get any hugging going at all. I was feeling quite grateful for this reunion, and that Keydell would now know his birth mother was out there if he needed to see her. Finally, Sue asked Keydell for a hug; he gave her his usual sideways version and quickly moved on. I took a mental note of that body language, and realized it wasn't just me he resisted affections from.

⇥⊢⊣⇤

The following week we had Keydell's 10th birthday party at Laser Gate, an indoor laser tag complex. He invited a bunch of his guy friends from school, plus the travel soccer team, so he was surrounded by his closest buds. They blazed into the giant warehouse space full of pinball games, a putt-putt area, party rooms, and the Laser tag arena as Jim and I set up at one of the orange plastic tables in the middle of the game room. They played a few quarter games, a round of mini-golf, and some foosball before going in for the tag game.

As I took my coat off, I noticed Sue coming in; we had invited her to this party before we left Chuck E. Cheese. She was accompanied by Kamaria and Patrick, who we expected, but also her husband and his son from another marriage. They walked in as one big happy family.

I started feeling very protective of Keydell's feelings in that moment, wondering how he would take in that scene of the family unit, but I couldn't do much about it. He was busy playing with his friends anyway, so when they came in he only said a quick hello and bounded back to his group.

You had to love his resilience.

Our group got called in for their Laser tag game, so the kids suited up with their electronic vests and guns and went in with

Jim, Henry, and Ella. Normally, I would have been right in there with them, but felt called to sit with Sue and her husband. It was an opportunity to get more information about Keydell's child-hood without him around. I curiously watched her mannerisms and body language as we talked, noticing how they mirrored Keydell's. Her face held very little expression, and she was poised and cordial.

"Thank you for inviting us today," she said, as I joined her and her husband at the table. Kamaria and Patrick had gone to the snack table with their stepbrother. She introduced her husband to me and explained that he was from Africa. He had a good job working with computers, but sent most of the money he made back to his family there to help support them and the daughter they had together. I'd wondered what happened to the baby Sue was pregnant with when I saw her at the group home; apparently, she was now living in Africa with his family so she could be raised a Muslim.

"Are you a Muslim, Sue?" I asked.

"Yes, I converted when I got married."

"So, was Keydell raised with any particular faith?"

"My aunt took him to church a few times, but not really."

I had asked Keydell once about his religion but all he could re-member was sitting still in the church pews and how hard that was.

"How often do you see your daughter?" I asked.

"We go to Africa about once a year and she's come here once," she said, with very little emotion. It was hard to tell how she felt about this situation. I couldn't tell whose decision it had been to send her there, but assumed it was the husband's. Or, maybe, knowing that she had a hard time raising children, it was hers.

"So, Sue," I said as I adjusted my seat. "Can I ask you some questions about Keydell? I would love to know more about his baby years."

"Yes, okay," she replied quietly.

"Was Keydell violent and angry even as a young boy?" I was so curious to know if he was born with these behaviors or if they developed due to his frequent changes in care and living situations.

"Yes, he was always a handful, climbing on everything and demanding my attention all the time."

"She was not a very good mother," the husband chimed in.

What the hell? Did he just say that in front of her? I looked at Sue to see her reaction but she sat there, still and expressionless. "She has a hard time disciplining the kids."

I wanted to reach out and hug her in support.

"How long have you two been together?" I asked.

"We've known each other for six years but have been married for five," Sue answered.

"So you lived together when Keydell was still with you?" I asked, confused. I'd thought she was a single mother for most of his early years when he was living with her.

"Yes," her husband answered. "Toward the end of his time with her."

I thought to myself, trying to hold in my judgments. *Why didn't you help her out, man? She was depressed and needed you! Are you a hands-off dad, or didn't you want to help because Keydell is not your child? Is it a cultural thing not to help with the kids?* Believe me, I was happy to have Keydell in our lives, and knew we were going to give him better opportunities than Sue and her husband could have, but it made me sad that he was not able to be with his birth family. Today, though, he didn't seem to care if they were there or not.

I excused myself after a few more pleasantries and joined the second tag game with Keydell and the other boys while Sue and her husband remained at the table. I chased Del all around the dark, cave-like play area as we shot laser beams back and forth, trying to out-tag each other. Keydell was having so much fun. When the tag games were over and we gathered in the party room for cake and pizza, he continued to focus on his friends and eating.

After we sang "Happy Birthday" and Keydell blew out his candles, Sue asked if she could take a few photos with Keydell and his siblings. I offered to do one of all of them. As I looked through the back of the phone to take the photo, I couldn't help but notice how awkward Keydell looked, even though his resemblance to them was so striking. He could have been standing with anyone at that moment, and looked like he wanted to bolt back to his friends as soon as possible. Patrick had his arm on Keydell's shoulder and a big grin on his face. *He* certainly was happy to be there with his little brother. Jim took a quick shot of me and Sue with Keydell in the middle. Keydell then had enough and went to finish opening his presents. His behaviors over the last two visits baffled me. He had screamed his head off to see Sue, yet seemed so disconnected from her. It was if all he needed was to just know she was out there.

We politely said our goodbyes and gave Sue and her kids the leftover cake to take home. We saved one giant piece for Keydell.

Life was busy that fall, but going along smoothly. Keydell focused all of his free time on soccer practices and games, and appeared to be less depressed. The Zoloft was doing its job. Ella was busy with drama club and soccer, not to mention all the school clubs she was involved in, so she was out of the house a lot. She needed her space. Keydell and I had gone back to Dr. Martin a few more times that summer and early fall, but were taking a break now. Most of our visits had not been very productive, and life was just too busy. The endorphins Keydell was producing playing soccer kept him more balanced than any talk therapy we'd done so far, so I kept what worked and threw out what wasn't.

One evening when Keydell and I were reading his favorite book together, *Treasury of Virtues: Courage, Love, Honesty*, I cuddled in nice and close. I felt the most bonded to him when we were doing simple mother-and-child activities like this. He loved the one-on-one, as did I, and he let me sit close and hold him for quite a while as we read. I cherished every moment. I got very melancholy thinking about how I had missed his baby years, and told him how I would have nibbled on his toes or blown bubbles on his belly if I'd had him as an infant. He asked me to do that now.

"Oh, yeah," I said. "Well, baby toes are cute, but there is no way I'm nibbling on your stinky big-boy toes." We laughed as I grabbed him and blew bubbles on his very ticklish neck. I sniffled around his ears acting like a dog sniffing out a biscuit. He giggled a heartfelt giggle and asked for more. We were having fun. As we settled down for sleep and he rolled over for his back scratch, I commented on his great mood.

"I'm happy to see you doing well these days, Keydell. You seem very happy and more content."

"Yep. I can't wait for our next soccer game."

"Oh, me too," I said. "You're going to be amazing out there." I squeezed him in a bit closer to me. "Have you enjoyed the visits with your mom, or do they upset you?"

"They're fine," he said as I continued scratching his very dry back. I was leaving white marks from my nails, but the harder I scratched the more he loved it.

"Are you okay seeing her with Patrick and Kamaria?"

He rolled back toward me and looked up at my face. "Can I meet with my mom by herself next time we visit?" he asked.

I took in the question, thought for a second, and answered, "Sure, you mean without your brother and sister, or without me?" He seemed to have a good reason behind his question and I was very curious.

"I just have some questions I want to ask her, and I want to do it when we're alone," he said.

"That's fine, Keydell. I'll arrange that for you, but I want to sit with you while you ask your questions if you're okay with that.

You don't have to have Pat and Kamaria there, but I want to be there."

I was feeling very protective after having asked my own questions of Sue at Laser Gate, because I found that sometimes her answers could be very vague and confusing. I wanted to see his reaction to her answers as well, and make sure he didn't get too upset. I believed that knowing the truth was best, but it could sting at first, so I wanted to be there to support him. I was proud of him for asking to talk with her, though, and happy to know he'd been thinking about her and their relationship. He hadn't shared any of his feelings about our visits yet, and when I asked him about it, he didn't seem to know what to say or feel. He might not have wanted to share with me as his new mother, and that was okay, but it was my right and duty as that mother to protect him.

I called Sue and explained Keydell's request. We decided that she should come to our house for this visit. Up to this point we'd kept our visits at a neutral location until I was sure she was reliable and wouldn't hurt or try to take Keydell back from us. It had been suggested by Angela that we do it this way until we trusted her. I'd come to respect and like Sue, and felt a lot of empathy for her. She was seeing Keydell in a good place now and I think she was grateful for us helping him, but at the same time, she must have wished it could have been her who had him. She was very kind and always thanked us after the visits for taking good care of him and letting her see him from time to time.

She showed up alone one afternoon, per our request, and we sat at our kitchen table. Keydell sat very quietly at the end of the table for a minute, trying to figure out how to start the conversation. He was flanked by two moms, but was looking at Sue.

"Are you okay?" I asked, reaching to gently touch his arm for his attention.

"I'm good." He turned back to Sue and said, right out of the gate, "Why am I not living with you anymore?"

I got the biggest lump in my throat. He was so brave.

Sue said, "I just didn't know how to be with you."

What? What did that mean? She didn't say she couldn't take care of him, but that she couldn't *be* with him. Confusing. I waited. She didn't add anything else to her answer, so I wasn't sure if Keydell understood. My protective side reared its head and I finally said, "Keydell, do you understand what she means by that?"

"Not really."

Sue then repeated, "I didn't know how to be with you. You were a handful, and I was having a hard time. Sometimes I would lock myself in my room and stay there, and you guys would be left on your own."

"Keydell, do you understand that your mom was having her own issues and it made it hard for her to care for you? You were not the problem or reason for her issues. Just because you were a handful doesn't mean you needed to go away, she just couldn't care for you. Remember that Patrick and Kamaria also left at times and stayed with your aunt or their dad."

Keydell moved on from that question.

"Who's my dad?" he asked.

Sue hesitated for a second and decided to tell him, "He's not a good person. You don't need to know him. I told him I was pregnant, but he didn't care." She didn't offer any more information.

Maybe it was best for now, but I think Keydell was very curious as to where he got his athletic abilities and often fantasized that his dad was a great soccer player. At least she seemed to know who the dad was, because we'd been told that she wasn't sure. Whether she knew him or not, Keydell had been an unwanted pregnancy from the get-go. I found out later that this kind of emotional detachment from a baby, even in utero, can cause problems in the baby's brain development—which explained a lot about Keydell.

That phrase, "attachment disorder," again, popped into my head.

Keydell then asked, "Do Patrick and Kamaria live with you now?"

She answered, "Yes." There was no further explanation. I could see where his cut-and-dry attitude came from. She was as black and white with her answers as he was. Keydell seemed done with all his questions, and was fine with the visit ending right then and there.

"Are you satisfied, Keydell? Did you get what you wanted out of that?" I asked.

"Yes," he said. "Can I go play soccer outside now?"

He was done with the hard stuff, and moving onto the fun. I had to admire him. He had accomplished his goal, and was ready to do something else. We chatted for a few more minutes, and then Sue left. The whole visit lasted about ten minutes.

CHAPTER 18
MY PRACTICE

"Love yourself and be awake -
today, tomorrow, always.
First establish yourself in the way,
then teach others,
and so defeat sorrow.
To straighten the crooked
you must first do a harder thing -
straighten yourself.
You are the only master. Who else?
Subdue yourself,
and discover your master."

—From The Dhammapada

The few additional visits we had with Keydell's birth mom and siblings were short and simple; we met once at the Starbucks at Barnes and Noble, where they sat quietly and played a board game while I read and sipped on a coffee at a nearby table, and once again at our house with the same activity. Because of her size, his sister couldn't play soccer with him, and Patrick had no interest in playing, so Keydell found little in common with them. They held conversations, but they were a family of few words. He didn't ask to see them after we'd had three or four visits, so although I e-mailed Sue with photos and updates, I didn't push for more in-person time. Keydell's meltdowns returned, so we knew there was still more to do.

I felt like I'd aged ten years since Keydell had come to live with us. Jim and I were fried. Ella managed to spend more time at school and with friends, which made me sad, but that's what she needed to do to keep her mind off the craziness at home.

It was 7:30 a.m. and the morning school rush was over. I quickly vacuumed the downstairs rooms, something I received a great deal of pleasure from doing, and finished my cup of coffee. I grabbed two pillows from the couch and sat in Henry's bedroom downstairs, my usual spot for meditation. The double bed was still set up for when he was home, but the room was sparse otherwise, and perfect for my sits.

Edo followed me in and sprawled next to me, knowing it was our time to be quiet. I think even he felt better when we meditated because he felt the stress of the household lately, too. During Keydell's outbursts he cowered, and if he could, he'd leave the house and find a place in the yard to hide. The latch on our back door was broken from all the recent slamming so he'd learned to push it open with his nose and escape. Once Keydell went off to school, it was our time to sit quietly, and then go for a walk before the workday began. After closing the door behind me, I stacked my two pillows and sat crossed-legged facing the window to the west. Breathing deeply, I began my sit. Edo let out a big sigh and plopped his head down on the carpet near my bare feet.

My back was straight, and my hands were lying in my lap with my right hand resting in my left, palms up. My eyes gazed gently down to the floor, slightly open as I said my vows to myself. "I take refuge in the Buddha, the Dharma, and the Sangha. Through the merit I create by the practice of giving, and the other perfections, may I attain Buddhahood for the sake of all sentient beings."

I repeated that three times, taking in the meaning, especially the part about "for the sake of all sentient beings."

"May I attain Buddhahood for the sake of *all* sentient beings." That was a huge and daunting task, but I didn't expect to do it overnight.

Expectations. That word came up for me often when contemplating Keydell. I could not *expect* to help him overnight. I could not *expect* him to find happiness and peace with us overnight, and I certainly couldn't expect him to be someone he wasn't.

I thought about what one of my meditation teachers had said to me when I was telling her about how difficult things were with Keydell.

"Kim, look at it this way. Your family is like an elephant family. You all act like elephants, walk like elephants, and think like elephants. Now, you've brought a tiger into your home and are expecting him to act like an elephant, too."

Wow, I was so moved by her words. She was right. Of course, Keydell was different from us, and we had to learn to understand each other. Since his time at Westwood and our experience at Hasbro, I realized it was up to me to help my little tiger, but before I could do that I had to let go of my expectations about who he was. He wasn't me, and he wasn't Jim, Henry, or Ella. He was Keydell, and existed as he was due to his karma and the life he was born to. He may have been a tiger, and I an elephant, but we were both smart, and had minds we could work with.

My little tiger was wearing me out. *But there is more to do, Kim, there is more to be done,* my heart screamed to me.

Another thought: *I know, but I need a re-boot so I can continue to be a helpful mom for Keydell and be present for the needs of my family. I could use more words of wisdom like my friend Elizabeth gave me, so I can reframe my thoughts around this whole situation and start again.*

"Change your thoughts and you change your world." I had heard that phrase a long time ago, and was beginning to see its meaning.

I sat, trying to accept our situation and asked myself this question. "How can I accept my tiger as he is—even with all of his temper tantrums, his badmouthing, and his crazy yelling and thrashing around?" This was what I hoped to learn after I first shook hands with the Dalai Lama. He seemed to love me unconditionally without even knowing me. Could I love Keydell without conditions? Did I have enough energy to work on that?

I took a few more deep breaths and closed my practice with my prayers for all sentient beings to be at peace, to be safe, and to be happy, and slowly bowed to my inner vision of the Buddha. The last phrase of my vow popped into my head just then, the part that says, "May I attain Buddhahood (or at least get close) for the sake of all sentient beings." I took that to mean that I had to help myself before I could help anyone else.

Edo knew it was time for our walk when I bowed so he jumped up from his own meditation (or nap) and we headed out for our walk.

That evening, I found a workshop led by Jack Kornfield that was being held at Kripalu in western Massachusetts in early December. Without a second thought, I signed myself up for my reboot.

⇌╫⇌

"Are you going to be okay with Keydell while I'm gone?' I asked as I packed my suitcase.

Jim and I were in our small bedroom with the big four-poster bed between us. He looked across the queen-sized mattress and said, "I'll be fine. Just go and relax."

I stared over at him for a few minutes, watching him put his laundry away. He would always say "I'm fine" whenever I asked him how he was doing. Sometimes I just wanted to crawl inside his head and get at his thoughts. I swear he could read mine, but sometimes I had no idea what he was thinking or feeling. I mean, for Christ's sake, I had never, in our twenty-five-plus years together, seen the man cry. How do you not cry? Even at his mother's funeral he was solid as a rock. I hoped he realized I was not running away from our issues, but going to this workshop so I could dig deeper and find the inner wisdom and strength to carry on. Perhaps he could use some deep digging into himself too.

I finished packing all my comfy clothes and went across the narrow hall to say goodbye to Ella and Keydell.

"Have a good time, Mom," Ella said, looking up from the laptop resting on her outstretched legs.

"I will sweetie," I replied. "I hope everything goes smoothly at home while I'm gone. Enjoy the snow if it comes, and do some fun sledding or something." I bent down to give her a kiss and headed to see Del. He was on his bed in the usual position; on his belly, game controller in hand, staring at the Xbox.

"Hey, buddy, I'm heading out for my retreat," I told him. "See you on Sunday."

"Where are you going again?" he asked without looking up from his game.

"To a meditation retreat in Massachusetts," I answered.

"*Okay*, bye." He rolled on his side and looked at me with his arm stretched out. He had his thumb and index finger touching to form a circle and held it out for me. I did the same shape with my fingers and we touched hands to connect the two circles to make an infinity sign.

We then said to each other "to infinity and beyond" as we pulled our hands apart in a dramatic motion backwards. This was our way of saying how much we loved each other.

Kripalu was a magical place—a beautiful old Jesuit seminary in Lenox, Massachusetts, that had been converted into a beautiful place to practice and learn yoga and meditation. The building sat high on a hillside, with a sprawling view of the mountains and fields below. It was quiet, tranquil and full of nice people.

Jack Kornfield, the mindfulness meditation teacher for the weekend, was a wonderful speaker and guide. He trained as a Buddhist monk in monasteries in Thailand, India, and Burma, and co-founded the Insight Meditation Society (IMS) with meditation teachers Sharon Salzberg and Joseph Goldstein. He was a husband, father, psychologist, and activist who had a great sense of humor and wisdom. I felt honored to study with him.

I checked into my double-occupancy room. I didn't know who my roommate would be, but I could see that she'd already gotten there and unpacked. I changed into my black yoga pants and loose, long-sleeved T-shirt, put my mala beads around my wrist, and headed down to the evening session. Those beads had come with me to the Dalai Lama teaching in Pennsylvania, and I wore them when I sat with the Rinpoche, so they were special for me.

The first evening, we all gathered in a large central room with a vaulted ceiling that was the main chapel of the converted seminary. We took our shoes off outside, and proceeded in to find a cushion on the expansive, open floor where the pews used to be. I picked a spot directly in front of where the teachers would be sitting. On the way up, I noticed my friend Alicia sitting on the right about halfway up. We knew each other from our meditation group in Middletown. She was sitting next to a lovely blonde woman, talking, so I figured we would connect later. As others rolled in, I wondered which one might be my roommate.

There I was, with about three hundred people whom I didn't know. I wondered why they all were there, but felt connected to them, knowing that they, too, wanted to practice and learn about their minds. Everyone was adjusting their seats and arranging their journals or tea beside them. Some added pillows or seat jacks for support and some were stretching to prepare for their sit. When Jack and the two other teachers approached from the back, we all turned our heads to watch. Jack had on a cotton vest and jeans; he was balding, with patches of gray hair at the sides of his head. He had wonderful, large ears (a sign, I once heard, of generosity), and a full mustache under a big nose. His face was friendly, and had an air of whimsy to it. He looked to be about sixty years old.

We all stared at the teachers, waiting for their wise words. Being a Buddhist practitioner and teacher takes a lot of dedication and years of study, so I was, honestly, quite in awe of Jack. The Dalai Lama often tells his students that he is just an ordinary monk and man, no different than us, but I was aware of his wisdom and dedication toward his own and others' enlightenment. Jack Kornfield also projected a great wisdom after years of study, and was ready to deliver that wisdom to us.

He began by welcoming and informing us of the format for the weekend. He'd teach some, and we'd meditate some, and there would be a few interactive exercises as well. He told us about his family and his own practice. He had a light and humorous attitude, one I hoped to reclaim for myself during this retreat. He then asked us to do a half-hour mindfulness meditation, paying attention to our bodily sensations.

Sitting with that group was powerful. It fascinated me to think about all the minds in the room thinking or behaving in very different ways, even though we were all doing the same thing: just sitting there. We each had our own unique perceptions—yet, again, we were connected through this practice.

Wait—I was supposed to be focusing on my body's sensations, not thinking about all this stuff! That's how my mind works; it likes to make connections. I was here to notice the thoughts come in, perhaps name them something like "planning," "worrying," "thinking," or "judging," and then move back to the point of concentration, which right now was my body. I was here to relax, to become familiar again with my mind that had drifted away from its positive self and lead it back to peace. I wanted to pay attention again, and be aware of the thoughts that no longer served me. I took a deep breath and tried to refocus.

I was hungry; it had to be time for dinner by now. *When is that bell going to ring so we can get up from our cushions? Where is the guy next to me from, I wonder? He sure breathes loudly. I have to pee. Uh oh, my stomach is growling. I wondered if anyone can hear that.*

And so it went.

⇒═╫═⇐

That night at dinner, I caught up with my friend Alicia, and her friend, Karen, who'd I'd only met once but was happy to get to know better. Alicia was a Yin yoga instructor and a woman I highly respected. She had a gentle and soothing presence that felt good to be around. Karen was soon to be a grandmother, and was excited to have this time for herself before her grandmotherly duties began.

The dining tables reminded me of something from a high school cafeteria, only there were wooden chairs to sit on instead of benches. The room was decorated with beautifully painted giant Buddha heads, but not much else. I'm sure they kept it simple on purpose.

"Kim, it's really great to see you here" Alicia commented with her big smile and giant doe eyes. She was an elegant, graceful woman who I really didn't know a whole lot about—and yet, I felt I knew her so deeply at the same time. "What made you decide to come?"

I replied after a pause. "It's been a tough couple years with our son Keydell, and I'm hoping to find some new energy and tools to move forward in being with him more peacefully, and to help him find his peace. I'm tired, and need a break from the past two years of therapy, managing his outbursts and, frankly, from my own patterns of thinking. I want to find a new way to look at things and change the way I'm dealing with all the stress," I explained.

Karen didn't know about Keydell, so I filled her in on how he came into our lives and the types of behaviors we were working with.

"Did you know he was like this when you adopted him?" she asked.

"No, not really," I answered.

"Wow," she said. "It's really awesome of you guys to do what you did. You've done a great thing helping this boy. You've changed his life for the good."

I couldn't fully absorb her compliment because, even though we'd given him a nice home, Keydell still might end up in prison if he couldn't get under control. If he could not find peace within, he might continue to hurt himself or others. Being the "fixer" that I am, I felt so unsatisfied with our progress that it was hard for me to take in her kind words.

I had very high expectations, I realized, and I was here to work on just that.

We continued to chat through dinner and as we cleared our trays. Then, it was time for the last sit of the first evening. We walked with full bellies back to the chapel and found our way to a cushion. My front row seat was still open so I plopped down with my thermos of tea and prepared for the closing talk.

Jack talked about the practice of opening our hearts and that it's upon our vulnerability that we should depend. If something is difficult, we should get curious. Opening our hearts allows us to acknowledge our personal sorrows and those more universal, like war, old age, illness, death, and hunger. As we sat in meditation, we would observe what arose or presented itself for healing. It could be past traumas, fears, or feelings we have kept in our unconscious.

We might find shame and unworthiness around those feelings. We might feel sorrow, anger, or loss.

"As Oscar Wilde wrote," Jack said, "'Hearts are meant to be broken.' We can heal through meditation as we let feelings run through us, recognize them, and allow them to sing their songs."

Our meditation for the next half hour was to pay attention to our hearts, sit with any sensations or feelings that may arise, and let them be as they were. "Just notice," he said.

My heart was aching. It felt heavy and wounded. If I was to open my heart, however, it meant I had to trust the process of acknowledging those feelings, and sit with them to see what arose.

I focused on the heavy part first. What came up was the weight of responsibility I was feeling for Keydell's well-being and the well-being of my family. I felt like I was so far away from helping Keydell find peace, and that I had made my family suffer so much by bringing him into our home. I knew it was the right thing to do, but felt at fault for their pain. The wounded part of my heart was sad. I had hoped Keydell would be happy with me, but he seemed more upset now than when he lived at the group home. I imagined holding my heart and telling it everything would be okay. I had to realize I was only responsible for myself and my healing, and could only be with others with my open heart. I could not control their feelings, their lives, or their own paths to healing. I have a very vivid imagination, so this visualizing worked well for me. I could see my beating heart in my mind's eye as if it were outside my body, right in front of me. I was holding it, caring for it, imagining it healthy, light, and happy.

The evening sit ended with the bell. We all quietly got up from our cushions and filed out of the room. It was only 8:30, but I was really tired. This healing stuff was exhausting. I decided to go sit in the community hot tub before going straight to bed. I walked to my dorm room, hoping not to meet my roommate because I wasn't in the mood to talk. It ended up that we barely spoke to each other all weekend and honestly, it was perfect. I was grateful for her silence as I needed to go inward after these meditations for my own self-reflecting.

⟞⟝

Our daily schedule included an early sit before breakfast, breakfast, then three hours of walking and sitting mediation with the teachings, lunch, yoga or a shake-your-soul dance workshop, three more hours of meditation and teachings, dinner and a final sit. It was a full day.

Each teaching from Jack was a heart-opening practice that included forgiveness for any harm we may have done toward ourselves, toward others, or toward those who may have done harm to us. We practiced compassion toward others and ourselves, we talked about our connection to others, and did a few partnering exercises that involved breathing together in unison or staring at each other for a full minute. That was intense, and made me feel close to the person looking at me. For years, I had looked at others through the lens of my camera with this kind of connection, but realized it was easier with strangers. When I knew someone and looked at them, or they looked at me, I was often triggered by an emotion, or a memory of an experience with them. I had a harder time looking at them objectively. Perhaps my practice should be to look carefully at Keydell with an objective eye. I needed to see him like I saw my photo subjects for the first time, so I could get a clear picture of who he was. Then, I could approach him with a more open heart, not one attached to an outcome from our interaction.

Jack talked a lot about attachments we have to our stories, and how a trauma or illness can become our identity. Yep, that was me. We become attached to our fears, our past, and even our things, and they become who we are. We allow these stories, fears, and physical things to weigh on us and cause us undue suffering. The thing he said that struck me in that moment, though, was, "If you get rid of the anger, for example, you have to feel the pain—and some are afraid of that."

Was Keydell using anger to keep from feeling his pain? Maybe his acting out or being angry was actually coming from fear, and it felt safer to be angry. Anger gave him power over his pain, which was just too much to bear.

What I took away from these heart-opening exercises was that, when we hold too tightly to a belief, to a fear, to our past, or to our physical things, it can cause us to feel a lot of pain when we lose them or they change. It's okay to have feelings, ideas, and things, but we need to hold them with a gentle hand and not let them control us. If we can loosen the hold and understand the impermanence of all things, we can gain some ease around our suffering.

Everything changes. Nothing stays the same. Nothing. My situation with Keydell would change. If I could lead with an open heart and let go of some expectations, fears, and attachments, perhaps I could find some ease in our relationship—and, perhaps, I could teach him to do the same.

Jack then taught us a meditation on death as a way to look at the impermanence of all things. I remembered reading in the Dalai Lama's *Illuminating the Path to Enlightenment* that "the significance of meditating on impermanence and death is not just to terrify yourself; there is no point in that. The purpose is to remind you of the preciousness of the opportunities that exist for you in life as a human being." That made sense to me. I understood that my body will die, but my mind is always expanding in this human life. I have the opportunity to pay attention and take in all my lessons, and to also have a positive impact on others.

As I sat with this meditation, I imagined myself floating out of my body and above the room.

"Step back, Kim. Give your issues some space, and don't get caught up in them," I coached myself as I floated above my body.

"Your family and Keydell are fully capable and whole, and if you just love them, even from afar, everything will happen as it should. They can find their own way."

I had purpose in my life, and I wanted to fulfill it by being a good mother, wife, friend, and person in general, but I could do it with a bit more ease. I could be vulnerable and live with an open heart. And so my thoughts went as I imagined myself floating all the way about the earth.

The last day of the retreat happened to be Bodhi Day, the day Shakyamuni Buddha became fully enlightened under the Bodhi tree and awakened as the Buddha. I felt gratitude for his wisdom and his teachings—of which maybe I had absorbed a bit more over this weekend.

The teachings got me thinking about how to bring all that I'd practiced into my real life. It was great to sit on my cushion and imagine and practice with other like-minded people; it was easy to be at peace when someone was feeding me and I was surrounded by beauty with nothing to do but meditate. I asked myself that evening how I could practice non-attachment, even before leaving the retreat, and keep that open heart as I travelled back to my family.

And then, I got an idea.

⚔⚔

The next morning, I came into the chapel room for our last sit and walked over to where Karen and Alicia were sitting. They were in the midst of a conversation so I stood there for just a moment between the rows of cushions. I wished them both a good trip home in case I missed seeing them again before the end of the day, and squatted down behind Karen. I began to unwind my black mala beads from my wrist. My heart was pounding, knowing what I was about to do. I loved my mala beads so much, and they represented times in my life that I wanted to hold onto; times of being with great teachers and learning the *dharma*. I got Karen's full attention and said to her, "Here. I want to give you something to celebrate your upcoming grandmotherhood," I said, as I handed her my black mala beads. Her mouth dropped open.

"They've been with me on many positive retreats and teachings, so I hope that they bring you good luck." I closed her fingers around them so she could not refuse and gave her a quick hug. My heart did feel open. I was going to miss those beads—but, in reality, it felt really nice to give Karen something that I knew she had admired on my wrist earlier. If I could let go of those beads, I could let go of some expectations around a perfect outcome with Keydell, some judgement toward myself, and some control over what I couldn't control.

Of course, after that sit I went right down to the gift shop and bought a new set of beads. I guess I still had some work to do.

Thank you, Jack Kornfield, for all your wisdom and thank you, Alicia and Karen, for your ears and your hearts. I'm sure the black mala beads are in great hands—and my new, colorful ones are pretty cool, too.

CHAPTER 19

INVESTIGATION

"The only way around is through."

—*Robert Frost*

February, 2011

I'd been back from my retreat for a month and was hunkering down for the cold Rhode Island winter months. Fortunately, Keydell's mood was usually better this time of year, and we got longer breaks between episodes. What we noticed, however, was that his disruptive behaviors around his peers were becoming more frequent. He tended to get overstimulated, and would do inappropriate things. Like with us, he didn't seem to understand his impact. He also got his first smartphone, which enabled him to talk to his friends without us hearing him.

I discussed this with Jim one night. "I swear you have ADD," I said to him from across the other end of the couch in the den. We'd been talking for a while, but it was a one sided conversation.

"Why do you say that?" he asked as he stared at his iPad, barely listening to my concerns about Keydell's iPhone. I often thought I bored him because he never seemed to be interested in what I was saying. Sometimes, when I was talking to him, he'd turn and leave the room mid-sentence. I knew he heard me, but it was challenging to keep his attention and get his feedback.

I sat quietly to see whether he would look up or notice that I hadn't answered. I was practicing patience. He was focused on what he was reading, so I just sat there sending daggers with my eyes to get him to look at me.

Finally, he stopped reading and looked over at me. "What?" he asked.

"Nothing. I was just waiting until you were done so I could finish the conversation."

He rolled his eyes in aggravation. I knew I could be passive-aggressive, and that it drove him nuts, but I really wanted to try a new way of making him aware of what he did in conversations.

"I was reading," he said. "I heard you."

"Well, I can't tell sometimes because you don't give me any reply or feedback in conversations. I'm talking into space. Do I bore you?"

"No, I'm just thinking about something else sometimes," he said.

"I know. That's why I think you might have ADD," I speculated. "You have a hard time focusing on what people are saying for more than a few seconds. It seems as though your brain is moving so fast that you move onto other topics in your head before the person you're talking to does. It comes off as rude, babe and it's not just to me."

He closed his iPad case and threw it down on the couch and left the room. He looked mad, and I wondered if he was masking his pain (or fear).

I loved going to workshops and coming home with all the answers. Yeah, right.

Just then, Ella and Keydell came back from the basketball game they'd gone to at the middle school.

"Hey, guys. How was the game?"

Ella was standing behind Keydell as they came into the kitchen and she was rolling her eyes and gesturing that something had happened with Keydell.

"What?" I asked, mentally preparing myself for what was coming.

"Keydell was texting a girl during the game and he called her a bitch," Ella said.

Keydell whipped his head around, threw himself down onto a kitchen chair, grabbed his head in frustration and yelled up at Ella, "You said you wouldn't tell, and you don't know that for a fact!"

"Yes, I do," Ella retorted. "One of my friends, who was sitting with the girl, told me you called her a bitch. And I'm sorry for telling, but Mom and Dad need to know, Keydell. You need to learn how to text right."

"I was joking," Keydell said, glaring at Ella for telling on him. Sometimes I wondered if she told on him to help him or because she was embarrassed for what he'd done and it was a reflection on her. As parents, we felt like that, too, sometimes. We believed people would look at us as bad parents if our child was screaming or throwing a fit.

"Well, it was not taken as a joke, Keydell," Ella continued. "She was upset, and you can't always tell what someone means in a text. He really needs to learn about using his phone, Mom."

His jaw had dropped open when we got him the phone for Christmas. Everyone in our family had one, and with Keydell's soccer and play dates away from the house, we felt it was time to get him one, too. More than that, I wanted him to feel part of the family in that respect. This was new for us, though, because when Henry and Ella were younger they shared a flip phone, and only brought it along if they were going to be at a sports game and might need a ride home.

Keydell had his forehead down on the table with one arm draped over it and his other hand on his phone as it lay face down on the table. I gestured for Ella to leave the room so I could talk to him. She went to sit with Jim in the living room.

"Del, you may not have meant anything rude by texting what you did, but it's never nice to call someone a bitch," I began as I sat down across the table from him. I suddenly felt far away with the table between us so I walked around to his side and bent down next to him.

"Why did you call her that anyway?"

"We were texting back and forth and then she said to stop texting her. I could see her across the bleachers laughing so I thought she was kidding," he said in a muffled voice from under his planted face. I could only imagine what the back and forth text messages were.

"Would you look up, please? I want to talk to you and it's hard to hear you with your head down."

"No, I don't want to."

"Are you embarrassed?"

"No, Ella's a jerk."

"I think Ella wants you to learn how to talk to girls in a nice way, Keydell. She, of course, is one, and can give you some good insight as to what might upset a girl," I explained.

"It's not nice, Keydell," Ella piped in from the other room.

"I've got this, Boo," I yelled back. "First off, Keydell, if a girl asks you to stop texting her, you need to stop texting her. If you have a real problem with someone and need to have a longer conversation to clear things up, it's best to do it in person so you can get a real sense of what they mean or are feeling. She may not have been able to tell you were joking by calling her that. 'Bitch' is a pretty strong word, and not nice under any circumstances. Do you understand that?"

Keydell lifted his head from the table, grabbed his phone, stomped into the living room, and threw it right at Ella's head.

"Bitch!" he yelled.

I could feel my body harden right away, bracing for the oncoming storm. Jim was already in a mood from me calling him out about not paying attention to me, and now he was feeling protective of Ella, so he followed Keydell up the stairs like an angry bull while I stood frozen in the middle of the living room, watching as he skipped steps to the top.

It was going to be a long night.

"Are you okay, Ella?" She, too, was frozen on the couch, looking confused and pissed off at the same time. I think she felt like I did when I was trying to help and Keydell reacted so defensively, so quickly, that it was shocking. I thought I had spoken to him in the kitchen very calmly but it just didn't matter.

"I just wanted you to know what he'd done, Mom," she answered. "He was pretty good most of the night, but I didn't know he was texting that girl until the end when my friend came over and told me. We'd been having a good time, actually."

"I think he probably feels guilty or ashamed, which is a good thing," I said hopefully. "It might mean he regrets doing it and won't do it again."

I leaned over, touched her arm, and kissed her on her forehead. I could hear Jim trying to keep his cool with Keydell so decided to go up and relieve him.

"You know it's going to get rough now, right?" I asked Ella.

"Yes, Edo is already hiding in Henry's room." We smiled. He always knew how Keydell was feeling.

"He can't throw things at Ella anymore; or at you." Jim yelled. "I'm so tired of this. I will not tolerate this anymore, Keydell. I am done, I am so done!" He was boiling as he held Keydell down on the bed.

I never understood what he meant when he said, "I'm done!" I think it meant he was just plain tired of all of it, not that he was done being Keydell's father. I was a little more refreshed after my retreat, but Jim had not had a break at all. It didn't matter how much "rest" we had in between meltdowns though, they still assaulted us each time. That's why the respite places made no sense to me. Pushing problems away never solved them: you had to bring them in close and examine them deeply to get to the solution, or they just keep coming back.

"We're going to leave you for a bit to think about what happened," I said to Keydell. "We can't talk to you when you're like this. Please breathe deeply and try to settle down and we can talk later."

"I am ready NOW!" he screamed.

"Del, you are obviously too wound up. Please notice this. Downstairs, I wanted to teach you about texting politely, and I think you took it to mean you were horrible. I don't think that at all, but we can't talk until you settle some, okay?"

"I want to talk NOW!" he insisted, as he grabbed a pencil from the side table and chucked it at me. I tried to stay calm and ignore it.

"Open your heart, Kim, and give this some space," I heard myself say. "See him clearly, and without a preconditioned view."

He jumped out of the bed, opened his door and started throwing things down the stairs one at a time at the back of my head. He threw them hard and with force, putting dings and dents on the hallway walls, thankfully missing me. His room was already full of holes, chipped paint, and dents in his door from smashing things against it. Screw looking at him in a new way. I needed to get out of his path. I felt as though my retreat lessons were miles away; I was right back to feeling like I had before I left.

"If you throw anything else, Keydell, you know we're keeping it, so please stop. You're going to hurt someone," I yelled up from the bottom of the stairs.

He then chucked his watch down at me. What is it with the goddamned watches? He kept throwing things that *he* loved, knowing they would break or get taken away.

This went on for another hour or so before things finally calmed down. Jim came downstairs after it was all over, tight-lipped, with a body slack from exhaustion. "He's sleeping now," he said.

"Good job, babe."

Jim sat on the couch with his head in his hands as I rubbed his back. "I'll talk to him later about what he did, but for now, let's just let him sleep." We both knew talking to him too soon sent him back into a meltdown. I kind of chuckled, thinking about the lunacy of it all.

Jim leaned on the back of the couch and stared up at the ceiling, not saying anything.

"Do you think I shouldn't have said anything when he came home tonight?" I asked, looking for validation on my parenting.

"No, it wouldn't matter. I just can't take this sometimes. He had no reason to get upset tonight. I'm keeping his watch." At least we were on the same side there.

"It's one thing for him to treat us poorly as he continues to connect with us," I said, "but if he starts acting out more in public, he's going to get into some real trouble down the road. We have to keep teaching him, whether he likes it or not."

Jim agreed but didn't say anything else. I don't think he had the energy.

Keydell slept for the rest of the night.

⋟⊹⊱

After his indoor soccer practice the next morning, we asked Keydell to sit down so we could go over what happened the night before. He instantly put his head down under his arm.

"First off, can we please try to talk without getting upset at each other? Will you lift your head please?" He obliged. "Thank you. Dad and I just want to be able to talk to you and teach you about things like manners, or how to be respectful to others, without you getting so angry. We still love you if you do something inappropriate, but we also want to help you get along in the world."

Keydell just sat there looking at the floor. Jim was leaning back in his chair with his arm draped over the top of his head. I could tell he was just there to listen. He was obliging me, too.

"Do you understand what I said last night about talking to girls or texting girls in a nice way, and not calling them names?" I prompted.

"I was just joking," he said.

"Yes, you said that, but it was not appropriate joking, okay? It upset the girl. Did you know that?"

"No."

"And, by the way, if you had just listened to us say that last night and moved on, then we would have ended it right there. What got us upset was that you threw the phone at Ella instead of talking to her, and then went into a fit. It ended up with you losing your things and us all being drained. Can we look at how we can avoid this next time, please? What do you think you could have done differently if what we said had upset you?"

"Given you the phone to take away," he replied sarcastically. Jim was looking even more impatient.

"Yes, but maybe something else. I want you to be able to use your phone, but I need you to learn how to use it respectfully."

He thought for a minute. I could see he was annoyed by the whole process, but I really felt he needed to understand.

"Keydell, if you make a mistake, it doesn't define who you are, the way you handle it afterwards does. Everyone makes mistakes now and then."

Keydell didn't have much to say.

I wrapped it up with, "You need to apologize to Ella now, and try just listening when we're talking to you about something rather than getting so defensive. It sucks the life out of all of us, and I'm sure you would rather put your energy toward more positive things, like soccer, than yelling and screaming all the time. Besides, that kind of behavior only hurts *you*. You end up losing privileges and your things. One thing I have learned is that all my actions have consequences, so if I don't want a bad consequence I do only nice things. Do you feel like you can work on that, please?"

"I try," he insisted. "Sometimes I can't stay in control. I get angry and my body just takes over."

Wow, that was the first time he said anything like that about his actions. I was impressed that he had that awareness.

"You know what, Keydell? Thank you for telling me that. I'm proud of you for noticing that. At least I know you are trying. I have often wondered what makes you act the way you do when I know how sweet you really are." I looked at my silent partner to see his reaction to Keydell's statement and saw that Jim was reading something. I'd lost him. I gave Keydell a hug and his watch back, and went to get some lunch. His apology to Ella was quick and sarcastic, but it was a step in the right direction.

As I reflected on the situation, I thought about how Keydell said he was trying, yet he couldn't control his outbursts. Was it just habit for him to react this way? If so, I needed to keep showing him better ways to respond. If it was a malfunction in his brain, then I needed to get better help.

Keep thinking, Kim. Keep thinking.

⪤┼┼⪥

Patrick, Keydell's oldest brother, was really missing Keydell, and asked if he could come for a visit. He said he would take the bus to our house if we were able to give him a ride home. Keydell came with me, and we stopped in to say hi to Sue and see where she lived. She, her husband, Kamaria and Patrick had a very tiny apartment in Providence with no yard, and I think when Keydell saw it he realized how good he had it at our house.

Patrick was very laid back. He spoke slowly and quietly, and his voice would often trail off at the end of his sentences, so you had to pay attention when he spoke. He was so different from Keydell. They certainly looked like brothers, but they had opposite energy.

When Patrick came to visit, we took him to the indoor practice at the Boys and Girls Club. It was a good opportunity for me to ask him about Keydell's childhood from his perspective. I was still curious about when all the aggression had started, and if there was an event that had shifted things for him.

Keydell ran to meet his buddies as we arrived at the gym so Patrick and I pulled out the lower seat of the bleachers and sat down. I filled him in on how his brother was doing and how much he loved soccer. Then I decided to dive in.

"Patrick, can I ask you a few questions about Keydell as a young child?"

"Sure," he said with a big wide smile and sleepy eyes.

"I know this is a hard question, and you don't have to answer if it makes you feel uncomfortable, but I often wonder if Keydell was sexually abused in any way because of the way he grabs at us, and touches Ella and her friends inappropriately. He also flinches when I go to touch him. " At this time, I thought being sexually abused led to repeat behaviors, but in most cases it does not. Children who have been raped or sexually molested in any way often turn to drugs or delinquent behaviors due to their feelings of poor self-worth.

"No, its fine, you can ask me whatever you want. I don't think that happened though." He was as straightforward as Keydell, but chill about it. "He's always been inappropriate, even as a very young kid, but I don't think anyone ever did anything to him."

"Really?" I said. "What else do you remember about when you guys were little?"

"My mom was sick," he said protectively, "so Keydell used to be up in the middle of the night just running around or watching

TV. He would find food, or I would get it for him. He would bug Kamaria a lot."

"Where was your mom when Keydell was up at night?"

"In her room sleeping," he said.

"Do you know his father?"

"Yeah, I hung out with him sometimes when he came over." He shrugged his shoulders like it was not a big deal.

"What do you mean?" I was really surprised to hear this. I wondered if Keydell had ever met him but just didn't remember.

"He was around, so we would hang out. He's kind of a hood. I don't see him anymore." Patrick was so matter-of-fact with his answers. He didn't seem ashamed or upset by anything I was asking, so I continued.

"Wow, I didn't know that you knew him." It gave me hope that if we ever did need to find him for medical issues or something, we might be able to find him through Patrick. "Did Keydell know him?"

"He might not remember him. I hung out with him when I got older."

"Well, thank you for answering my questions, Patrick. Keydell's been having a hard time with his anger control and frustrations and I'm trying to get to the root of his problems. I know leaving you all has been very traumatic, and I'm not trying to blame your mom or anything, but just seeing if there is something I've missed."

Patrick and I continued talking about Keydell's progress and what Patrick's plans were for his future. Did he want to go to college? Did he do well in school? He was a very kind boy and I hoped Keydell could maintain a relationship with him. Before Patrick left, he wanted to take lots of pictures to show his mom.

"Let's take some 'pitchers,' Keydell," he would say. "Mom will like to see them. It will make her happy."

The more we got to know Patrick, the more we saw how close he was with Sue. He acted like Henry did with me. He was thoughtful about her, and attended to her feelings. It was sweet. What was different for Keydell? What kept him from feeling bonded to Sue or to me? I felt like I was growing on him, but it surprised me that he never asked for Sue after our first few visits. And of course he didn't ask for his father; he didn't know who to ask for.

I was becoming more convinced that Keydell had this "attachment disorder" that Sonya had mentioned and that he hadn't properly bonded with his mother or other caregivers. I had looked it up several times, and seen videos online of kids melting down just like Keydell did, but there were no links to information or resources. "Keep reassuring them that you love them, they need to feel safe and trust you, etc.," the advice said. We were doing all of this but seeing no improvement. We thought we were getting somewhere during the off-seasons, but as spring or fall would roll around his behaviors would ramp right back up again. He had it as badly as Sonya had thought.

I was talking to a friend at one of our Buddhist group meetings that next week and, surprisingly, he told me he'd grown up in the foster care system and had battled depression and other issues similar to what Keydell was displaying. He told me he'd done some neurofeedback recently to help him with his lingering anger and depression.

"I read about neurofeedback," I said, "but don't really understand how it's used."

"You should check it out," he suggested. "It helped me a lot. I was a mess, and now I can cope much better. My meditation practice helps, too, but the neurofeedback really helped me get under control and started on a more peaceful track."

That was all I wanted, too. I would love to get Keydell on a more peaceful track.

I stored this information in my library of things to explore.

⋟⋞

Spring was in the air, so we braced ourselves.

After one of the first early spring, outdoor games, I got a frantic call from Tim. He was the parent of one of Keydell's friends and had given Keydell a ride to the game that morning.

"Calm down, Tim, and tell me what happened" I said.

"Keydell opened the door as we were coming back from the game. I mean we were driving down the road, on the bridge and he just opens the door! Jesus Christ, he could have fallen out."

"Tim, I'm so sorry you had to deal with that."

"He's never riding with me again," he yelled.

"I get it. I'm sorry," I apologized. "I'll talk to Keydell."

Good lord. You'd think he would understand how dangerous some of his actions were. He was going to kill himself! I hoped he could make it through the soccer season and stay on the team.

After Del got home, I decided to wait a bit before talking to him about what happened. He was so happy from his game, and I needed to take a minute anyway. I thought about how to approach it so he wouldn't get defensive but just explain himself.

"Keydell, can I talk to you for a minute?" I was looking up to the top of the stairs bracing myself for what was to come. *Stay calm, Kim. Deep breaths. Speak with compassion and patience.*

"Yes," I heard from his room.

I climbed the stairs. He was sitting on his bed, playing on the Gameboy.

"Hey, Tim Jones just called me and I wanted to talk to you about what happened," I started.

"What happened?" Keydell asked, still looking at the game screen.

"Hey, can you put that down for a minute so we can talk please?" Keydell played a couple more seconds on the game, and then put it down with a sigh.

"He told me that, on the way back from the game today, you opened the car door while the car was moving. Can you explain that to me? You got pretty scared the last time you did that."

"Michael and Tyler dared me to do it," was his reply.

I breathed deeply, and tried to speak slowly and calmly.

"Mr. Jones was really scared for you, and very upset. He doesn't want to drive you to any more games."

"So?"

"So, that's a problem. Dad and I are very busy. We want you to be able to play soccer, but we need to carpool sometimes with other parents. If you do things like this, it won't work," I explained. "Also, I think you need to call and apologize."

"I'll get a ride from someone else."

"No you don't get my meaning, Del. When you do something that is harmful to someone else, you need to take responsibility, and fix it or apologize. And if you continue doing things like this, you might not get to go to the games at all. No coach is going to want to take responsibility for your dangerous behaviors that could lead to injury. It puts them in a very awkward position."

Keydell took his covers and pulled them over his face. "I'm stupid," he spat out. "I should just kill myself. It would be so much easier for you. You wouldn't have to take me to soccer and everyone would be happier."

"Del, please look at me," I begged. "I love you and we're practicing talking nicely, remember? I want you to be alive ... and safe. If you were dead, it would be a hundred times worse than this. My sadness would be overwhelming. This I can handle. I just want to help you realize how your actions affect others. You might have just been goofing around, but Mr. Jones only saw the car door open and the possibility of you falling out. How do you think he would feel if you fell out on his watch?"

"He would be happy?" he gruffly said from under the covers.

"No, he wouldn't, and you know it." I tried to take the covers off his face and look at him.

"Hey, let me tell you something," I continued when he wouldn't let me see his face. "You're perfect just the way you are, but you have to decide whether how you behave is working for you. I know you want to be able to play soccer and get to the games, so is it worth it to do things that you know are not helpful toward that? You can continue with all the crazy behavior you want, and live the rest of your life like this, but you won't get what you want. Or, you can see which behaviors no longer serve you, stop doing them, and get better results. The anger and outbursts never get you anywhere, Del. They hurt you and they hurt others. If you hurt you, you're making an unhappy life for yourself. If you hurt others, you get sent to jail and again you have an unhappy life for yourself. Get it?"

"Yes."

"So think about that—and please don't open the door anymore when the car is moving, even if you think it's just for fun or to entertain your friends."

Oh, God, now I had to worry about peer pressure. What next?

I left Keydell after giving him a hug through the covers and he seemed to be okay. Whew. Maybe we're getting somewhere. That was actually a normal conversation and he didn't flip out.

"Maybe the Zoloft is really helping Keydell's depression," I said to Jim that evening after dinner. "Even though he still has fits, he's happier in between more."

"Yeah, he seems a lot happier these days. I tried one of his Adderall today," Jim announced. Just like that, like it was no big deal. I turned away from doing the dishes to face him.

"What? Why?"

"Hey, I wanted to see what we were giving our child." Oh, was that the reason? It surprised me that he would just pop one of Del's pills but he looked right in my eyes as he said it so I knew he wasn't kidding.

"And, what happened?" I asked as we stood facing each other.

"It was pretty cool actually," he replied. "It kind of cleared my head. It got rid of the white noise."

"The white noise?" I questioned. "What white noise?"

"I always have a kind of static in my head, and it made it go away," he said with a tilt of his head as if he was realizing something.

Well, what do you know? Maybe Jim was having one of those "a-ha" moments.

"So the Adderall cleared your head, huh? Maybe you *do* have ADD"

"Maybe I do," he said as he wandered out of the room. "Maybe I do."

CHAPTER 20

DILIGENCE

*"No matter how hard the past, you can always
begin again."*

—Buddha

Spring, 2011

"Hey Del, I have something different I want to read to you tonight, it's about how to take care of your anger like it's a baby," I said with a smile as I came into his room for bedtime.

"What?" he said, looking at me with a curious eye and a grin.

"I'm reading a book by a Zen Buddhist Monk named Thich Nhat Hanh," I said. "It's called *Anger: Wisdom for Cooling the Flames*, and the way he talks about it is pretty cool. I mean, I'd like to be less angry at times—how about you?"

He looked right at me, trying to get a read on what was happening. Was this going to be another discussion about his anger, or something fun like most of the other books we read at night together?

Finally he shrugged his shoulders as if to say, "Okay, what the heck."

I opened the book to the page I wanted to read as he leaned into me.

"It says here that it's a good practice to get to know your emotions so that when they start to arise, you can look at them like they are separate from you and say, 'Hey, I know you, you're Anger' or, 'Hi, I know you, you're Joy.' This will help you notice when joy, anger, fear, or excitement are coming on, and where they produce sensations in your body. For example, when you are angry, take notice if you also feel tight or sick in your belly. When you are happy, notice if you feel relaxed or energized."

Then I asked Keydell, "Have you ever noticed how *you* feel in your body when you're angry?"

He sat still for a minute and didn't say anything. I hoped he was thinking about my question.

"I don't know," he said hesitantly. "Tight?"

"Well, it's good to know how the emotions feel so you can notice how they affect you physically. You might not like feeling tight or agitated, especially during a soccer game," I smiled, miming the feelings by balling up my fists, "so when you feel that sensation coming on, you can take deep breaths to relax or change your thoughts to something more pleasant instead of letting the emotion take you over." I was dramatically taking deep breaths to demonstrate and animating my words to make it fun.

"The more you practice doing this, the quicker you can turn the emotions around if you don't like them," I explained.

He was shaking his head up and down like he understood and agreed, so I went on.

"Thich Nhat Hanh says when you notice your anger, you should talk to it, pretend to hold it like a baby, and rock it slowly. You should take care of it, and put it to sleep slowly and gently."

"Like this," Keydell said all of a sudden, as he folded his arms like he was holding a baby, and began rocking them back and forth.

"Yes, perfect. Now what would you say to *your* anger Keydell?" I asked him as we turned to face each other.

Keydell looked down at his invisible angry baby and said, "Shhh, baby. Go to sleep. Take a deep breath and go to sleep."

It was so stinking cute. I heard my own words in his, and thought that maybe some of what I'd been saying over the years might have sunk in.

"So maybe next time when you start to feel angry, Keydell, you can remember this, and see if you can calm that baby," I said as he cuddled back into me and smiled.

"Maybe," he said. I believe he wanted to make the promise, but just wasn't sure he could keep it.

"I don't expect you to do it the first time. It takes practice— just like getting good at soccer takes practice. I'll try, too, and of course, if we feel joy or happiness we should rock that in our arms and love it just as much. All of our feelings are important, but maybe this will help us keep the ones we like awake, so the not-so-good ones can take longer naps."

Keydell thought that was pretty funny.

"Sleep, Anger," I barked at my invisible anger. "Sleep for a long time." We both giggled and I closed the book.

I really liked how playful this was, and how understandable for him. Maybe he could learn to see his emotions as something outside of himself that he could touch and work with like a soccer ball. Maybe he could work with the anger, versus the anger controlling him.

I read one more story from the shelf and tucked Keydell into bed. I turned on his lava lamp so the room would not be completely dark (we would work on that fear later) and kissed him goodnight. He was asleep in less than a minute.

<hr/>

It was a chilly, crisp, blue-sky day in May. Spring in Rhode Island can be quite cold, and often comes with rainy days, but every once in a while we get a good one. New Englanders are hardy people. As soon as it hits forty-five degrees, they put on their shorts—but, today, up at Wyatt soccer fields, the wind was whipping up the hill, so it was very raw. All the parents were bundled up, preparing for the first travel soccer game of the spring season. It'd been a long winter of indoor practices so it was nice for the kids to be outside.

Jim and I were excited to see Keydell in his happy place but, honestly, my biggest concern today was that he might get upset during the game. He'd had a rough couple of weeks; even Coach Teeters had noticed, and was careful to keep him under control. Keydell could be manic and overly aggressive at practice, but still had not shown too many people his completely defiant or violent side. I wanted to keep it that way for his sake. I couldn't help but want others to see him as the beautiful, talented, smart kid he was, and soccer really helped that part of him shine. I prayed he could keep it together today and just have fun out there.

Keydell was wearing his royal-blue uniform and sporting his fancy new haircut. He loved going to his barber, who'd put a lightning bolt in the side of Keydell's short hair yesterday. He had on his number ten jersey and his game face, and was looking sharp.

The game started. Keydell was playing striker on the left wing. He went after the ball right away. He was still one of the smallest boys out there, so it was a good thing he was fast. He was a force to be reckoned with and looked confident and happy.

Then he got knocked down. Hard. *Oh, please don't get mad, please don't get mad. Just get up and keep playing.*

And he did.

I looked at Jim and said, "Oh man, I thought that was going to be a problem."

"He's tough," Jim said. "He doesn't let up, so he's going to get defended hard."

The whole team was very talented and had great teamwork. Keydell was handling the pushing and shoving well enough, but when he got a call for fouling another player, he lost his composure.

All of a sudden, in his mind, he was being called "wrong."

The whistle blew, and Keydell and a player from the other team were told to stop. We saw him turn to the ref, who was just a young kid himself, and say something that we couldn't hear. The ref stopped in his tracks and glared at Keydell, so we knew whatever he'd said must not have been good.

"Oh, God. What just happened?" I asked Jim.

"He got called on a foul, and he doesn't like it."

Oh please Del, just take the call and move on. Don't yell at the ref, I said to myself.

Then we heard Keydell say something else to the ref, very loudly this time.

"I didn't foul him. What are you, his bitch?" and he turned to walk away and get back to the game.

"Oh man, really? Did he really just say that?" I put my hands over my face to see if I could make it go away, but it didn't work.

One of the other dads looked over at us and laughed. "Keydell's not happy," he said.

"Yeah, this is going to be interesting," I retorted as I crossed my arms and squinted to see what Keydell was doing.

Then the ref took the red card out. Not the yellow, which is a warning, but the red card. Keydell was being kicked out of the game. He stormed off the field, but not toward his team bench. He ran to the corner on the spectator's side, and sat down in defiance. I waited a minute to give him a chance to settle down. He then got up and started to walk away from the field, so I decided to try talking to him.

"I'll be right back, Jim. I'll see where his head is and try to get him to at least sit with his team. He needs to understand that he can't just do what he wants."

"Good luck," Jim said, happy I was the one handling it.

"Ha, yeah, thanks." I said over my shoulder as I jogged over to where Keydell was walking away.

I felt like everyone was watching what I might do, but I had to let that go. I didn't want to embarrass Keydell, and I had nothing to prove to any of the other parents, so I just kept my cool. I was upset for Keydell. I really wanted soccer to work out for him.

"Hey, Del. Stop. Come here, buddy. Let's just sit for a minute," I said as I got closer to him. He dropped down on the grass with his knees up and his hands grasping around his ears. I sat next to him, quietly trying to get a feel for his energy. The grass was cool and I could feel the dampness seeping into my jeans. We were about twenty-five yards from the parents on the sidelines, so we had some privacy. Keydell was crying, and his warm skin was damp and smelly. I realized in that moment that getting kicked out of the game for something he didn't understand must have triggered feelings of other abandonment he'd gone through and not understood.

"Let's just sit here and settle down for a sec. Sorry this happened."

The end-of-game whistle blew. Everyone started folding up their chairs and blankets, and moving toward their cars. We just sat there. Coach Teeters came over to talk to Keydell, but I stopped him.

"Coach, do you think he could call you later and talk? He's upset, and it would be very unproductive right now."

"Yes, that's fine. I just wanted to check in."

"We'll call you later."

Keydell and I got up and met Jim at the car.

"You okay, bud?" Jim asked.

"I didn't do anything wrong. That was a bad call," Keydell barked back.

I'm sure you can guess what happened next. Yes, another upset. The worst part about the afternoon's meltdown, however, was that

Keydell came very close to really hurting himself on purpose. He had smacked himself in the face before, but had never tried to use an object to draw blood or hit his head with.

I went upstairs during the bout between Keydell and Jim right at the end of round two, and rang the bell. It was time to tag in and relieve my hubby. The room was a mess from the things Keydell had thrown around during the fit, and Jim was picking them up saying, "These are mine now. I told you to stop, and now they are mine."

"Take them, take everything. I don't want them anyway," Keydell was still screaming. "I want to be dead!" he yelled as he grabbed a pencil off his desk. He held it against his chest and applied some pressure while glaring right at me. I dashed over to him and grabbed the pencil out of his hand and tried to hug him tightly to see if I could calm him down. "Shhh, Del, it's okay, let's try to breathe and calm down."

God damn it, he scared me some times. Would he really poke himself through the skin?

"Keydell, take that anger and try to put it outside of you. Hold it like a baby, remember?" I said, soothingly.

He wiggled out of my hold and spit at my face with a big wet one. Well, that was one thing he took out of his body; a big ball of spit. Nice. I thought Jim was going to strangle him after that little stunt.

"I'm fine," I said quickly. "He's really wound up, and so are we. We need to get under control. This is nuts."

"I can't take this anymore," Jim said as he threw all the stuff he had picked up back on the floor in disgust." I wondered if he wanted to die, too. It sounded kind of peaceful, actually. I was remembering my visions of floating above the retreat center, outside myself, and the relief I had that I was free.

Oh, God, I was going down. Maybe I was in some sort of depression now, too.

I wiped the spit off my face and held Keydell again as tightly as I could. "Take it easy. It's not worth killing yourself over, that's for sure. We love you, we love you, and we love you. We want to help you continue doing what you love. It's all right. You're good now."

He began to soften.

"I want to call coach." His face was puffy and wet with tears, and his tiny ten-year-old body looked so lost. He was still wearing his uniform and cleats. My little warrior was ready to win. I was very proud of him in that moment. I hated the meltdowns, but it was great that he was recovering and making it right. It was a big step. He went downstairs in front of Jim and me as we followed. I looked back at Jim as if to say, "Okay, maybe we're getting somewhere," but he was drained of any expression.

We dialed Coach Teeter's number, and Keydell got on the phone with him.

"Hi, Coach. I'm sorry for swearing and not coming back to the sidelines," he blurted out without even saying "Hi, it's me, Keydell." It was so touching.

I could hear Mr. Teeters talking on the other end but couldn't make out what he was saying. It really didn't matter I guess, because I was so proud of Keydell for calling him and saying his part. I looked at the lightning bolt haircut again, and thought about how quickly he went from being a warrior on the field to a very different kind of warrior at home. On the field he was determined, focused, and confident in his abilities. If he could be like that out there, I knew he could be like that at home. We had to just keep coaching him, working on his skills, and practice staying calm under pressure. Wow, what a good sports metaphor. Our family was a team, just like his soccer team—and we had to work together, all of us, to win.

Later that night, when things had settled back to normal (whatever that meant these days), I asked Keydell if he could tell me why he'd gotten so upset over the referee's call. I felt like this was a great opportunity to reflect on what happened: for one, he didn't get in trouble with us, so he might not feel as defensive; and two, the way he acted wasn't out of character for a lot of boys who play sports. Lots of kids get upset at referees and swear. Overall, even though I prefer good sportsmanship, I thought Keydell handled it very well, and I wanted to acknowledge that to him. I also wanted to focus our conversation on getting to the root of his distress by showing him how to reflect upon the event and practice his recovery around it, so next time he could stay in the game.

I approached the topic softly, in a supportive, conversational tone. We sat on the couch with him sprawled next to me.

"Keydell, you were amazing tonight," I began. "You got upset, but you recovered much better, and even when you got called out of the game, you didn't run away or hit anyone. You just sat down on the sidelines and took some space. I'm proud of you for that."

"Thanks, Mom," he replied. "Sometimes I just need to be left alone."

"I can see that," I told him, "and I think it's great that you recognize what you need. How do you think you could stay in the game next time though? I know you love it."

"I shouldn't have gotten a red card. I didn't foul that guy."

"Yes, but sometimes, Keydell, the referee can't see everything, and right or wrong, they make the call as best as they can."

I put my arm around his shoulders. He leaned in tighter and said, "He wouldn't listen to me when I tried to explain that I didn't foul him, though."

"The ref is just another component of the game. Some days he will be really good, and some days not so much. Some days you will play really well, and some days you might not. It's just how people are. It's not about you, personally. The ref is not out to get you or anything. They're looking at individual plays, not individual players. If you noticed, there were other kids who also got called on fouls, not just you."

"But they did foul. I didn't." I had to laugh at his confidence.

"Think of it this way, Keydell, the game is made up of many parts, just like you are made up of many parts. One foul, or one bad call, does not define your whole game. And, by the way, that's like life in general. We're the sum of *all* that we do. When you have a meltdown, that's not all of you. You also have times of real kindness, love, and happiness. When I have a bad day, it doesn't make my whole life bad. In Buddhism they talk about the impermanence of everything, so if I'm having a bad day, I know it will change. If the referee makes a bad call, the next one might be good. If the sun is shining, a cloud might come over it and upset us, but it moves on in time and we are happy again. See?

"Life is always changing," I continued. "We have to be careful not to get stuck in how things *should* be, and just work on the things we can—like our own actions or responses."

"So I can't control the ref, but I can control my kicks," he offered.

"You got it, buddy. That's exactly it. So next time if the ref makes a call that you can't control, look at what you *can* control."

"My mouth, so I don't get kicked out," he said.

I had to laugh at that. "You're funny Keydell, and right. You know, that ref from the game today is adopted, too, and has had some similar issues to yours. You're lucky that, when you called him 'someone's bitch,' he didn't go all Keydell on your butt." I tried to tickle him to let him know I was kidding around.

Keydell smiled at me and took it in stride. I put him to bed and felt happy. We'd had a really nice conversation. I felt I had paused more before going in for the big talk; I needed to do more of that. He said he needed some space, and I had to remember that too.

I was beginning to believe that Keydell was grasping what I'd been teaching him about cause and effect, and about the difference between what is real (based on fact) and what we *believe* to be true (based on emotions.) The fact is, the referee made a bad call.

Keydell's belief was that the referee was someone's bitch, and that's *why* he made the bad call. That belief made him angry; he then acted out of anger, and it got him into trouble.

Equanimity is a state of mind that does not resist the truth of how things are. It's born from wise attention—and, through that, we recognize that there will be pleasure and pain, gain and loss, happiness and sadness—and that it all changes. If we resist these facts, or take them personally, then we react in the same old ways: with hatred, fear, and delusion, and by grasping tightly to our beliefs (like, "that guy is an asshole" or "he's someone's bitch"). Alternately, we can be open-minded, relaxed, and balanced. That's deep for a child, I know; I hoped I'd broken it down to his level. I hoped he could always feel with passion, and express his feelings as openly as he needed to—but in a way that was helpful, rather than harmful.

Keydell was a good boy with a big heart, and he truly wanted to be good. I would continue to plant seeds of wisdom as best as I knew how.

The next day Coach Teeters stopped over to chat. He was so dedicated to his players, and I was really impressed with his efforts toward Keydell.

"How's it going, Mr. Teeters?" I asked as I met him outside.

He got out of his car, and we stood in the driveway, talking.

"I just wanted to see how Keydell was doing. He called me last night to apologize," he said.

"Yes, I heard him talking to you. Thank you for that. I wouldn't be surprised if you wanted Keydell to take a break from the team. I know this isn't the first thing he's done to disrupt things, but I hope you can still give him a chance. We had a long talk last night, and I think we're making some progress."

He gave me a big smile, probably remembering some of the crazy things Keydell had done over the past few weeks. One day at practice, he peed right in the middle of the field. He thought it would be funny, and told me later that his friends had dared him to do it. Coach asked him to sit out and he threw a fit so I had to come get him.

"Keydell's an excellent player," Coach responded, gesturing with his graceful hands. "He's a real leader on the team, so I'm trying to impress upon him that he's a role model for the other boys. They look up to him, and if he acts that way, he's not setting a good example. I'm willing to keep him on the team, but he has to understand that he'll get taken out of the game if he can't stay in control."

"Yes, I get that, and I think he does, too," I said, as my eyes got a bit teary. I was still drained from the night before, and feeling very emotional about the possibility that this might not work out for Keydell. "I can't guarantee that he won't lose it again, but I really appreciate you giving him such support and keeping him on the team. If it's any consolation, Coach, he only acts up around people he cares about."

The coach smiled.

"I'm not kidding," I continued. "Up until recently, he's only shown bad behaviors around us. The people he's loved or trusted in the past got rid of him, so if he gets too close to someone he cares about, he gets scared and pushes them away. I could be wrong, but that's my theory. He may not trust that we've all got his back. You're showing him that, even though he can be difficult, you're not going to throw him out. I don't mean to say that his mom threw him out, but in his mind it may feel that way."

I felt like I was sharing too much, but the coach seemed genuinely concerned.

"Well, as long as he doesn't hurt himself or anyone else, I will work with him," he said. "He's worth it."

"Yes, he is." I thanked him for coming by, and walked back to the house with a lump of gratitude in my throat. I'd been a coach before, and when you have one or two kids who act up, it disrupts the whole practice and sometimes the game (or in my case, the track meet). I felt like I had an advocate outside of the family, someone who was on my side.

I went up to my room and cried my eyes out. I wasn't sure if I was relieved, or what—but I felt I had crossed another hurdle on our road to recovery.

Henry came home from college in mid-May.

I was standing at our kitchen sink looking out at our backyard. The old-fashioned, deep ceramic sink felt cold against my hips. The cracking paint on the windowsill reminded me of what I'd let go over the years. The fact that it needed painting seemed trivial, so I didn't give it a second thought, except to take in the beauty of the texture, and the color underneath the chips. The layered paint showed the history of the house, and of those who'd lived there before us. The window reminded me of the wears and tears life brings, yet in such a beautiful way.

I looked past the window to my two handsome boys playing soccer in the yard; one who'd come from my womb, and one who'd come from another's. It was nice to see them hanging out together. They were such opposites physically: Henry was tall, blonde, and fair-skinned and Keydell was small, dark, and brown-eyed. But none of that mattered today. Today, they were just brothers.

Both boys were enjoying themselves and bonding with each other. Henry was excited to be home for many reasons, but a big one was to be able to be a brother to Keydell. Managing him or pinning him down during an upset was not his idea of a good brotherly relationship, and that was mostly all he'd had before leaving for college. Now, Henry was out there coaching and motivating Keydell while they played soccer. I heard him tell Keydell that, if he wanted to be great at something, he had to practice it for 10,000 hours. Like most ten-year-old athletes, Keydell *did* want to be a pro soccer player, so he decided to start keeping track of all his practice hours starting right then. He was certainly determined to do what was needed to become who he wanted to be.

Keydell came bombing in the back door and saw me standing at the sink. "Oh, you scared me!" he said as he popped back into the moment. I had to laugh. He always moved at ninety miles an hour.

"You having fun out there?" I asked, knowing he was by the look on his face.

"Yep. How many hours do you think I've practiced so far in soccer?"

"Oh, I don't know. Let's see if we can figure it out. How many days a week do you practice with Coach Teeters, and how many for rec soccer? And let's say you've been at it for two years now?"

"I need to have 10,000 hours to be pro, Henry told me, so I have to go calculate how many I've done already and then make a plan for how many hours a day to practice and then how long it will take to get to the 10,000 hours and I can keep the journal on my phone!"

Whew, I was out of breath just listening to him.

"Well, that sounds like a great strategy," I agreed—and off he went, up to his room to start his calculations. Henry was standing right behind him that whole time, proudly smiling at his little brother. Henry had always been a very determined athlete as well, but was amazed at Keydell's natural talent and drive to improve.

"He really is amazing, Mom," Henry said after Keydell blazed out of the kitchen.

'Want to sit?" I asked Henry. Talking with him was one of my favorite things to do. I missed just shooting the shit with him.

"You two looked so great out there," I told Henry. "I think Keydell missed you, even though I know you never got a whole lot of quality time with him before you left."

Henry looked at me with his sweet blue eyes and said, "He's a good kid Mom. A really good kid."

"I agree Henry. We just have to keep letting him know that. Now tell me how your first year went, I want to know all the juice."

"It was great," he said with a grin. "I really missed you guys but I'm so glad I picked Chapman. I think because it's a smaller school I don't feel like just another fish in a big sea. I've made some awesome friends and what's not to like about the weather?"

"I'm so happy you like it there, Hank, it's a good fit for you. But, man, I've missed you."

Henry got that thoughtful look on his face that I'd seen before and leaned across the table toward me a bit. He took my hands in his and gave them a squeeze.

"How are *you*, Momma?" he asked with concern. "How have things been with Keydell since Christmas?"

I tried not to get emotional and keep it together all the time, but when someone asked how I was doing, especially my son, I lost my composure. I got a little teary from his question.

"Ah, where do I start?" I leaned back in my chair, letting my hands pull gently away from Henry's. My instinct was to tell him things were fine and that we were all doing great. I knew, however, that Henry really wanted to hear the truth. He enjoyed thinking things through with me. I think he was as interested in the human psyche as I was. He was studying to be an actor, after all, so he loved getting into the heads of others, and knowing their stories.

"I did read more about attachment disorder," I said as I noticed the light outside disappearing to night. I got up and turned the overhead light on. It gave me a minute to get the lump out of my throat. "Do you remember when I mentioned that Sonya, the social worker therapist, thought that was what he had?"

"Kind of," he said, wobbling his hand back and forth in front of himself.

"I found an article online about it, and out of the fifty-eight symptoms listed on a check list for attachment disorder, Keydell has about fifty of them. All the *reasons* he might have it pertain to him, too."

"What kind of symptoms did it list?" Henry asked, very curious to know.

"Anger, self-destruction, inappropriate sexual conduct, being argumentative, being hyper, having a lack of remorse or a conscience, lack of cause-and-effect thinking, being depressed or sad, hoarding food, eating strange things (you know how he eats cardboard?), developmental delays, avoiding physical contact ..." I was out of breath.

"Sounds like him."

"And you know me, Hank, I'm all about hugs and kisses. I have to approach him thoughtfully and carefully with my affections."

Henry was looking up at the ceiling, thinking. "So what were some of the causes listed for attachment disorder, Mom? I mean, was he born with it, or what?"

"I'm not sure when he started to show all the signs, but according to his birth mom, it was quite early. It can come from things like an unwanted pregnancy, maternal ambivalence, and prenatal exposure to drugs or alcohol, neglect, emotional abuse, abandonment, having multiple caregivers, frequent changes in caregivers, poverty, and separation from the mother. Most of those apply to Del," I explained. "I am determined to get to the root of all this, but it's draining, for sure. I haven't found any therapies for attachment disorder, per se, or heard any other therapists mention it when I describe his symptoms, so I don't even know if that's what's going on. His ADD might be causing some of the anxiety, too, who knows?"

We both paused, taking it all in. We could be so cerebral sometimes—but, for us, it was fun.

"You know what?" I said as I snapped back to the conversation, "I feel like there's something wrong in his brain, like something switches on and off when he goes in and out of his meltdowns. It's not like he chooses to be a pain in the ass, even though once he's there he seems to enjoy it in an odd way. It's like, to him, it feels *good* to be mad. It's his comfort zone, like a bad habit might be. But, I mean, one minute he's his sweet and funny self, and the next he's a raging tiger. It just makes me think something's not firing correctly in that head of his."

"What do you think his number one trigger is?" Henry asked.

"His self-esteem. When he feels he's done something "stupid" or wrong, it seems to upset him more than anything," I replied. "When I was at my workshop last winter, I learned that anger is a mask for fear. He may be masking his fear of rejection with his anger."

"Interesting, Mom. That is really interesting and makes a lot of sense." Henry was shaking his head up and down, leaning on his elbow, thinking.

Then he declared as his mission, "I am going to work with him as much as I can this summer to make him feel really good about his soccer. We are going to build that self-esteem up."

I smiled at his enthusiasm. "Sounds good, Henry, although, it might be nice to give your sister some brother time, too. This has not been an easy year for her, even though she's been amazing. I think she could use some normalcy."

"I will, Momma. I know you and Dad are tired from it all, so let me help sometimes."

"I know, sweetie—but you should enjoy your summer, too." The lump was back in my throat. "You worked hard this year, and we're very proud of you. It's time for your own break. Thanks for talking, Hank, I really appreciate it. You have some good insights being a boy, and just being you."

I got up from my side of the table and walked over to give my six-foot-tall man-child a big hug. He was much narrower than Jim, so I could get my arms all the way around him. He hugged me back fully and with great intention. I really needed that.

That night, as I lay in bed thinking about our conversation, I rolled over to Jim and said, "There is more. I know there is more we can do."

He just smiled at me as if to say, "We will figure it out" and fell asleep. Jim was reminding me to stay open-hearted and present, and that all would be revealed—whether he knew it or not. I stared at him for a second, feeling grateful I had him for a partner. Even though things had been very tough over the past two years, he and I were still good. Both of us were very independent people but in raising our kids, we were a team, one hundred percent.

There was more. There was more investigating to do. My little cake was only half-baked, and an ingredient was missing. But what was it?

CHAPTER 21

MY ANGER

*"Our prime purpose in this life is to help others. And if
you can't help them, at least don't hurt them."*

—Dalai Lama

Summer 2011

"Oh shit! Jim, he's out on the roof! He's out on the roof!" I
screamed. "Go outside and get underneath him in case
he jumps."

We were putting out fires like this all the time now. Keydell's
impulsive actions were continuing to be dangerous. He had just
come off another meltdown where he had screamed he wanted
to die, so when I saw him on the roof, I panicked. After we finally
coaxed him back inside I grabbed him for a hug.

"During your meltdown, Keydell, you were saying you wanted
to kill yourself. I thought you were going to jump off the roof! You
really freaked me out!"

He didn't say anything as he pulled out of my grasp. He just looked at each of us, as if wondering what was next. Again, he didn't see the impact of his actions.

"You cannot climb out there ... ever! Do you understand?" Jim commanded.

Jim had been with me during Keydell's earlier meltdown and had been holding him down for a while to keep me safe, so we were both spent.

I looked at Keydell as if to say, "You'd better listen to Dad," and then said, "Let's get ready for bed, Keydell." I had a slight tone of annoyance that I think Keydell picked up on.

Really, you pick up on that, but not the fact that you scared the shit out of me two seconds ago? I thought to myself.

He jumped on the bed and threw the covers over his head.

Jim looked at me and whispered, "He thinks he disappointed you. He needs to know you forgive him."

We'd been noticing lately that he demanded forgiveness after he did something like call me a name or misbehave. He would badger me to give him a hug or an extra kiss goodnight and wouldn't stop until I did. I was probably the toughest on him of anyone—but I was his mom. I'm sure if I'd let him do whatever he wanted all the time, we wouldn't have had as many meltdowns—but he also would've had to live as a hermit to stay out of jail! I knew I rode his butt but sometimes, it was because I believed he could do what I was asking.

I didn't overly praise my kids or do the "everybody wins!" thing: they were too smart, and would have known it was shallow praise. Instead, I hoped to help them take charge of their lives, and not to expect their successes or happiness to come from outside of themselves. Keydell even told me once not to compliment him after a game if he didn't do well. (Of course, his opinion of how he did often differed from mine so I started asking him "How do you think you did?" before making my own comments.)

I swear, though, sometimes he upset me just to see if I would forgive him. It was very controlling, but I thought, at the time, it was a sign that he was developing a conscience. I learned later that he did it because he was seeking reassurance that I was there for him, in good times or bad. It was his way of securing the bond he was forming with me.

"Look Del, first and foremost, I'm glad you're safe," I began. "You scared us because we didn't know what your intentions were up there, and we love you. I would have been sad if you'd jumped and hurt yourself so please realize why I'm upset. It's the same reason I get upset when you do anything to hurt yourself. It's over now, and you are good, so let's read a book and go to sleep, okay?"

I'm not sure I convinced him I was over it, but he was tired and agreed. While reading the book to him, I heard none of my own words. I could hear my voice, but my thoughts were elsewhere.

What would we do if he really killed himself? Maybe he was just exploring out there on the roof, but what if he wasn't? Can we ever really help him? Is his destiny set in stone? It can't be: everything is impermanent, right? This will change. Everything changes, so even his destiny can change.

I didn't know what his destiny was, but before he came to us, it hadn't looked hopeful. I had to believe, in some small way, that his life was better with us than it would have been if he'd stayed in the system. In this moment it was hard to see, but there was nothing more to do than keep trying in every moment.

I brought myself back to the storybook and focused on what I was doing, just being with my son, in a loving, caring way. I laughed inside, thinking about the workshop I had to lead the next day: it was about how to live peacefully by changing our thoughts. How ironic.

I researched attachment disorder and found a website that listed therapists around the United States who worked with kids exhibiting signs of this condition. I called the one office that was listed for Rhode Island and left a message for them to call me back. I reached back out to Dr. Martin as well, and he called me back first. We scheduled an appointment for late August when he returned from vacation. We would give talk therapy one more try.

July 26th, 2011
"Keydell you've got to calm down! I have nowhere to pull over, sweetie."

I had his collar in my right hand and the steering wheel in my left. We were stuck in bumper-to-bumper traffic on our way back from Maryland, where Ella had been at lacrosse camp.

"Motherfucker," I said out loud. There was that trucker mouth again.

Ella was in the passenger seat with her headphones on, and had been trying to mind her own business and relax when Keydell lost the battery power in his iPad. We'd already been in the car for about three of the eight hours of the ride so it was time for another break. I just couldn't get off the road.

"Keydell, please stop hitting Ella, and calm down." I had him in a full-on grip under his armpit now, practically pulling him into the front seat so I could control him. He had tried to open the door already, and had been smacking Ella and me from the back seat so things were getting crazy.

"As soon as I can, I will pull over so you can run around, Del. There is nothing I can do right now so PLEASE SIT DOWN! My God, Keydell, what do you want me to do?"

Where was the happy kid who I just spent four awesome days with? And what the hell had triggered him?

While Ella was at camp, Keydell and I stayed with our friend, his wife, and their two young children, who lived just outside of Washington D.C. I was excited to be spending some one-on-one time with Keydell, and knew he would really enjoy seeing the museums in Washington. Plus, he would be the older child for a change.

The ride down was smooth. We had very little traffic, made stops for stretching and dinner, and kept the iPad powered up. We arrived at our friends' house around 10:00 p.m., ate a light snack, and went to bed. We got up early to get Ella to camp the next morning, and get her checked in to the dorm room at the college where the camp was being held.

Ella was really growing up. My kids never did the whole sleep-away-summer-camp thing, so this was a first for her. She was a great lacrosse player, and had been so patient with Keydell all summer, so I wanted to give her something special. I got a pit in my stomach, thinking about how close she was to leaving the nest, too. Soon it would just be Keydell at home, for four more years after Ella started college.

I let that thought sink in for a minute. *Hmmm.*

Moving on.

Keydell and I had a fantastic few days together. We took the train into D.C. twice, and saw the Museum of Natural History, the Science and Aeronautical museums, and several monuments. We had so much fun running up the Lincoln memorial steps and seeking out the best ice cream sandwiches. (We decided we liked the ones made with Tollhouse cookies.)

On the morning we visited the Natural History museum, something funny happened: Keydell was mistaken for one of the camp kids touring the museum. Ninety percent of the kids were black, and they were all wearing red T-shirts. They must have been from the same summer program. Keydell was also wearing a red T-shirt (the Spiderman one, of course) so he fit right in with the crowd of kids.

Keydell and I were looking at two different things apart from each other, when an older woman, who was one of the camp chaperones, yelled over to Keydell, "Come on, sweetie, we're movin' on."

She was trying to get him to return to the group of campers.

I looked over at her with a big smile and said, "Oh, he's with me."

She laughed. "Oh! I saw that red T-shirt and thought he was part of our group."

"Nope. He's my son, he's with me." I found myself feeling very proud as I said that. Our friends from home knew our new family member, but no one here did. He was my son, and I wanted to show him off. I was proud of him, proud to be his mother, and we were on a cool trip together. *Yeah, he's a pain in the ass but he's my son, our son. He's smart, he's talented, he's black, he's white, and he's my son.* I wrapped my arm around his shoulder as I reclaimed him from the camping group and gave him a hug.

"That was funny," Keydell said. "She thought I was part of the group because of my red T-shirt."

"Yeah, you match." I said. We laughed about that for days. He looked more like the campers than me in many ways, but I was starting to forget that.

After our two days in D.C., walking and touring, we grabbed Ella at her camp. It was about ninety-five degrees outside, and humid as hell. The mid-day sun was blazing down and I could see all the lacrosse girls sweating bullets. I certainly felt irritable.

When we finally got in the car after the last game, ready to roll back home, I cranked the air conditioning and tried to cool us all down as quickly as possible.

Ella was beat. "I am so tired, Mom. They worked us hard," she said as she melted into the front seat. Her hair was in a matted braid, and her face was red from the heat. She was ready to sleep.

"Well, we have a long ride home, so just rest and take a nap if you want. Del, you ready to go, babe?"

I looked over my shoulder to the back seat. He was already asleep. So cute. The heat was taking its toll on all of us. His relaxed, puffed lips stuck out when he slept, and I swear it looked like his neck was made of rubber. It contorted and hung forward, balancing his perfectly round head. He was comfortable, I guess, because he would stay that way for a while before he needed to adjust. His large eyelids were softly framed by long, dark lashes. He really was a handsome boy.

"Do you mind if we drive for a bit before we get food, Ella? Keydell just fell asleep and we might hit traffic so I would like to get going."

"Sure. I have snacks from the camp and I'm tired, too, so I'm just going to put my headset on, listen to music and pass out," she said. "Did you and Keydell have fun in D.C.?"

"Yeah, we had a blast." I filled her in on what we'd done, and our little red T-shirt incident.

We chatted for a few more minutes until she fell asleep. The car was quiet now, and I drove along blissfully for about an hour, soaking in the fun we'd all had over the past few days and starting to cool off. I was really glad I'd gotten to create some good memories with Keydell. I didn't want his childhood to only be filled with memories of his damn meltdowns.

Keydell woke up first—and, as always, was starving. Ella came out of her sleepy stupor soon after.

"Looks like we're hitting some major traffic, guys, so hang in there with the hunger. I will plug an alternate route into the GPS and see what we get," I suggested to them.

Things were going along fine, even though we were in bumper-to-bumper traffic, but there was no other route to take. Keydell played on the iPad, and Ella was blissed out with her music.

Then the iPad battery died.

"Mom, can we stop somewhere and charge the iPad? And I'm really hungry," Keydell asked in frustration. We didn't have the right car charger for that thing.

I was in the middle lane and tried to move to the right in case I found a spot to pull over, but even that was slow going. There wasn't much space on the side of the road anyway.

"I'm working on it but you may have to find something else to do for a bit. This traffic is not moving. Can you read? Do you want to play the alphabet game?"

"No."

"Okay, well, hang in there. I'll get off the road when I can."

He lasted about ten minutes before he got bored. He started bouncing around in the back, making the whole car shake. He started kicking the back of Ella's seat. She tried to ignore him.

"Keydell, please don't kick the seat, buddy, and maybe move behind me so you don't bother Ella," I said.

That was basically a cue to bother Ella. He was bored now, getting hyper, and he wanted out of the car. He started poking Ella on her ears and messing with her headphones.

"Please stop, Keydell. I just want to listen to my music," she shouted.

"Eeeeekkkkk," he screeched at the top of his lungs. I'm sure he was heard by the surrounding travelers, even though their windows were shut to keep the cool air in.

"Del, honey, is that necessary? Let's play a game, sweetie." I could feel myself tighten, knowing he was beyond hope. I was trying to breathe, relax, and keep my voice steady. This was going to be rough if he really got going. There was nowhere to go in this traffic. My hands were gripping and twisting tightly on the steering wheel. He continued to scream and reached for the door to open it. I quickly hit the lock button for all the doors so he couldn't and then locked the windows as well. Why hadn't I locked the child safety lock on the door before we left? How could I forget how fast things could rev up? I was trying to focus on the road and keep him from climbing out of the car, and was basically freaking out inside.

He could hear the doors click to locked position, which ticked him off, so he started lurching forward in between the front seats, poking Ella and me each time, then throwing himself back against the back seat to then propel himself to the front again. He was out of his seatbelt and going nuts. Ella was crying, but being very patient, and just kept adjusting her headphones back on as the yelling and screaming, both mine and Keydell's, escalated. He was constant with his screaming so I had to scream just so he could hear me. Totally pointless. Finally, the next time he lurched forward, I grabbed him with my right hand, under his armpit and held him there. He was being so dangerous.

"Keydell!" I screamed. "I have nowhere to go. I know you are frustrated and hungry but I cannot get out of this traffic."

I could only imagine what the cars next to me saw. They must have thought I was a child abuser. I kind of felt like one at the moment, actually. I had a death grip on his shoulder now, as I tried to keep him still and from hitting us, but could also feel myself wanting to twist his arm off. I was so fucking angry—which meant I was afraid. He would break my grip and then just start all over again with the poking, hitting, kicking, and screaming. It was nuts. Poor Ella was sobbing as she could see how upset I was and how I was manhandling Keydell.

"I'm sorry, Boo, I have to hold him. He's not stopping, and I don't know what to do."

"Just let him go, Mom, you're hurting him. I'm fine. Just pull over when you can," she said with a quiver in her voice. She loved her little brother and could see that I was losing it.

I tried to inch my way over to the side of the road—but, man, it felt like I was treading through cement.

"Fuck," I yelled. I was crying now, too, and just trying to maintain some kind of sanity. I had never been so upset and afraid for our safety. I knew I was holding him too tightly. I had to get a hold of myself. When I let go, he tried breaking the windows. I was so conflicted about how to keep us safe. I was shaking, looking around for a solution and just felt stuck. I felt like the worst mother ever.

I took some deep breaths and tried to calm myself. *Please, Universe, send me a roadside space.*

Sure enough, I noticed a pull-off up ahead that led to what looked like an abandoned diner with a parking lot. It took another ten minutes to get to it, but when I finally was able to get to the off-ramp I tore out and screeched to a halt in a parking spot. We were facing a woodsy lot, and to our left across the pavement was a small ravine below a hill. I stopped the car and looked over at Del.

"I'm going to unlock the doors, Keydell, but please stay nearby, okay? We're not far from the road and I want you to be safe. Run around the car or something," I said.

The second the doors clicked to the unlocked position, he threw his door open and took off toward the ravine. I was too upset to chase him. It didn't look like there was much over there anyway, so I figured he was safe enough. He needed to get some of that energy out, and I needed to breathe.

"I'm so sorry, Ella. That was not one of my finer moments." I burst into tears again, putting my hands over my face in shame.

She came over to comfort me. "Mom, it's fine. He's being an asshole," she blurted out.

I stood, shaking my hands out, trying to get rid of my own negative energy, and walked in circles as I kept an eye out for Keydell. Ella and I walked over toward the ravine, calling his name. I couldn't see him at all. The lot was empty, and the old diner on the property looked decrepit, so no one was around, thankfully. It would have been quite the scene for someone to come upon.

"Keydell," I yelled out. "Where are you? Can you please just yell out so I know where you are?"

Nothing.

"Del," Ella called. "Come this way. Everything is okay."

We walked a little closer and could just see over the wall into the gully of the ravine. Then I noticed Keydell crouching down looking at something. He turned his head and saw us.

"Look," he said, in his calmest and most centered voice. "There's a squirrel over there on the rock. I think he's looking at me."

Ella and I just stood there with our mouths open. Really? A squirrel. He acted as if nothing had happened. He was over it, moving on, and observing the goddamn squirrel. What the hell?

At least we knew he was okay—but were we? I knew I should forgive him, but I didn't want to at all.

He climbed back up the hill and gave me a look, showing me he was the one in control. I wanted to smack him.

After fifteen minutes in the abandoned lot and some laps around the building, we all climbed back into the car.

"Are you feeling better?" I asked Keydell as I started up the Prius.

"I'm hungry."

"Yeah, I bet you are. We all are. Let's go get dinner, try to charge the iPad, and then move on. You have to know though, Del, that what you were doing was scary. I'm sorry I had to grab you so hard, but you were out of control. I can't drive like that."

"Sorry," he said.

That was it. Over. Done. All he had to say. At least he apologized.

Whatever. Moving on. All my strength and desire to work through this issue was gone.

We made it home around 11:30 that night. Keydell did fall asleep after dinner for the rest of the ride, as did Ella. I was wiped out, however.

After we carried Del up to his room, Ella said goodnight, and I fell into Jim's arms and bawled my eyes out. He held me quietly, trying to calm me down, and then pushed me back so he could look at me.

"You okay?"

"Not really," I sobbed. "I don't know how much more I can take. We had such a great time in D.C. but then all hell broke loose in the car. I don't have much left in me."

"What do you want to do?" Jim whispered, as we stood in the bedroom. The air was still sticky from the summer heat, but I felt cold and shivery. I just wanted to go to bed.

"I don't know. I really don't." The table lamps made the light dim and dreamy, and my puffy eyes made it look even more so. I wished this was a dream, but I knew it wasn't. Finally, after a few seconds of silence, I said, "I need to keep looking for more help for him. I've got another appointment with Dr. Martin, but who knows if that will even help. Let's talk in the morning. I can't even think."

I slumped out of his hug, wiped my eyes, and dragged myself to my pillow without even washing my face or unpacking. I really wasn't sure I could keep going with Keydell. I had nothing left. Jim curled up behind me in the bed and spooned me with his big, cozy body. Thank goodness I had him.

Thank goodness I had him.

The next morning, I felt angry. My blood was boiling, my back was tense, and I was stuck in the thoughts of our car ride. Del and I had had a great weekend in D.C., so why did he do that to us? That was my story: he was "doing it to us." I couldn't understand it. He wasn't being punished for anything, and we hadn't said anything to set him off, so he basically was just acting like a spoiled brat. He couldn't get what he wanted when he wanted it, so he flipped out.

I had been so patient over the past two years, so compassionate for his situation. I had supported and loved him as best as I could—and what did he do? He shit on me! That's what it felt like: as if he'd taken me for everything I had, and then taken a big, fat dump on me. He didn't care if we suffered, as long as he got what he wanted. He was happy as long as he was fed, got to soccer, and was left alone. He didn't seem to give even a tiny little shit as to how *we* felt.

This was my story, and I was sticking to it. So much for letting things go.

"Generally speaking, if a human being never shows anger, then I think something's wrong. He's not right in the brain."

—*Dalai Lama*

CHAPTER 22
RELIEF

"Character cannot be developed in ease and quiet. Only through experience of trial and suffering can the soul be strengthened, ambition inspired, and success achieved."

—Helen Keller

According to the Buddha's teachings, our actions can never be divorced from the state of mind from which they spring. What happened after the D.C. trip was not one of my finer moments. Some people, especially from the old-school way of raising kids, may not see it that way—but for me, it was a new low point.

The morning after our return, Keydell was throwing the f-bomb around (wonder where he got that from?), calling me a bitch, and going on for about an hour, all because I asked him to unpack and clean his room. He wanted to play video games instead. Jim was angry, I was still reeling with tension from the car ride, and we both seemed to fuel each other's desire to kick some little Keydell ass.

Have you ever noticed that if you're angry, and someone agrees with you, it kind of gives you permission to act on it? Well, in this case that was just how it was. I was angry at Keydell, Jim was angry at Keydell, and we just went for it.

"Jim, I can't take it anymore," I complained. "I am getting the soap and we are washing his mouth out with it. I'm going hard-core. Fuck it. He needs a good lesson."

When I think back on this, I can't even believe I said that, or wanted to do that. Our friend in Maryland had mentioned, while we were down there, that his parents had done it to him when he swore, and it had honestly sickened me, so why did I think it was okay now?

Well, because I was angry—and anger can be a powerfully negative feeling that puts powerfully negative actions into play.

I grabbed the dish soap and put some on my hand. Then, I grabbed Keydell by the arm and put my hand in his mouth and swiped the soap down his tongue. I was on fire.

"You want to curse at me, Keydell? Keep it up and this is what you will get. I will wash your mouth out until you stop," I screamed at him as Jim came over and held his other arm.

"Fuck you, bitch!" Keydell spit from his foaming mouth. "Fuck you!"

"Okay, you had your chance to stop." And I added more soap to his mouth. He just spit it out in my face, wiggled from our hold, and ran away, cursing back at us with his bulging eyes. He ran out to the side of the house where the garden hose was and tried to rinse his mouth out.

"Oh, no you don't. Not until you show me some respect. I mean really, Keydell. Just stop. I know you don't want this soap in your mouth."

"Oh, I love it. It tastes great," he retorted sarcastically. "Stupid bitch. I hate you guys, I hate you guys and don't want to be here anymore."

He was screaming at the top of his lungs while the soap foamed from his lips. Jim grabbed him again and held him by the shoulders and shook him hard. He looked directly into Keydell's eyes and said in a firm, low, direct tone, "Stop, Keydell, just stop. Settle down or this will continue."

"It's in my eyes, you assholes. It's in my eyes. I can't see," he accused.

"I'm getting more soap," I said.

Keydell was screaming so much that his voice started to get hoarse and raspy. "My throat is burning!" he yelled. "You're killing me."

"Then stop swearing at us, for Christ's sake. Stop calling us names and this will end."

"Fuck you, fuck you, fuck you … and *fuck you!*" He started to cry as I came back out with more soap.

Jim looked at me and said, "Give me that, I'll do it."

Jim grabbed the soap bottle from my hands, but just as he was about to jam it into Keydell's mouth, he stopped. His arm was raised, hovering over Keydell's face. It was as if everything moved in slow motion right then; as if we'd both been hit over the head with a bat, and jolted out of our power trip.

Jim lowered his arm and put the bottle down slowly, still holding Keydell to the ground.

He looked at me and asked, "What are we doing?"

I looked back at him, stunned and in shock at my own behavior. Here was the most caring and kind man I knew—a man who would never hurt anyone—and here I was, the practicing Buddhist. At this moment, neither of us were those things. Or maybe we were, and that's what stopped us.

I took the soap bottle from Jim's hand and chucked it across the yard. "We have to stop. This is not us. God, what *are* we doing?" I collapsed to the ground.

My whole body was shaking, and I could see that Jim and Keydell were, too. There was a weird stillness in the air, filled only with the sound of Keydell choking for air. His throat was dried out from the harsh dish soap, and his lips were white from the lack of moisture. I sat there on the grass next to Jim and Keydell, and started to sob.

What were we doing? How had we allowed Keydell's behavior to affect us in such a horrible way? I'd gotten angry toward him before, but neither one of us had ever hurt him like this. We were literally stripping his throat. I was so ashamed of myself. All the years I'd been practicing kindness, compassion, and patience went down the tubes. Putting soap in Keydell's mouth was not doing anything to teach him: it was just plain abuse. It was fire fueling fire.

In that moment, I understood how parents could end up hurting their children; how episodes get so out of hand that, if the parents don't get themselves under control like we just had, things could go very wrong. I hid my face behind my hands and sat there frozen. Jim released Keydell from his hold, and took him over to the hose to rinse his mouth out.

As I watched the love of my life helping the boy who sucked the life right out of me, I wondered how we were going to recover from all this. How could I get back to square one and be the fun, happy, loving mother I once was for Henry and Ella? How could I find the Kim who was strong, in control, and had compassion and empathy for Keydell? And where had my sense of humor gone?

Jim took our now-calm (or just stunned) little boy up to his room. I stayed on the grass, sobbing out my shame.

After a few minutes Jim came back outside to find me. "He's lying on his bed, resting," he said.

"Of course he is," I said with some sarcasm. "What are we going to do, Jim? I can't even believe what we just did. What *I* just did. I am so sorry I led you down that path."

"Hey, I was out of control, too. Let's just talk to him later and calm down right now. My parents used to wash my mouth out with soap, too; he'll be okay."

"It wasn't just washing his mouth out. I was on some kind of power trip or something. I was afraid he would never stop, or get better, and my fear turned to rage and anger. That's just not right. We were really wound up," I said. "I'm feeling out of control, and his threats toward me are getting scarier. When you're not here— and after Henry leaves for school—I worry that he's going to hurt me or Ella. I can still hold him down, but not for long, Jim, he's going to get big."

"I know, I know." Jim reached for my hand and squeezed it tightly. We sat side by side on the grass. "We can't afford a military school or anything like that, and I don't really want him to go to another Westwood type place."

"God, no. Me, either," I replied. "I'm just getting nervous about his strength. I don't know what to expect, or how long he'll act this way. I don't like how I am acting, either. I'm hitting a breaking point. If this is going to be the way he is, then we are not safe."

I had a rock in my gut. I felt defeated. I was so sad, and I knew Jim was, too. We loved Keydell and wanted him with us, but we were both starting to wonder how to do it. I couldn't risk Ella's safety. She loved Keydell but had taken a lot from him this past year and a half.

Jim and I moved to the lawn chairs to sit quietly in the setting sun, lost in our own thoughts. Henry then came out and crossed the side yard to where we were. During that whole episode he and Ella had locked themselves in their rooms. This kind of upset was so common now that they just had to tune it out and get through it. His tall body stood towering in front of us. He looked at both of us back and forth for a minute and in a low pleading voice said, "Mom, Dad, whatever you do, please don't put him back into the system. Please."

He knew something needed to change, but he couldn't bear to have us send Keydell away. I felt like I was sitting in one of those tiny child-sized chairs with my teacher hovering over me, scolding me. I could tell Henry's heart was breaking.

"God, Henry, we don't want to do that at all." Or did I? I was still shaking thinking about how far we might have gone if we hadn't caught ourselves.

"We need more help, Henry, that's all."

"He will die back out there, Mom. You can't send him away," Henry said with tears in his eyes. I stood up and took him into my arms.

"We aren't going to right now, Hank. Yes, we are depleted, confused, and scared, but for now I can still manage and so can Dad, so we will get through this. We love him, too, and he's been sent away enough already."

I just can't do it, I thought. I just could not send him away. I often wonder where my strength came from, but somehow I found room in my heart for more. Or maybe my heart was telling me I had more. I had to trust.

Jim and I both gave Henry another big hug and we all sat there as the sky turned orange and pink as the day turned into night. The colors shifted ever so gradually, and eventually dimmed to black. Tomorrow, we would start all over again.

Then, music started pumping from the house. It drew the three of us back inside. We followed the beat toward the living room to find Ella and Keydell having a dance party. Ella loved putting on her tunes and just moving around the room. It must have gotten Keydell up from his bed. She was lifting with the grace of a butterfly to the flow of sound, while Keydell was low and heavy with the beat, his feet flat and grounded. His body was relaxed as his arms waved toward the earth; his eyes were closed in full joy.

If he learned to tune his mind as acutely as his body, I thought, *he would be powerful beyond belief.*

I was so proud of Ella for bouncing back and making some fun out of this crazy evening. Nothing could bring her down for too long. I was a lucky girl, even with all that life was bringing at the moment. Everything I needed was right in front of me.

My family. That was all my heart needed.

⊨⊨⊨

End of August 2011

The summer was ending, and we all said our goodbyes to Hank as we dropped him at the airport. He leaned over to Keydell at the last minute and said, "Have a good year at school Little Bro, and go kill 'em on that soccer field. Text me when you have a game and let me know how you do. I will give you a dollar for every goal you get."

Keydell was beaming. He and Henry had practiced a lot this summer, and Keydell was working on those 10,000 hours alone every day as well. He was ready for the fall season. Ella grabbed Keydell's hand in hers as they waved Henry back to college. I gripped Jim's arm and quietly cried behind them. My easy boy was leaving, and my challenging boy was staying.

Did I want it to be different? No. It was just something I noticed.

⊨⊨⊨

September 3, 2011

I stood at the edge of the creek, watching the water flow ever so gently. I was at the Norman Bird Sanctuary, leading a Wabi Sabi retreat with Rachel. Our students were out on their own, reflecting on the lesson from the morning, and I was doing the same. I'd hiked out to the bridge that overlooks a small creek and stopped to look at the water flowing by. It was a beautiful place to find some quiet.

As I edged closer to the shoreline, I noticed two small rocks. They stood side by side with a bit of space between them, but that space was blocked by sticks and leaves which had created a dam. The blockage was tight; what came to mind was the old phrase, "Stuck between a rock and a hard place."

I chuckled to myself. These days, I felt like that damp clump of leaves and sticks. My life had been flowing along, rocking and rolling through the years with a fair amount of ease, but lately, my leaves, sticks and mud (by which I mean my emotions, responses, and actions) were all jammed up. I was being tested by all Keydell put in front of me. Everything he did challenged my patience, my will, my need to control, and my Buddhist practice in general, and I was losing ground. My life was not flowing any more smoothly than that clump of leaves between the rocks. I watched as the water continued to pass around the clump, just as life continued to pass by me, and wondered what it would take to release the dam.

I like to look at nature as my guide. Nature exists with such ease. It ages, it grows, it produces bright color, and then it fades. Trees, wind, sun, air, and water all work together to help each other continue on through each season. It's a beautiful thing to watch the world move though the year with grace.

I wanted a message from nature now, to help me through my "stuckness." *Show me, Mother Nature. Show me how to unblock the dam and have some of that ease and grace.*

It was going to take a mighty storm. The water would have to rush by with enough force to release the jammed bits and allow things to flow freely again. I thought about how sometimes the greatest upsets (storms) are our greatest lessons; when we come out the other side, we gain freedom through the wisdom we have developed through the process. The storm or upset might give you a great beating, but if you can be strong and patient, pay attention, and understand that this, too, will change—if you can, above all, continue to love yourself, and be kind to yourself and others—you will survive.

"What doesn't kill you makes you stronger." Wise words from my father.

I watched the creek flow for a few more minutes, and tried to let go of my need to "fix" Keydell. I needed to trust, and be with the "storm" that Keydell was. Perhaps I needed him in my life in a way I had not realized before. I reminded myself that I had asked for this suffering, and that being tested in this way was an opportunity to grow, gain wisdom, and eventually receive a better understanding of who Keydell was, and who I was.

Learning about others' minds has always been interesting to me—and right now, I was learning about my mind and his. Mine was solid and healthy, but got triggered when I felt imperfect, just like his. His was unhealthy, yet smart, with much more room to grow. We were growing together, and that was what mattered. He truly was a great spiritual teacher for me, and as I acknowledged that, my heart felt softer and more open. I hoped I could keep it there—at least a little bit longer, until the next storm came.

I went home that afternoon and thanked Keydell for being such a pain in my ass. We laughed about that as I explained what I meant.

"I want you to know, Keydell, that I am very sorry for putting all that soap in your mouth. That was not helpful to the situation. I also want you to realize how hard it's been for our family, including you, during your transition here. We are frustrated because we love you and it's hard for us to see you in what seems like a lot of pain. We also don't understand why you do what you do. I personally feel helpless sometimes, and responsible as your parent. I have this need to "fix" you when you are not broken. You are hurting. You are a perfect human being and have a great purpose being here just as you are. I promise to keep trying if you will. Is that a deal?"

Keydell put his hand up with his thumb and pointer finger in a circle inviting me to do the same. We connected and completed the infinity sign with our hands touching, and pulled away, saying, "I love you to infinity and beyond."

We had our appointment with Dr. Martin a few days later, on a Tuesday so it wouldn't interfere with soccer practice. I'm not sure what made me go back to Dr. Martin, because I really didn't believe in my heart that talking to someone was what Keydell needed, but it was all I knew. However, going back to Dr. Martin set in motion a series of events that led to a big breakthrough.

As we waited in the office, I could see that Keydell was not happy to be here.

"Hey, it's okay, buddy," I said to him as he paced around the living room waiting area.

"Just go in and tell him how you've been feeling. It might help you to just get it out and let someone neutral hear you."

"Are you coming in?" he asked.

"I will if you want me to but you know I don't like the part where I have to tattle on you so I want you to say what you want about the past few weeks. Not me, okay?"

"Okay, but I don't want to talk about it."

"Then don't. Talk about something else."

Dr. Martin came out to get us and we went into the familiar room and plopped on the couch. I sat in silence and let Keydell lead, which meant more silence. Dr. Martin then asked me to go wait in the lobby, so off I went (once Keydell gave me a look to say it was okay).

After about five minutes, I heard banging going on in the office. I put my magazine down and tried to listen. Then, I heard Keydell scream.

He came running out to the lobby in a rage.

"What happened?" I asked, standing up to meet him.

"I want to go home," he was visibly upset, versus angry.

"Hey, just tell me what happened."

Dr. Martin slowly and calmly came up behind Keydell and said, "Keydell did not want to calm down, so I asked him to leave. If he cannot stay calm, he cannot come back."

Was he kidding?

Just then, Dr. Martin's cat came walking into the room, and Keydell kicked it. I was so confused at that moment I didn't know who to respond to first. I was angry at Dr. Martin for kicking Keydell out of his office, and angry at Keydell for kicking the cat. What the hell?

I grabbed Keydell by the arm and led him out the door. "I'm sorry about your cat, Dr. Martin, but we are never coming back. Keydell has been kicked out or given away because of his behavior too many times. This is the last thing he needs from a therapist!"

It just wasn't the right fit. He didn't understand what Keydell needed. I felt so protective of my son, and ashamed for the time we'd put him in Westwood. Even though our intention wasn't to kick him out for his behaviors, it must have felt that way.

"Keydell, this isn't working. We're not going back to Dr. Martin. I'm sorry that happened, and I should've trusted my gut on this. I was out of ideas. But damn it, can you not hurt animals? I don't care how mad you are. Don't take it out on an innocent animal."

A voice in my head echoed, *Keydell is the innocent animal.* I was losing it.

We drove home in silence. I guess I just had to live with my innocent tiger, as he was, for a little longer.

Then something magical happened. My cell phone rang. The caller ID read, "Delta Consultants West." It was the therapy office that I'd found on the website for attachment therapy.

Why I bothered to answer the phone, I have no idea. I was fed up with therapists and, at this point, wondered if Keydell would ever go again. It was too painful for him to be rejected again and again.

"Hello, this is Kim," I said as I pulled in our driveway.

"Hi, this is Dr. Vicki Moss from Delta Consultants," said the voice on the other end. "I specialize in working with adopted children and families. I got your message about … Keydell? Did I say that right?"

"Yes, he's our adopted son."

"Sorry to take so long to get back to you. We were away on vacation. Can you tell me a bit about Keydell and what's been going on?"

Keydell had already gotten out of the car and run inside so I gave her our quick history and told her about our situation.

"I'm not sure talk therapy will be what Keydell needs. We haven't had much luck with that so far, but maybe we can come in and you can see what you think." I was surprised by what was coming out of my mouth, but my heart was telling me to stay on the phone and keep talking.

"I work with a lot of adopted families," Vicki said. "We do more than just talk. I would like to meet you guys, at least. Will your whole family be coming in?"

"No, just me and Keydell," I replied. "Most of the issues we have seem to be centered on the two of us."

"Yes, I completely understand," she said. And somehow I knew she did. We scheduled an appointment for two weeks out. It just felt right.

＝⊰┼⊱＝

Dr. Moss's office was about forty-five minutes from our house. Over the bridge and through the woods, to the therapy office we go. I was getting a little loopy. I had to entertain myself on these car rides because Keydell just slept.

We found the office in a long strip mall without any trouble. The lower half of the building had a cool coffee shop called Brewed Awakenings, a name I loved, and thought was perfect for what we were doing. Buddhists say that, when you become enlightened, you have an "awakening" to reality. I needed that—and maybe some good coffee would help, too.

Dr. Moss's office was on the second floor. There was an elevator and a set of stairs—so, of course, Keydell wanted to race to see who would get there first. He took the elevator and I took the stairs. I raced to the top of the stairs and stood right in front of the elevator doors, so when they opened, I startled him. He jumped and screamed with joy. We walked along the outdoor hallway to the Delta Consultants door, and went in. The venetian blinds on the door's window clanked against the glass as it closed behind us.

The waiting room smelled like old wallpaper and looked a bit outdated—nothing like Dr. Romero-Bosch's fancy office. There were a few toys on an end table, the typical magazines, and a plastic table set. Keydell went right for the puzzles and figured out the sliding tile puzzle in about one minute. The kid had brilliant spatial reasoning.

Dr. Moss came out from her office to greet us. She was about sixty years old or so, blond and smart-looking with a straight bob haircut. She spoke with a touch of a Rhode Island accent.

"Hi, Kim, I'm Dr. Moss. You can call me Vicki. Hi, Keydell. How are you?" She said as she leaned toward his kneeling backside. He was still playing with the puzzle at the low table.

"Hi."

"How about we go into my office for a minute and get to know each other?" She encouraged.

"Come on, Del, let's go," I said.

"I want to finish this," he said, without looking at us. I had mixed up the puzzle again for him.

"You solved it once, and we can do it again after our visit, okay? Let's go now."

"Fine." He tossed the game onto the table.

Vicki's office was like a big living room with the typical layout of a therapist's office (I had seen a few now). There was the couch, and then two single chairs, one for the therapist. She had a desk on the other side of the room with a lamp and writing accessories, and a bookshelf filled with what looked like kids' books. There was a lot of natural light from the three windows along the side wall.

Keydell walked around, touching and looking at everything, taking it all in.

I sat on the couch, watching him to make sure he was careful. Dr. Moss asked Keydell where he wanted to sit. I liked that.

"I can sit anywhere?" he asked as he sat on the floor to see if that was okay.

"Well, I would like you to sit with your mom, but today you get to choose." She explained to me that he would sit right next to me for most of the sessions as a way to encourage bonding.

He gave a manic smile, jumped up off the floor, and sat next to me at the edge of the couch. He immediately picked up a plastic bird toy, the kind that you balanced on your finger so it looked like it was flying. He was moving in spurts and fits, so I could tell he was nervous or agitated. He was keeping his mind busy so he wouldn't have to face yet another therapist.

We began chatting, getting to know each other, but Dr. Moss didn't ask about his behavior or anything threatening. She said she would talk with us both for a few minutes and then we would take turns being with her alone. That seemed to be the norm, but never had a doctor talked to me alone, just Keydell. I liked this idea because I wouldn't have to talk about his bad behaviors in front of him like before.

Dr. Moss looked at Keydell and asked him a personal question. I don't remember what it was exactly but he turned toward the back of the couch and started doing a headstand on the seat cushion. He was basically sticking his rear end in the air with his head down.

"Keydell, honey, turn around please. That's not a polite way to sit and Dr. Moss would like an answer to her question," I said as I touched his shoulder to prod him to turn back around.

"I can answer from here," he said.

"Yes, you can but again, it's not very polite the way you are sitting right now. Can you please turn around?"

All of a sudden, he leaped up and ran over to the desk on the other side of the room.

"What is this?" he asked as he started picking things up off the desk. He kept doing that to avoid any more questions.

Vicki said, "Keydell, you can stand while we talk but please don't play with the things on the desk. Those are my work things."

He completely ignored her and threw a pencil across the room. Then in one quick movement he knocked over the lamp. I jumped up to grab him as the light crashed to the floor.

"This is what he does," I said. "He just all of a sudden goes into these fits."

Vicki was very calm and just said, "Keydell, come sit down please. We don't have to talk but you need to calm down."

Again he ignored her. He was rolling on the floor now as I stood over him, waiting for some guidance. I was not sure what to do. I let things unfold without intervening so she could see what happens. It was easier than explaining it.

Keydell looked up at me in that moment and screamed bloody murder, wide mouth, bulging eyes and all. He tried to kick my feet from his laying down position so I jumped out of the way. He sat up and tried to grab my legs.

"Keydell, please stop," I implored. "We're just talking sweetie. There is nothing to get upset about right now." I tried to go in for the hug-and-hold method of calming him.

He was gone, though. He was in that weird place, and I knew it.

"Dr. Moss, what should I do? This is where I need help. I don't know what to do when he gets like this, and it's so hard to deal with." I could feel the tears building and the lump in my throat hardening.

"You're doing fine," she said. "He's what we call dysregulated right now. You can't do a whole lot of talking when he's in this kind of state. They are not themselves."

"Yeah, I've noticed—but what *can* I do? He gets like this all the time, and it is getting to be too much," I responded, corralling him away from her desk. He'd broken away from me. He was getting so much stronger.

Vicki could see that Keydell was really getting violent so she told me she was going to get her husband for some help. He was in the next office.

Keydell was screaming and trying to find other things to throw. As soon as Vicki opened the office door, though, Keydell got up and bolted for the exit. Vicki didn't even get a chance to leave the room to get her husband.

"Whoa," she said. "Keydell you need to slow down. Come back here." But he was already out of her office and through the main door we'd come in.

"I'm not going to chase him," I said. "He runs off a lot, but doesn't go far."

I explained how he'd had a violent meltdown at our last therapist's office and gotten kicked out because of it. "He told me Keydell could not come back until he could behave in the office," I said in disgust.

"Well, no wonder then," Vicki said. "He's testing me. He wants to know if I'm going to kick him out if he acts this way." She was so calm about it.

"Oh, I didn't even think of that," I said. "It makes so much sense though. What should we do now?"

Just as I asked that, Vicki's husband, Dr. Bob Raphael, came out from his office to see what was going on. Then Keydell came blasting back into the office and slammed the door behind him. He turned away from us, toward the door, and started plucking the blinds trying to break one of the slats off.

"Keydell," I said "Anything else you break, we have to fix and pay for so please help me out here and stop doing that. I love you, bud, and really need you to calm down."

Vicki reassured him, too, saying, "Keydell, I know you are upset but I want you to come back in the office." She was not asking us to leave.

"What should I do Dr. Moss? Should I carry him back to the office, or just leave him here? Should we go and come back another time?" Just then I noticed another mother and child in the waiting room watching the whole thing. *Great. This is either really familiar to them, or it's scaring them to death,* I thought.

"Just keep talking calmly. You're doing a really good job. You've stayed calm and you are telling him you love him. That is very important," she said.

It made me feel good to know I was doing something right, because honestly I had lost faith in myself.

"Keydell, we still have some time in our session, so let's go back and finish," Vicki said to Keydell.

He looked at her and as if it was a last test and screamed at the top of his lungs at her; just a plain old ear-piercing scream. I could see he was getting tired. He'd slid to the ground with his back to the door and was panting like a dog. His eyes were wild and staring, darting between all of us. He'd probably been running around outside before returning. I was hoping he was processing her words and that he realized he was not going to be asked to leave. No matter what he did, we were all there for him.

"Do you want to stay out here while I talk to your mom for a bit?" she asked. "You can do your puzzle with Dr. Bob. This is Dr. Bob right here." She quickly pointed him out to us and I gave him a quick smile.

Keydell didn't say anything but got up and went over to the puzzle table, stomping his feet the whole way to show us that this was his decision. Vicki and I went back to her office as Dr. Bob stayed with Keydell. I hoped the other clients out there would survive.

"Are you sure this is okay?" I asked as I collapsed back on her couch.

"Bob is out there with him, and he's great with the boys. It's fine." She walked to her desk and got things back in order.

"He should work off the money to pay for the lamp," she said.

"Oh, I know," I agreed. "The hard part is getting him to do anything. Anything we ask of him that looks like punishment for something turns into a two-hour rage. My older kids never did that. We barely had to punish them, so this is crazy. I was raised with taking responsibility for my actions and mistakes, but he just doesn't get it. Once he's done with his mean or angry act, it's over in his mind. Done. Moved on."

"He needs natural consequences," she said.

I didn't quite understand what she meant by that, but I was too tired to go into it.

"He doesn't seem to have a guilty conscience at all, or any feelings about how his actions affect others. He often asks why we care what he does. He doesn't seem to care how or if he hurts me while he is in this 'dysregulated' state you just mentioned, yet when he comes out of his state he is upset, like he's sorry. No one has been able to help me find tools to work with him on this."

"Does he get this violent often?" she asked.

"Yes, maybe two or three times a week lately. We can go for longer periods, but the past few months it's been more often."

"Well, here's what we'll do, Kim. We will work on a lot of bonding exercises. Keydell may be suffering from attachment disorder," Dr. Moss explained.

Did she just say that? Had I really found someone who works with kids with attachment disorder? Woot-woot!! I wanted to cheer out loud. The website information was for real!

"Attachment disorder is complicated, and can have varying degrees of seriousness," she said. "Because of the neglect he experienced as an infant, his brain may not have developed properly, and he has remained in fight-or-flight mode essentially."

Whoo-hoooo! I was dancing inside, hearing this. *I knew it! I knew it! It isn't his fault. He is a good kid.*

Dr. Moss continued, "If the child is neglected, moves from caregiver to caregiver, or has other similar traumas, they don't feel safe or trust adults to take care of them. They don't form a good relationship with the mother or caregiver, and so feel separate and disconnected. They essentially don't have normal bonding with them. This can lead to confusion, frustration, anger and even violence. Sound familiar?"

"Oh, yeah." I nodded my head vigorously. I can't even explain how this was making me feel.

"He needs to bond more with you so that he can develop a normal connection, feel safe, and know that you are there for him no matter what," she explained.

"That sounds really good," I wanted to cry with relief. "It makes a lot of sense. I love him so much and want to have a better mother/son bond with him. What kind of exercises will we be doing?"

God, I was excited. This was something. This was really something.

"Well, some doctors consider the exercises controversial, but I've found them to be very successful. For example, I want you to spoon-feed him, sing lots of nursery rhymes at bedtime while rubbing his back, watch Disney movies together on the couch that have good themes and messages in them, and spend as much time as you can looking into his eyes and cuddling."

"I do the singing thing, but I never thought about spoon-feeding him and focusing on eye contact. I'm not sure he will go for that!" I said, skewing my face in wonder. I was reminded of the staring exercise we did at Kripalu with Jack Kornfield. Maybe it would make Keydell feel seen and acknowledged.

It seemed kind of silly, but I was up for anything at this point. I realized, too, that when Henry and Ella were little, Disney films were a big part of their lives. They both loved them, knew the songs, and always danced along, even the millionth time we watched them. With the amount of energy Keydell had, though, he really didn't watch much TV.

"While you're in your visits with me, we're going to have you sit closely on the couch together while you read some books to him. The stories have themes on dealing with your anger, making friends, or being helpful around the house."

"Well, hopefully he will sit with me like that," I said. "You saw how he is. Once he decides he's done, he's done."

Vicki then said, "I think he felt threatened, and that will send him into that fight-or-flight mode. He will enjoy the books because as we read, we will casually pause and talk about the theme in a more objective way, versus making him feel attacked."

I really liked Vicki's methods, and was ready to try some of these new things with Keydell.

It had been pretty quiet out in the waiting area so I was guessing he had calmed down. These guys were good. They seemed to completely understand what we were dealing with, and had actual concrete tools and experience to help us. *Whew.*

It was time to go. "Thank you, Vicki. I'm sorry about your lamp and the whole meltdown. I will, of course, replace the lamp. Hopefully our next session will be better."

It was. He never acted up that way again with her.

I didn't say too much on the way home, just let us both settle down. I wanted so badly to talk about the lamp, but I knew from past experience that it was not the time. I didn't want another ride of screaming. I'm such a control freak sometimes, though, and I wanted to figure out and fix things right away. I'd recently read a quote by Pema Chodron, a Buddhist nun who said, "I equate ego with trying to figure everything out instead of going with the flow. That closes your heart and your mind to the person or situation that's right in front of you, and you miss so much."

I'd been trying for two years to fix and figure things out, so maybe now it was time to let go of my ego and finally just open my heart. Let him fix himself.

I was lost in my own thoughts, trying to grasp the idea of natural consequences for his actions. It seemed in line with going with the flow and letting things unfold naturally. Did she mean that he would see from others what happens when he did something bad, versus receiving punishment from us? That was what had happened with the whole soccer ref incident, I suppose; I would have to wait and see on that one, but he was going to work off the expense of that damn lamp. I had plenty of chores for him.

Patience. Patience.

Keydell, too, was quiet all the way home. He fell asleep, of course. I was grateful for the quiet, and invited my body to relax and drive with ease. I was shaking from the experience, as I always did, but now it was time to chill.

That night at bedtime I did my normal reading to him and made sure to cuddle in tight. Then I gave him an extra-long back scratch and sang some new nursery rhymes to him, inserting his name in the song where I could. Instead of singing "Baby Beluga in the deep blue sea," I sang, "Baby Keydelly in the deep blue sea, swims so wild and he swims so free ..." Henry and Ella had loved that, too.

I started thinking about all the things he must have missed as a young boy. He probably never bathed with his mother as an infant, hence his curiosity around my body. He probably hadn't been fed much by his mother, and either did it himself or got help from his brother. Sue told me he had been colicky; I bet she just let him cry it out instead of trying to soothe him. Ella was also colicky, so I knew what that was like. We were constantly holding her, bouncing her and swinging her, trying to calm her down.

Just before he fell asleep that night, I asked him to roll over so I could talk to him. I wanted to look at his face.

"Sweetie, I know that today was hard, but do you think we can go back? I really like Dr. Vicki and Dr. Bob, and I think they understand what's going on. This is the first time I have felt like someone can help us. They were very patient and kind today, and that felt hopeful to me—and hopefully to you, too."

He seemed to be reading my new light-heartedness on my face as much as hearing my words. He replied, "I'll go back."

I gave him a big hug, and told him I loved him and was proud of him.

Then I looked right into his big brown eyes and said a line from the book "The Help" that I always loved. "You is kind, you is smart, and you is important."

He watched me as I explained. "When I look at you, I see a smart, funny, energetic boy with curious, open eyes that are like pools of chocolate" I acted like I was going to eat those chocolate eyes. *Nibble, nibble, nibble.*

"I see beautiful skin so young and smooth and soft. I see perfectly shaped lips that are pink and full. People pay big money for lips like that," I laughed.

"I see a boy who I know wants to be happy—and I hope you see a mommy who wants to help you get there."

"I do," he said. "And you have a mole on your cheek that looks like a bug."

I cracked up. Straight from the mouth of a babe.

We just stared at each other for a few seconds more. We were bonding. I kissed him goodnight on his forehead, wishing I had known him as a baby. He was so innocent, even now, but as a baby I could have made him feel safe, and given him all the attention he deserved. I could have played and nibbled on his toes, blown bubbles on his tummy, and held him close for hours. Every child deserves that.

I felt an ache in my heart for his birth mother. Sue had tried her best, and knew it was not enough for him. She must miss him terribly now.

CHAPTER 23

HOPE

"It is better to conquer yourself than to win a thousand battles. Then the victory is yours. It cannot be taken from you, not by angels or by demons, heaven or hell."

—*Buddha*

The morning after our first visit with Dr. Moss, I decided to try spoon-feeding with Keydell. He'd just made some oatmeal in the microwave and we were alone in the kitchen, so I thought I'd give it a shot.

"Hey, Keydell, can I feed you like I used to do for Henry and Ella when they were babies? I never got to do that with you."

I wasn't sure what his reaction would be. He paused at his seat, looked at me for a few seconds, and then his face broke into a big grin.

"Really?" He said it with excitement, and not a pre-teen "Are you nuts, Mom?" look.

"Yeah, I mean just for a spoonful or two." I leaned in to make more of a physical connection with him.

"Okay," he shrugged and handed me the baby spoon that he liked to use all the time. I noticed the irony in that.

He liked mini things, in general. I scooched around in my chair to his side of the table, filled the spoon with the oatmeal, and looked him right in the eyes like Dr. Moss had suggested.

"Down the shootie." I said as I lowered the spoon into his open bird mouth.

We both began to giggle, which made him spit some of the oatmeal out through his nose. Then we lost it. We both started cracking up as he asked me to do it again.

I'll be damned, I thought with joy in my heart. *He is loving this.*

I fed him a couple more bites as we laughed and looked at each other. He then fed me a couple of times, pretending to be the parent. This really was a great bonding moment. I got the greatest feeling of hope that just maybe we were going to make some real progress with this new therapist. It was nice to see Keydell having fun in relationship with me. We'd had lots of fun together before, but nothing quite this intimate.

"Thank you, Keydell," I said sincerely. "It made Mommy feel really good to be able to feed you like a baby, even though I know you're not one any more. I missed that part of your life and would've really loved knowing you then. So thank you, thank you." I leaned in for a very quick hug that was tensely returned.

Baby steps.

End of September, 2011

Keydell's birthday was coming up soon, and we wanted to get him a new bike. He'd been riding around on an old stunt bike that Henry had used for years, and it was getting too small for him. We found a good one and gave it to him early so he'd have more time to ride it before it got too cold. He loved riding around the neighborhood with me, and down to the airport. He never minded wearing a helmet, like some kids, and I didn't even have to remind him to put it on. Maybe it felt like a uniform for bike riding. He loved his bike and he knew we loved watching him enjoy it—so, sadly, one day he used it to try to push my buttons. Or maybe he felt he didn't deserve it.

Del got upset the week after we'd been to Dr. Moss', but I remained calm. In fact, I was maintaining my cool so much that he didn't like it. He needed to step up his game, so he tried to do something that would upset me. He stormed outside, yelling, "I am running away on my bike!"

He was getting smarter. He would've actually been able to get further on a bike, and worry me more. I followed him out the door to keep an eye on him

Just as I got around the side of the house, I heard a screech.

Oh, my God, I thought. *He's been hit.*

Keydell was standing at the end of the driveway at the road, not hurt, but with his arms limp at his sides. He was staring at the road, stunned. He turned around and began to run up the driveway toward me. Following him was a very large, angry, hairy man.

I grabbed Keydell and held him close to me, watching the man carefully.

"He just rolled his bike out into the middle of the road! I thought there was a kid on it," the guy screamed. His face was red, his fists were clenched, and I could tell he was really scared.

"Sir, I'm so sorry. He didn't mean to frighten you."

Keydell was the one who was frightened now. This guy was on fire.

"Are you okay?" I asked him.

"Your kid almost made us have an accident," he yelled again as he moved toward us. "What are you going to do about it? He needs a good punishment!"

"Yes, I'm so sorry. I can see how upset you are, and you have every right," I placated him. "Please understand, sir. He was angry at me and made a mistake. Please forgive him. We'll take care of this so, please, just go back to your car."

I was shaking but tried my best to speak calmly. I knew that if I acted aggressively, it would only fuel his anger. I was doing okay, and I could see him starting to calm down.

Keydell was clinging to my side. I think he thought the guy was going to punch him. I was glad he felt safe with me. Bonding.

The man stared at us as if thinking about what to do next. I had acknowledged his anger/fear and I was not fighting back, so he had nothing to push up against. His fists were loosening and he turned to go back to the car.

"Again, I am sorry, sir," I repeated as he drove away.

Anger really does come from a place of fear.

After the man and woman drove off, I looked down at Keydell and plucked his fingernails out of my leg.

"So, Del," I began. "How was that for you? Can you see now what I mean by your actions having an effect on others?"

He shook his head yes.

And there it was: a natural consequence. It was just what Dr. Moss had talked about! I can't make this stuff up.

I didn't need to do anything else in that moment. We got the bike from out of the road and wheeled it back to the garage, where I think it stayed for a couple of weeks until Keydell decided for himself that his punishment was over.

I was excited for our next visit with Dr. Moss a week later, and for once not dreading the therapy. Keydell and I arrived a little early, so we stopped in at the Brewed Awakenings coffee shop. He asked for a big piece of lemon pound cake but that would only spin his sugar levels out of control, so I told him we could get that after our visit if he could try to sit nicely during therapy. Once upon a time, I had vowed never to bribe my kids with food—but here I was. Oh, well. He settled on lemonade for the time being.

We finished our drinks and raced again up the elevator and stairs, but this time Keydell took the stairs so he could "scare" me. When he reached the top, he jumped in front of the elevator doors, poised for the attack. The doors opened, but I had hidden off to the side so he couldn't see me. The elevator looked empty. I could hear him say, "Hey, where did she go?" and I jumped out and grabbed him. He screamed with delight and ran the rest of the way down the outdoor hallway to the office.

Once inside, he bolted right for the tile puzzle game. I sat next to him, in awe of his skills as he solved it in less than a minute. He handed it to me so I could mix it up again as we waited for Dr. Moss.

"You are unbelievable, Del. So smart," I said, meaning it.

Dr. Moss came into the waiting room, and finished up with another mom and child before motioning for us to follow her into the office where all hell had broken loose last week. I felt like I should smudge the room with sage to cleanse it of all the negative energy we'd left behind. I laughed as I pictured myself walking around with a big bone of sage, smoking the place out while everyone coughed.

I sat down on the couch as Dr. Moss reminded Keydell to sit next to me. She didn't mention last week's visit, which was awesome. No need to rehash that, and it put Keydell at ease to not have to talk about it. She didn't ask him to tell her about his feelings, but went right over to her bookshelf and pulled down a book called *Don't Pop your Cork on Mondays* by Adolph Moser. It had a great illustration by Dav Pilkey on the cover, an image of a boy with clenched fists and a big cork-bottle head that was about to blow. Dr. Moss asked Keydell if he would like to read to me, or whether I should read to him; we decided to take turns for each page.

"It happens every day: some people come unstrung. They pop their corks, they start to yell, and they begin to act like animals," we read. The illustrations showed monkeys, lions and other animals losing their cool. We read how some don't lose their cool, but bury their heads in the sand instead. Keydell was enjoying the story and pictures.

Dr. Moss asked, "Do you understand what stress is, Keydell?"

"Kind of," Keydell answered.

"Well, let's keep reading, and see if we can get some clarity around what it is and see how this little boy deals with his." I loved how we were examining the book's characters and not Keydell himself. By doing this, I thought, he would connect or learn to feel sympathetic toward the characters and what they were going through in the story. Keydell might relate and not feel alone or separated from others around him. One of the pages even warned that, if an adult's stress turns to violence, you should back off. I never hit Keydell, but I sure wished he had backed off a few times when I was stressing out. In the story, the boy learned to handle his stress by dancing or exercising with friends and family, and taking deep breaths to calm down so that he felt better.

This was such a wonderful way to ease into our therapy sessions. Keydell was having fun; it didn't feel like the other therapy we had been to, so he relaxed and opened up more. Dr. Moss had us stop on certain pages, and ask Keydell what he thought about what was happening. With all of our pauses and discussions, the reading took up most of our half hour—but it was a fun half an hour.

After we finished the book, Keydell asked, "Can we read it again?"

We read through the book again, a little quicker this time, as we continued to cuddle on the couch. Dr. Moss asked Keydell what sorts of things made him feel stressed. He talked about losing his pencils, and forgetting to do his homework and only remembering it at the last minute. It seemed so small to me—but obviously it was big to this ten-year-old.

We met with Dr. Moss one more time before school started. Once school started, I had to pick him up about twenty minutes early to make it to our appointments on time, which stressed him out. He hated missing school, but it was the best appointment time for our overall schedules. Our sessions continued to be peaceful, but at home, things were still on fire. It was fall, after all, and therefore one of the worst times of the year for Keydell's mood. He was having fit after fit, impulsively ripping up homework if he didn't like it or understand it, throwing his game controller around if he lost his video game, and continuing to drag me into his fits by swearing at me and then wanting forgiveness.

In early October, I asked Dr. Moss if I could speak with her on my own.

"Keydell, I'm going to have you sit with Dr. Bob for a few minutes while I talk with your Mom some more," Dr. Moss said, after Keydell and I read a book about adoption together. "You remember him from the first time you came here right? His office is right next to mine."

"Okay, can I play with the puzzles?"

"Well, I'll let you ask Dr. Bob."

Vicki went to get her husband as Keydell and I sat waiting. I noticed she'd put the new lampshade on that we replaced. She came back in after a minute or two, followed by Dr. Bob.

I noticed this time, since things were calmer than last time, how friendly and handsome he was. I remembered his calming presence.

"Hey! I hear there's a guy named Keydell in here who likes puzzles," he said as he came in and pretended to look around the room for Keydell.

"Kim, this is Dr. Bob Raphael, my husband."

"Hi Dr. Raphael. I remember you from our first visit. How are you? I'm sure you remember Keydell," I winked at him. How could he forget?

Dr. Raphael put his hand out to shake Keydell's and I was proud to see Keydell grab it and give a firm shake back.

"Oh, great handshake!" Dr. Bob said as he vigorously shook Keydell's hand up and down, just long enough to make it comical.

Keydell was laughing. I loved this guy.

"I hope you're feeling smart, Dr. Bob," I warned him. "Keydell's good at those puzzles, and he will keep you on your toes if you play a game." He smiled and guided Keydell out to his office as Vicki and I sat back down.

"So how has it been at home, Kim? And how are you holding up?" Dr. Moss asked me. It was nice to get a bit of my own therapy here.

"I've been doing the bonding exercises," I said with some confidence. "I did the spoon-feeding you suggested, and he loved it. I've been making sure to cuddle in really close with him when we read or watch cartoons, and I even held him like a baby once and rocked him back and forth. He's only sixty-five pounds, so he wasn't too heavy." I laughed. "While I was doing that, he looked in my eyes like Henry and Ella used to do, and started sucking his thumb."

It happened very organically one evening on the couch. Keydell sat down and I playfully grabbed him for a big hug and started talking to him in a baby voice while rocking him back and forth. I said, "Oh, what a cute wittle baby I have. Mommy loves you." It was silly and lasted about five seconds, but he went along with it.

"Oh and then, you won't believe this, but I think I now understand what you mean by natural consequences." I proceeded to tell her the story about the bike incident.

"Well, first of all," she said after hearing the whole story, "you were good to stay calm. The more Keydell sees that, the more he will learn from you. Also he saw how anger looks on someone else and how it could have affected you both negatively. Great example for him."

"The biggest issue we still have is the violence and the outbursts," I explained. "I love what we are doing here for the bonding, but he just can't stay in control. What you saw in your office a few weeks ago happens almost every other day at home. It's extremely frustrating."

Dr. Moss was nodding her head, understanding just what I was talking about. This was obviously not her first time hearing a story like this.

Vicki had already added helpful parenting tools to my toolbox, but Keydell was still so reactive to the smallest things. Today, though, she threw me the best hammer, screwdriver, wrench, and saw ever—all at once.

"Kim, have you heard of neurofeedback?"

Oh, there was that word again. Neurofeedback. I felt excitement bubble up in my chest, although I didn't know why.

"Kind of," I replied. "I have an adult friend who grew up in the foster care system, and he mentioned he'd done neurofeedback. Why do you ask?"

"Well, I think Keydell would be a good candidate for it. Based on how he was at the first visit, and what you've told me about his behaviors at home, I think he will really benefit from it."

I was stunned, trying to process all that was being said. I had so many questions, and was feeling really excited about a treatment that could help him with his control.

"Wait, do you do that here? What is neurofeedback anyway? Oh, my God, I'm really excited for some reason."

Vicki smiled at me and replied, "Bob does it in the office next door. We have found it to be very helpful with kids who have ADHD, attachment disorder, or anxiety, and even kids with autism. We actually had an autistic patient who didn't speak his whole childhood. After about six months of neurofeedback, he began talking."

"What, are you kidding me? That's amazing. Why don't I know more about this?"

"We just started doing it here last year. It is a fairly new therapy for children who have attachment disorder, ADHD, or depression. I'll ask Bob to come in and tell you about it before you decide if it's right for Keydell. He will give you all the details. Insurance does not always cover it, though, because it's considered 'alternative therapy.'"

Of course it was. Every treatment I had ever done that actually helped me was considered "alternative" therapy. I had used acupuncture to help my hip and elbow joints heal, and massage for back pain. Neither was covered by insurance, yet both worked better than any drug.

"So what happens next?" I asked, practically jumping out of my seat, ready to take action. I wasted no time.

"I'll see how Dr. Bob and Keydell are doing, and get them back in here so we can talk."

When Keydell came back in, he was happy and bouncy. Dr. Bob was good. Neither Dr. Moss nor Dr. Bob talked about how "bad" Keydell was. They knew what he was dealing with, and that it wasn't his fault. Now, he was going to get some help for it. God, this was exciting.

Dr. Bob sat in the chair across from me, and Keydell sat back on the couch.

"Bob, can you explain neurofeedback to Kim?" Vicki asked.

"Sure. To put it simply parts of Keydell's brain may be over- or under-active due to some very early developmental issues, most likely caused from his childhood traumas of neglect and frequent moves from caregiver to caregiver. If you decide you would like to do neurofeedback, we would like Keydell to have a QEEG, a Quantitative Electroencephalogram. This is a trace of his brain waves over his entire cerebrum, the outer layer of his brain. The results will be compared to thousands of others in the database.

Then, we will have a better idea of what frequencies to look at and the best strategy to implement the changes we are looking for. I have a pretty good idea right now, based on his history and behaviors and my own experience of working with kids like Keydell. When we start, the goal will be to re-regulate, to bring his particular brain waves to a less agitated state."

I *knew* it! His brain was the issue, not who he was as a person. It was a physical issue, not a spiritual one.

"I just knew there was something going on in that head of his." I said. I had so many questions, but was ready to start this second. Keydell was listening quietly, too.

Bob continued, "I will sit with Keydell during the therapy and monitor his brain activity while he plays a game or watches a movie."

Keydell was smiling now. He liked this idea. "I get to play a game?" he asked. "A video game? That's my therapy?"

"Yep," Bob answered. "You will have electrodes pasted onto your head, probably one or two on your temples, and we will be able to see your brain waves on my monitor. As you play and your brain waves change, I can adjust the degree of difficulty of the game to give you more or less feedback. The more feedback you get, the better the game will play. It is something like going to an exercise class for your brain: the more you do, the easier it gets."

This all sounded so cool. Keydell wanted to start immediately. What was so exciting for me was that it reminded me of meditation. When I meditated, I practiced calming my mind and concentrating, and that sounded just like what Keydell would be doing. I loved this. We would be doing the same thing with our brains—him through science, and me through my mindfulness practice.

How freakin' cool was that?

"Are the results permanent? How long will we have to do this, and how often? Are there side effects?" I asked. Yep, lots of questions. And since this was his brain we were talking about, I wanted to be sure it was safe.

"Essentially, we will be gently shifting his brain waves toward a more regulated state. This will reduce his over-arousal and decrease his tendencies toward impulsivity and agitation. The feedback helps create a pathway back to the original ratios between brain waves that were disrupted by his early trauma. There is no electrical energy going into his brain; all we are doing is monitoring and providing feedback. Side effects are minimal to non-existent. He might become sleepy during or after a session. There are reports of some clients experiencing headaches, but they are rare."

Dr. Bob continued, "This is not a 'quick fix.' At first, I want to see him twice a week for several weeks. The sessions will get longer as we proceed until they are about forty-five minutes long. You will be providing me with feedback regarding his behaviors following each session, so I can make any necessary adjustments as to where and at what frequency we are working. The positive effects tend to be cumulative."

I was out-of-my-mind curious, fascinated, excited, and hopeful for Keydell. This could be big for him, and my homework would allow me to report the bad *and* good behaviors. Dr. Bob explained that, of course Keydell, would mature and continue to develop physically, and we could not predict what challenges he might encounter in the future, but he thought we would see a greater ability to control his impulses.

Dr. Bob continued explaining the challenges. "One major difficulty will be identifying events that *do not* occur. What I mean is, it is difficult to notice when something *doesn't* happen. For example, you have learned how to navigate many of Keydell's triggers, but there are many you cannot. When you say 'no,' he is going to be disappointed; when his schedule changes unexpectedly, you know that a negative reaction is imminent. When that does not happen, or when it occurs with less intensity, those are the times you need to notice. By doing your homework, you will have a better handle on those changes."

Dr. Bob got Keydell's full attention and told him, "Keydell, this will be your work to do. This will not be your Mom and Dad doing it, or me, or Dr. Moss. This will be *all you*. You will get your scan done, and then you will come back to my office and get started. Do you think you can do that?"

"Yes," Keydell answered. "What games do you have? Do you have the movie *Clone Wars*?" He was smiling and as excited, as I was. He thought this was going to be fun.

Vicki said, "I'm going to set up an appointment at the Neuro Development Center in Providence for the QEEG. As soon as we get the results, we can start."

"Keydell, do you understand what we are going to do here?" I asked him. "It's going to involve a lot of time for the first few months, but wouldn't it be great if it helped you?"

I could see Keydell thinking.

I continued, "I will try very hard to not have it interfere with soccer or school but we may have a couple times when it will."

He was still thinking and we all gave him some time. Then he finally said,

"I play a lot of video games at home anyway and that takes up time, so this will just be the same thing." We all laughed at his practicality. I also truly believe he wanted to get better.

"You know what, Keydell, that is a great way to look at it," I said as I gave him a quick hug. "Will we still do the talk therapy Dr. Moss?"

"The neurofeedback only takes about forty-five minutes from setup to finish, so once a week you and Keydell can talk with me for the first fifteen minutes of our sessions. Then, Keydell can go with Bob, and you and I can continue to talk. You might benefit from some therapy of your own," she said with a smile. I agreed. "On the other days, he can just come in for the neurofeedback."

Well, I cannot lie. I was excited. I was so encouraged leaving their office that day, mainly because I had seen the changes in my own way of thinking through my meditation practice, and the neurofeedback seemed similar—but quicker, and something Keydell could actually have fun with. And, he would be doing it for himself. His healing wouldn't come from me, from drugs, or from a therapist. He would be working on healing himself. If he learned or practiced working with his mind like I had been doing, perhaps he could find some peace in that head of his. This gave me a jolt of encouragement to carry on. My heart, which had felt like the clump of leaves and sticks wedged between those rocks at the Norman Bird Sanctuary, was finally loosening.

Keydell and I went downstairs after our appointment, and we both had a very large piece of that lemon pound cake. I tasted every bite like it was the first time I had eaten something sweet. I couldn't wait to get home and tell Jim about neurofeedback. My mind was spinning.

CHAPTER 24

SELF

*"The bodhisattva is like the mightiest of warriors
But his enemies are not common foes of flesh and bone.
His fight is with the inner delusions,
The afflictions of selfishness and ego-grasping...
He is the real hero, calmly facing any hardship
In order to bring peace, happiness, and liberation into the
world."*

—*The 13th Dalai Lama (1876-1933)*

Early November, 2011

The Neuro Development Center in Providence was big, modern, and busy. The scan only took about an hour, and Keydell told me it was painless and relaxing. Not surprisingly, he fell asleep during it. The following week, when Dr. Bob got the results, we started Keydell's treatments. His scan showed excessive beta waves and transient slow waves in the frontal lobe. This gave Dr. Bob an indication of where and how to start.

It was November 16, 2011. Keydell was days away from turning eleven, and it had been almost two and a half years since he had moved in with us.

I was very curious about how the neurofeedback worked, so asked if I could watch the first session. I had read once that our brains have neuroplasticity, which means they have the capacity to change even throughout adulthood. The brain can reorganize itself and create new neural pathways to adapt as needed. Neurofeedback helps the brain develop more efficiency in how neurons fire by giving it "feedback"—like an audible or visual signal—that encourages the brain to reset or self-correct. I couldn't wait to see this process in action.

Dr. Bob said, as he sat Keydell down in a comfortable leather chair in front of a monitor and placed an electrode on his head, "I'm glad you wear your hair short, Keydell. It makes it easier to put these on your head."

Keydell laughed and asked what would happen if his hair were longer.

"Your tight curls would push the sensors off," Dr. Bob answered. "They are only stuck on with a little bit of paste."

He placed one on each ear, and one on his right temple.

"What do the electrodes do?" I asked Dr. Bob.

"These will send information to my monitor as Keydell is playing the video game. I will be able to see his brain activity."

"So there's no input going into his brain, it's just outputting information to you?" I asked.

"That's correct," he said. Then he sat down at his monitor, just behind Keydell over his left shoulder, as Keydell faced his game. It was a spaceship race game. As Keydell played, Dr. Bob watched his monitor. The computer program would beep whenever Keydell's brain waves were within the parameters Dr. Bob had set. When his brain waves strayed from the desired profile, the beeps stopped, and the game slowed or stopped. The reward elements were the beep and the smooth operation of the visual action. Over the course of twenty minutes the beep was heard hundreds of times.

Keydell's brain was slowly moving from occasional bursts of chaos, caused by years of dysregulation, to a more regulated, less agitated state where the necessary demands of the environment were met by more appropriate levels of arousal. His brain would make these transitions more smoothly and accurately as time went on. Essentially, that is what I worked on in my meditation practice. The practice of concentrating calmed my mind, and rid it of chaos and agitation so that I could have more appropriate levels of arousal and better respond to my environment.

I have since learned that one of the areas of Keydell's brain that Dr. Bob was working on is called the limbic system.

The limbic system, which is made up of multiple parts of the brain, is located in the temporal lobe. It's where our emotions—like love, fear, anger, and desire—are carried out. This system contains the amygdala, hippocampus, and hypothalamus. The amygdala is the lead character in controlling our emotional responses and, if it is not functioning properly, may lead to unusual or abnormal responses to our emotions. If it's overstimulated, we can have excessive reactions to our emotions.

The hippocampus talks to the amygdala, and sends it information about our memories and the emotional ties that correspond to them. So, for example, if Keydell had feelings of loneliness or unworthiness around his memories of being neglected or moved from place to place, that message was sent to the amygdala and a response was activated. If his amygdala was overstimulated instead of balanced, the response was one of aggravation, fear, or even rage and violence.

The hypothalamus feeds the information that the hippocampus has processed to the amygdala, and acts as the regulator of our emotions, controlling levels of pleasure, aggression, anger, and even sexual desire. Whew. What a complicated system we have up in that head of ours. Basically, Keydell's limbic system needed a tune-up, and neurofeedback was the tool Dr. Bob was using to do that. Keydell's brain, however, was doing all the work.

Another area Keydell was working on was the prefrontal cortex of his brain, located near the front of his head. It's where our decision-making processes live, and it controls what decisions we make when faced with an emotional reaction. It also regulates our anxiety. I think of the prefrontal cortex as our "moral compass" in social situations; it's where our fight-or-flight instincts are. Keydell's never calmed down as an infant, due to his lack of feeling bonded or safe with an adult. His social cognitive abilities were skewed, which caused his inappropriate social interactions (such as invading people's personal space) and his inappropriate language. When faced with feelings of insecurity, he either wanted to fight or flee.

But *why* was his brain like that?

Dr. Moss helped me understand a lot of that during our sessions together, so the information I am sharing is from Dr. Moss' wisdom and based on articles and videos written by or produced through studies done by Dr. John Bowlby and Mary Ainsworth, the parents of attachment theory.

Keydell was emotionally and physically neglected, maybe even as early as in utero. Based on my conversations with his mother, I guessed she had very little bonding with him when he was an infant, and gave him very inconsistent care. This process of bonding is extremely important for a baby's development and, if it doesn't happen, can negatively affect him for the rest of his life, depending on the level of neglect or trauma. Attachment disorder is the effect of this lack of bonding with his mother or other caregiver to the extent that he needed.

When a mother or father bonds with a child through touch— gazing in his eyes and smiling, and responding to burps, farts, and giggles—and through general care like feeding and bathing, the child develops what John Bowlby and Mary Ainsworth, call a "safe haven and secure base with the adult." They feel they won't be abandoned by that caregiver. They will also feel distressed or anxious if they are separated from that caregiver.

If a caregiver shows inconsistent attention, a child can form an ambivalent attachment, which leads him toward being insecure or clingy, yet also fearing neglect. The child does *not* have that secure base or assurance that someone will be there for them if they need something. He may continually ask for something (like, in Keydell's case, more ice cream), and when you say no because he has already had a large bowl and it's almost dinnertime, he doesn't understand. He has no confidence in the caregiver (in this case, me) and wonders if he's done something wrong. A child might think you don't care about him, or that there is a problem with the little bond he does have with you, so he continues to cling and seek reassurance until you give it to him. He might even call you names, just to see if you will forgive him.

Well, how do you do! That sure sounded familiar. Keydell also showed signs of this when he didn't ever want me, or anyone, to stop playing with him or when he jumped all over people for attention. It would trigger his fears of rejection if I left him. He had not formed enough of a bond with me yet to feel secure in the fact that I would always be there for him. Interestingly, at the group home, he always had someone with him so he may not have had this issue there.

If a caregiver rejects or is insensitive to the needs of a child, or is completely ambivalent toward that child's needs, the child forms an avoidant attachment. The child tends to not seek out attention at all. He will spend time alone, will not seek or accept any comfort, and will see strangers no differently than he sees a caregiver. He often won't accept praise, and feels it's patronizing. He appears to accept what you have said, yet walks away because he really has no confidence in you. He will avoid discussing anything with you, and will not seek your comfort or approval. Keydell also showed signs of this at the group home, and with us. During our kickball games, he couldn't accept the praise we were giving him. Often, he would sit by himself, playing video games for hours when allowed.

Here's where the fun begins. Some children, like Keydell, lean toward both ambivalent attachments and avoidant attachments, but may snap in the middle somewhere. This is called disorganized attachment. It is also called Reactive Attachment Disorder or RAD. This disorganized attachment can come from the child taking on the role of the caregiver who neglected or abused him. Sometimes it can also be because they saw their caregiver being abused and it was frightening. A child with disorganized attachment may show symptoms of ambivalent attachments as well as avoidant attachments, but will lean toward extreme insecurities, confusion, frustration, and anger, which in turn bring on rage and violence toward himself and others. He does not feel he has a secure base or safe haven anywhere, and will show no loyalty toward a caregiver. Such children tend to lose empathy for people and animals, struggle to feel remorse, and feel alone, disconnected, and very misunderstood.

If I was scared or intimidated by Keydell's behaviors, he felt misunderstood, and it reinforced his belief of being disconnected from me. If I didn't forgive him right away after an upset, it confused him and frightened him regarding the little bond we had together, and it disconnected him from me even more. Keydell lost his sense of self because of his unhealthy relationship or bond to others.

Our first sign that Keydell was benefiting from the neurofeedback came on Thanksgiving Day.

We were spending the holiday with our friends, Terri and Chuck. They'd been through thick and thin with us, and were of great support as we were raising Keydell. Chuck was a huge soccer fan, so was very interested in Del's soccer progress, and had taken him to a few games when we couldn't make it. Our goddaughter, Savanna, was there, too, along with Ella and three of Chuck's nieces and nephews who were about Keydell's age. It was wild, with lots of tag games, soccer in the yard, and dogs running circles around everyone. We were having a blast.

Toward the end of the day, Ella came bombing upstairs from the basement TV room complaining about Keydell's behavior.

"He's being a pain, Mom, and won't stop yelling."

I thought for sure our time here was coming to a close. Usually if Ella and Keydell started fighting, it ended in a meltdown.

I called down the basement stairs and asked Keydell to come up.

He yelled back up the stairs, "What, I know Ella was just telling on me."

"Can we just work this out please so we can stay a bit longer? Come up here, please." I wanted to make sure he wasn't driving the other kids nuts either.

Ella started in on Keydell and I thought for sure he was going to lose it.

"You are being wild and won't listen to me," she said. "You're making everyone crazy down there."

"Ella, please, honey, I really want to stay, and if you guys don't work this out you know how this might go." I was waiting for Keydell to show his frustrations or lash back at Ella's comments but ... nothing happened.

That's right. *Nothing happened.* Keydell sat there quietly, listened to her, and that was it. I looked at Jim, stunned, as I waited for the explosion. But Keydell said nothing.

I whispered to Jim, "Maybe this neurofeedback stuff is working already. I thought for sure we would be leaving now with a massive meltdown on our hands."

"Yeah, he's doing really well," he replied, leaning in with a shoulder bump, acknowledging my delight.

I mean, Keydell was not only spoken to by Ella, but he was probably overwhelmed and tired from all the activity of the day—and he was being still. I was amazed. Only three or four sessions in, and we saw more control in this moment than ever before. I was impressed. Ella looked at Keydell with a surprised and pleased look and said, "Thank you for not arguing with me right now. I didn't want to get you in trouble, but can you please try not to be so wild downstairs?"

Everyone was staring at them in this moment. Eggshells were being stepped on lightly. Terri, Chuck, and Savanna certainly knew what could happen right now, but Keydell just agreed to calm down and apologized to Ella.

Holy cow, did that just happen? I was so stunned and happy. They actually had a normal encounter with each other.

"Did you see that, Terri?" I asked as Keydell and Ella moved on from the kitchen. "He didn't freak out. I might need another glass of wine."

She laughed and gladly got me a glass. It was a big moment.

That night, as I was putting Keydell to bed, I sat next to him and told him how proud I was.

"Keydell, do you realize how in control you were today? When Ella spoke to you, you listened, didn't react, and moved on. It was really great."

Just then Ella came in his room to say goodnight and echoed my comment. "Yeah, Keydell, you were just a normal bratty little brother today." She laughed as she bent down to kiss him on his forehead. He was beaming.

We continued with the neurofeedback twice a week—which was a lot for an active young boy of eleven, but Keydell was beginning to see some positive changes in himself and it motivated him to keep going. Plus, he loved Dr. Bob, and they developed a wonderful friendly banter. Keydell's sense of humor was really starting to shine, and he would often try to trick Dr. Bob into playing the Clone Wars movie over and over again because he loved it so much. They were having fun and working on Keydell's brain at the same time. The neurofeedback did not "fix" Keydell's attachment disorder, but he was finding more control over his anger and other extreme emotional responses, which allowed him to put his energies toward his more positive traits. We spent once a week with Dr. Moss, and the more Keydell settled down, the more he was able to reflect on his issues with her and me.

After a few months, we saw some big changes in Keydell's mood, reactions and behaviors. He had a few meltdowns here and there, but they were fewer and farther between, and less intense. He had a few issues at school for being too gregarious and distracted because he often got his work done quickly and was bored—but he was, after all, still a very active and smart young boy. I had to go into the school often to update his teachers and counselors on the work we were doing and how they could best help him. I asked if they could give him in-school suspension if needed (versus at-home suspension) so that he didn't feel "kicked out." He would still understand the consequences of his actions, but could take the punishment in school as long as he behaved while on the suspension. They agreed and he actually sat very quietly during his suspension time in a side office and did his work alone. The neurofeedback didn't change his personality; it simply helped him with his emotional control, which helped his self-esteem. He was more at peace, and happier.

I think for the longest time Keydell identified with being an angry, "bad" boy, one who was separate from others. He felt alone in the world. Now, he was starting to see that he was able to control his negative or unhelpful traits, and we were responding to him in a more positive way. He was not bad; he just had some bad behaviors that he could now work with. His mind became calmer, and he was able to process his thoughts and ideas without so much frustration. He even said to me one day, "Mom, I lost my pencil the other day and didn't get mad. I remembered what you said about whether I could do something about it in this moment or not, and I couldn't. I had to wait until tomorrow to look for it, or buy a new one later, so I didn't get angry, I just made a plan."

I was so proud of him, and he felt good about that. He was learning to be patient and present to the reality of his situation, and he was telling me because he knew I would be happy that he understood. It showed me that he was bonding with me.

After about six months of neurofeedback, we had an appointment with Dr. Romero-Bosch, his psychiatrist. He was showing such improvement in his behaviors and mood that we decided to start taking him off the antidepressants and his ADD medications. Since there are no medications for attachment disorder besides love and security, we decided to keep him on that regime. Anything else was just putting a Band-Aid on his symptoms.

Notice you are suffering, find the root cause of the suffering, find the path to relieve the suffering, and then take that path: these again are the four noble truths in Buddhism. You must dig and look at yourself from all sides, or you end up treating the symptoms versus healing the problem. This is a more holistic approach.

For so long, we were stuck on the second noble truth as to the cause of Keydell's suffering—but once we got to it, we were on the path to relief. Dr. Romero-Bosch was so surprised by Keydell's positive changes that she asked him if he thought she should recommend neurofeedback to her patients. He wholeheartedly agreed that she should.

At the end of our year of neurofeedback, we were down to just one session per week. I had stopped sitting in with Dr. Moss after the first six months or so, and was continuing to do as much bonding as I could with Keydell on my own. That was the easy part, because he was letting me get closer now. He was more talkative; he shared his excitement and replayed all his moves with me after his soccer games, and he still liked to cuddle to read books or watch TV. We ended our time with the amazing team at Delta Consultants just before Christmas of 2012.

I think my family and I did a good job with Keydell, even without knowing what we know now. We loved him, showed him we were there for him, and gave him a safe and secure home life. I often wonder, however, how long it would have taken Keydell to heal had we not found neurofeedback—or if he ever would have. After all, he had been with us two years without any signs of behavioral improvement. Attachment disorder is curable for most children over time, especially if recognized early on, but he had such an extreme case that I'm glad we got the help we did when we did. The control he gained enabled him to stay in our home safely.

When I met the Dalai Lama for the first time at Salve Regina University, my heart opened to a new way of being—one that came from working with my mind and my thoughts to create equanimity in my life. He showed me what it looks like to be present for all humans equally. Meeting Keydell and adopting him challenged that practice, and brought to light what it takes to get to a place of peace and calm within myself and with others. I have asked myself, on occasion, if I would have done what I did without having met the Dalai Lama and studied Buddhism, and I always answer yes— but my practice supported my decision and helped me get through some very tough times.

We are works in progress, and at the time Keydell arrived in my life, I was working on my mind—my analytical, busy, monkey mind that was curious to find peace in that crazy space called the consciousness—and he had a mind that was ill, anxious and unhappy. I was searching for ways to be at peace with people who bugged me, ways to find inner peace beyond a temporary fix. He was searching for a home. I aimed for an inner peace that came from a place of knowing reality, and not one clouded by what I made up about life. He aimed for control and safety. I was not unhappy, but unsettled and interested to know and understand why some people are happy and some are not. He was very unsettled and unhappy. I felt there was more in my life to be done—and I don't mean "doing" as in physical activity, but more of an inner exploration of myself, of others and how we all fit together on this planet and why.

Recently, I went to sit with Alex, an intuitive who is also a good friend of mine. She said to me, "Kim, I am seeing you in a past life as a young black boy, maybe in Africa or at least in the jungle. You look to be about fifteen or so, and you are hunting. You are not alone, but the other people with you are spread out, and you can't see them. You have to be very still and patient. What I am sensing about this vision is the importance of that stillness, and really being in the moment so that you can be present for the hunt. It's as if your life depends on it, because you are hunting to feed your village, and it's a big responsibility."

This was so cool. I have always loved African culture so it was kind of fun that she was seeing this. I was getting chills about practicing patience and stillness, as it's what I do now with my meditation practice. Then she said something that really blew me away.

"Kim, I am seeing that you are hunting a tiger."

"What?" I said. "Are you kidding me?"

"No, I see that you are hunting a tiger, and that is why you have to be so still and quiet. The main message I am getting for you is that in this life—and I know that you already do this, but, I'll tell you anyway—your task is to stay quiet and still, and always in the present moment. That should be your main focus in this life. I know you do this with your photography already, but if you stay in the present moment, everything you need will come to you. You don't have to do anything else."

I was blown away. I've been taught for lifetimes by my tiger to be patient and present; if I do, everything I need will come to me.

Thank you, Keydell, my tiger. I am forever grateful that I hunted you down, and that you came to me when I was ready for you.

AFTERWORD

Before I began writing this book, I said to Keydell, "I want to write a story about you, and how you have been my greatest spiritual teacher. Some of the parts will not be very flattering or pretty for either or us, but I am so proud of how far you've come, and I think it will inspire many kids who are going through the same things you did. Are you okay with me sharing all of that?"

He paused for a few seconds, thinking, and then looked at me and said, "Yeah, it's fine. Everyone knows what I did."

No shame. He is confident now, and he is happy.

I decided to write this book because it was such a relief to gain some wisdom about Keydell's disorder. When I have wisdom, I have insight. When I have insight, I see the reality of the situation—and when I see the reality, I let go of my story. That letting go brings peace.

I saw Keydell's beautiful heart very early on, but often found myself stuck in who I *wanted* him to become—someone more like me, Jim, Henry or Ella. I couldn't see him for the tiger that he was. Now, as I have moved forward in my mindfulness, I practice seeing him and others for who they are, even if I don't have all the information about them, by letting go of what I make up about them and just being with them, as they are with me, in each moment.

I also wanted to write this book to share what I have learned about attachment disorder so that perhaps, if you have a child who is suffering with the symptoms I have described (or if you see a child who is suffering), you can help that child, or at least find empathy for her or him. Perhaps any judgments you may hold about someone's parenting style can be set aside, and you can show compassion for the struggles they are having, knowing something deeper may be going on with their child.

This book project called me like no other project I have ever taken on—and, as a visual artist, writing was a real stretch for me. Keydell showed me what it meant to be both fearless and diligent. He persevered, and didn't let his past define him. When he plays soccer he is all in, and never backs down from an opponent. At age fourteen, he is now just over five feet tall and weighs about 110 pounds, but he has learned to use his body and speed to control the ball and move through his plays with skill and ease. If he gets knocked down, he gets right back up and keeps playing. He doesn't miss a beat. He is a leader on the field and motivates his teammates. He hasn't reached his 10,000 hours of practice yet, but he is getting closer. (Since that conversation with Henry, he has literally practiced every day. In the warmer months he goes to the school turf and gathers his friends, and they play for hours. If they are not available, he goes on his own. In the winter, we take him to the YMCA where he practices his skills in the racquetball court. The Y staff are like a second family to him now, and they love seeing him come in. Not a day goes by that someone I know tells me they have seen Keydell pedaling his bike with his ball in tow, or practicing out on the turf late at night. He's a legend in town.) He continues to play with Coach Teeters on the travel team, and made the Premier Rhode Island soccer team for Bruno United two years in a row. He also does his homework without having to be asked, and gets straight As in school. If Keydell could overcome his fears and be diligent and strong, so could I.

I only know so much about Buddhism at this stage of the game, and had some concerns that if I tried to explain the teachings I would be inaccurate, but I didn't want to let that stop me from sharing my story. I hope that, if the teachings I've shared interest you, you will seek out a qualified teacher to learn the dharma and bring the practice into your life.

I know our family is not alone in our situation, and hope that in some way people can learn something from our story. Life can throw you some curve balls—but if you stay open-hearted and aware of all that is presented to you, even the toughest situations can help you grow, gain wisdom, and bring light to something or someone you didn't know before. If you let your sufferings define who you are, then you will stay in that suffering and feel unhappy. Let go of your story. Look at reality. Something happened. If there is nothing to be done, there is no need for worry. If there is something to be done, do it. And remember, everything is impermanent, even happiness, so find equanimity in your life through all of your ups and downs. See the good for the good and the bad for the bad, but practice being with all of it versus fighting it. Feel fully, but don't let your emotions overtake your actions. We can learn from all of our experiences if we remember these things.

I think in many ways, Keydell's early traumas molded some of his good qualities as well as his struggles. They taught him to be independent, but now his independence is a choice instead of a forced state. He can call on us to feel that "safe haven and secure base," or he can be alone or out on his own with confidence. He is bonded to us now, and we to him. I think his tenacity and diligence developed in part because of his strong desire to please others and search for positive attention. He wants to be "good" so he will get the positive feedback that he desires. He wants to make others happy now, which is so encouraging because it shows his growing connection to others.

Children who grow up untreated for attachment disorder have a very difficult time in relationships. They can have intense, violent anger issues, an aversion to touch or physical affection—which Keydell still has; he flinches every time we go to hug or touch him—and a difficult time showing affection. They can also have an undeveloped conscience—which is a characteristic of a criminal in the making, if you ask me. Imagine how many children have been abused, neglected, or moved from caregiver to caregiver in this country, who are battling the same issues Keydell did, but without the help or loving support that they need.

There are approximately 600,000 children in the in the U.S. foster care system—many of whom suffer from attachment disorder—and thousands of people in prison who came from the foster care system. They grew up feeling disconnected from society, feeling no empathy toward others, and lacking a realization of consequences. If their disorders had been recognized earlier, they may have gotten the treatment or care they needed and been able to stay out of prison. As kind-hearted and loving as Keydell was underneath all of his behaviors, I think he, too, would have ended up hurting someone and landing in jail had he not gotten the proper care and love from us. We were very fortunate to have had the means to help him, and that, through my own self-care and spiritual practice, I was able to stay patient and calm enough to get through it myself.

In a recent meeting I attended about the group home situation in Rhode Island, the lead coordinator told me that they are bringing neurofeedback into the group homes and trying to work with some of the kids. Hearing that gave me hope that this disorder is becoming more widely recognized and talked about.

My family is forever changed, for the better, since Keydell arrived in our lives. We watched him struggle, work hard to recover, and become the wonderful brother, son, friend, and teammate that he is today. He knows he has to create his own life, and he continues to do so by being positive, working hard to achieve his goals, and never giving up. We have a refrigerator magnet that reads "Anything is possible." It is something he has said to us from very early on. His nature is to be kind, hardworking, and diligent. He just had to rid himself of his demons—and he did it. He has created the life he wants in connection with us, his forever family.

Henry graduated from college with a degree in business and acting, and is now creating his young life in California. As he fine-tunes his acting craft, he talks about how he embodies Keydell when he needs to get in touch with a part of himself that is not familiar: his deepest fears and anger. He saw how Keydell felt, and applies that awareness to his dramatic scenes. He and Keydell were not close for years, but each summer he's come home, he's bonded more and more with Keydell, and says how inspired he is by Keydell's drive and talent as an athlete. They text often, and Keydell updates him on all of his games.

Ella. Where do I even begin? She is truly an extraordinary young woman who navigated her young life with authenticity and grit, and continues to do so as she works her way through college. She also ended up at Chapman University. She endured some very rough times in our home, but only complained as a way to vent. She totally understood why we adopted Keydell, and never questioned keeping him. She kept her head down when needed, and brought us all back up with her dance parties, laughter, unfiltered humor, and general love of life. We always know where we stand with Ella, and she keeps me in check if she notices my anger coming on too strong, or if I am being too hard on Keydell. She loves Keydell and they now have a very close relationship. She often picks out his outfits and shares her insights about girls, making sure he is kind and thoughtful to them. She wants him to have a loving relationship someday and make cute little babies that she can love and help raise. She has ADD as well, but stays centered with the help of yoga, medications, deep breathing, and pausing to stop and think clearly when she finds herself feeling anxious or scattered.

Henry and Ella were both tested in so many ways during those first few years with Keydell. They learned how strong they are, and what they could endure, and I'm sure found some new gratitude for the lives they were blessed with. They have never been ungrateful children but, like myself, they had never known anyone with a severe mental illness, or had to deal with being separated from their family. My kids knew they had it good, and wanted to give that same life to Keydell.

Jim, my wonderful amazing husband, is still with me. He was my rock through all of this, and never once blamed me for bringing such difficulty into our home. He loves Keydell and knew we were doing a good thing, even if it was hard, and he supported all my efforts and strategies for helping Keydell. He loves to cook for Keydell, who appreciates his food wholeheartedly, and goes to as many of his games as he can. Jim started taking ADD medications not long after he tried Keydell's that day, and continues to use them when he feels distracted (so, almost every day). Jim and Keydell both love math; they talk about math problems like I talk about art. It's fun to listen to them, even when it goes right over my head; It's like they have a secret language. Jim is, and always has been, an amazing father. He has been an example of what it means to embrace all people, from all walks of life, with open arms and an open heart. Jim is the kindest, most nonjudgmental person I know.

Jim and I struggled during those years to keep our marriage strong. We were always on each other's side about things, but we were under a lot of stress. I think we both had some depression or a form of PTSD after things settled down, but we made it through after a short time in counseling.

Keydell's birth family seems to be okay. He doesn't ask to see his birth mom much anymore, but they text each other around birthdays and holidays. He cares about her and loves her, and I hope one day can have a relationship with her again. She told me once that she hopes that Keydell understands why she put him up for adoption, and that she loves him just as much as her other children. I often wonder if he feels torn about asking to see her, thinking he will hurt my feelings; I try to reassure him that I understand, and am not offended in any way. I send Sue photos of Keydell now and then, and she seems very grateful for how we have raised him. She lived with Patrick until a short time after his high school graduation and still lives with Kamaria. Her baby, who is now six, resides in Africa with her husband's family. She sees her once or twice a year.

I continue to study the Buddha Dharma with Khensur Rinpoche Lobsang Tenzin from Middletown, Connecticut (the monk who first came to Channing Church in Newport) and his translator, Jeffrey Allen, who comes to Newport to teach now that Rinpoche's travel is limited by age and health issues. Jeffrey was given the blessing to teach by Rinpoche, so we invite him to our Buddhist group and he shares his humble wisdom with us. I am so grateful to have both Jeff and Rinpoche to learn from. I also still sit with my wonderful meditation group from Inner Light.

Keydell continues to teach me about myself. I practice patience while waiting for him to leave soccer practice after everyone else has already gone, or when he forgets things like his watch or sweatshirt at the field and we have to go back and look for them. These are normal things, and easy to let go of after what we have been through. I am reminded of the impermanence of life as I watch him stay in control when he gets frustrated, knowing that at one time he could not manage that control.

Things were so intense for a while that it was hard to feel the good even though I tried. Now, I have found my laughter and sense of humor again. Keydell and I have fun together, laughing, riding in the car listening to music, talking about his schoolwork and soccer games. He asks me about my day, and is helpful around the house. That little boy I saw the first day at the group home is still in there—but now, he is happy, safe, secure, and shines brighter than ever.

I am forever grateful for my life and all that it brings me every day.

May I stay present to all the lessons in times of difficulty, and in times of great joy and ease.

May I remember that all things are impermanent and will change, so I should not hold too tightly to any expectations, things, or people.

May my life be about seeing the beauty in all things and all people, and may I always remember to be kind and compassionate toward all sentient beings.

I am responsible for my own happiness, and by ridding myself of my delusions and cultivating a clear mind through meditation and mindfulness, I am able to find happiness more often.

Thank you for reading my story. I would not be who I am without you. I wish you happiness. Have a wonderful day.

> *"Just as you are intent on thinking*
> *Of what could be done to help yourself,*
> *So you should be intent on thinking*
> *Of what could be done to help others."*

> —*Nagarjuna, Precious Garland of Advice*

ACKNOWLEDGEMENTS

I've heard it said that it takes a village to raise one child, so I have a village worth of people to thank.

First and foremost, I thank my family. Jim, you are my one true love, soul mate, and grounding presence. I love you forever. Henry, my strong handsome son, you make me feel like a queen: your kindness is endless. Ella, my beautiful, smart daughter: you light up any room you enter with your energy, spirit, and gift for living fully; your thoughtfulness fills my heart. And, of course, Keydell: thank you for letting us adopt you. You have changed our lives for the better, and I am so proud of you. I can't even imagine my life without you in it.

To my sister Amy, who has always been there to listen to my drama and support me with her love and straight-shooting approach to life: thank you for the month in Florida so I could work on the book. To my sister Lisa: thank you for your sensitive ear, and for a shoulder to cry on. You both have been so kind to Keydell, and wonderful aunties to all of my children.

To Mom and Dad: thank you for your undying support for all the crazy things I take on in life. You have never doubted me, and I have always felt safe and loved by you. To my aunt Flo and uncle

Gary, who would have been wonderful parents if they could have: I thank you for loving me and supporting me through all of my child-rearing years. Gary, I know there is a joke in there somewhere. ("Rearing!") To my grandfather Bob, who is no longer in this life: you have always shown me what wisdom and humility look like, and I appreciate all the kindness you have shown me over the years. You were the best grandfather a girl could ask for.

To all of my girls: Kelly, Lorraine, Lisa, Rachel, Carolyn, Michele, Monica and Andrea. You have my deepest gratitude.

To Mary Edwards, Bryna René Haynes and Matt Haynes: thank you for all of your guidance and suggestions.

To the staff at Child and Family, especially Denise DiGangi: huge thanks to all of you for keeping Keydell safe and supported while he lived in the group home. I am eternally grateful for all that you do.

To Coach Teeters, and all of our friends who supported and loved Keydell just as he was: thank you. Thank you.

And finally, to "Sue," Keydell's birth mom: you are a brave and kind woman who gave up her son so that he could have a better life. I hope you know I hold you very dearly in my heart, and I wish you only good things.

ABOUT THE AUTHOR

Kim Fuller has been a freelance photographer for over twenty-five years, and practices mindfully observing her world and the people in it every day. She teaches a class called "The Mindful Photographer" because she finds her gratitude increases as she carefully takes in her views, and wants to share that process with others.

After practicing Buddhism and meditation for many years, Kim now leads workshops to share what she has learned about handling the emotional stresses of raising a child with a mental illness, specifically Attachment Disorder, and of dealing with difficult people in general.

Though she is an artist, writing this book has been a stretch for her—but her adopted son Keydell taught her about determination, and what it means to strive for your goals no matter your circumstances.

Kim lives in Rhode Island with her husband Jim and son Keydell. She misses her two older children, who now live in California.

Contact Kim

Facebook: Kim Fuller and Kim Fuller Photography. Follow her page FINDING.

Web: www.kimfullerphotography.com
Instagram: @kimfullerphotographer
E-mail: kbfphoto@cox.net

Made in the USA
Middletown, DE
30 January 2017